Corporate Networks, International Telecommunications and Interdependence

Corporate Networks, International Telecommunications and Interdependence

Perspectives from Geograpy and Information Systems

Edited by

Henry Bakis, Ronald Abler and Edward M. Roche

BELHAVEN PRESS
LONDON

Belhaven Press
(a division of Pinter Publishers Ltd.)
25 Floral Street, London WC2E 9DS, United Kingdom

First published in 1993

Distributed exclusively in the USA and Canada by St. Martin's Press, Inc., Room 400, 175 Fifth Avenue, New York, NY10010, USA

British Library Cataloguing in Publication Data

A CIP catalogue record for this book is available from the British Library

ISBN 1 85293 142 6

Library of Congress Cataloging-in-Publication Data

A CIP catalog record for this book is available from the Library of Congress

Typesetting Consultant James Cosby
Page layout, design, processing, and index Edward M. Roche

Typeset in Monotype Baskerville and Headline Bold
Delivery of text through the *Internet* – use of optical character recognition for non-automated text; Swedish, German and French characters processed by custom glossary.

Printed and bound in Great Britain by Biddles Ltd., Guildford and King's Lynn

Contents

Preface

It is clear that telecommunications is changing the way in which human society is organized, including towns and cities. Large industrial and service companies, organized as multinational corporations are also feeling the change.

As measured in costs/byte of information transmitted, telecommunications is decreasing in cost at 40% per year, whereas information technology is decreasing at "only" 30% per year, as measured in price/performance ratios.

If these trends continue, telecommunications and *not* computers may do more to change the organization of society in the next century than any other social force.

What is really happening?

Telecommunications is increasing the velocity of information flowing through different organizations. Increases in the velocity of information imply that the effective "information space" of an organization is dramatically expanded over greater distances.

Many concepts of geography and geographical space have been based on distance. After all, early geography was concerned with charting the world, and providing useful guides to those wishing to traverse the physical space of the planet. Until the middle of the 19th century, "information space" was a close analogue to the "physical space" of the geographers. Telecommunications has changed that relationship forever, and broken the close relationship between *physical space* and *information space*.

The rapid increase in information velocity brought about by telecommunications has changed the geographical distribution of information by making physically remote information appear very close.

It has been the geographers and not the information systems professionals who have helped us to visualize these new relationships.

The accelerating phenomena of telecommunications raises important questions about regional and national autonomy, as well as the interdependence between countries, organizations and other actors, including multinational corporations.

The editors are pleased to present this book based primarily on a Symposium of the *Commission C18 of the Union Géographique Internationale*, held in Washington, D.C., during August of 1992.

1 Economic and Social Geography – Toward the Integration of Communications Networks Studies

Henry Bakis

The telephone has long been ignored in university textbooks and courses on geography, as has also been the case for other urban infrastructures. However, telecommunications shows the relationship and hierarchies between geographic spaces. Even more, they have consequences on the spatial organization of transportation, industry, and cities. Economic geography, like regional development, is thus especially implicated, especially in developed countries. Is it still necessary to distinguish between utopias and dreams and the reality of present or predictable spatial relationships?

At the end of the 19th century, the communication of information was seen in the university as falling within the framework of the "geography of circulation" (Verkher in German) and of geopolitics. But the growth of geographic research on transportation reduced the attention given to telecommunications, in France as elsewhere. Despite individual attempts it was necessary to wait until the middle of the 1960s, and especially after 1970, for studies to become more numerous.

It is recognized today that telecommunications is an integral part of geographical research. The geography of telecommunications isn't a separate field beside a number of other geographic subfields (rural, urban, industrial, transportation, etc.). It is rather a more generalist theme, that plays a role in all human and economic geography. This is not surprising given the distribution of the usage of new information and communication technologies in both professional and domestic settings. How can one treat today the geography of transportation without considering the fundamental role of telecommunications networks (the reservation of places, the management of deliveries, the organization of time and space)? How to treat urban geography without considering the role of telecommunications (international functions, zones of advanced telecommunications capabilities, the circulation of information that allows the function of diverse infrastructures, etc.)? How to treat industrial geography without taking up the logistics of firms and of telecommunications networks (public and private) that support the requirements of a new organization of production ("tight flows", "zero stock")? These are the ideas of interest to telecommunications geographers, who have published a great deal in the last ten years, notably in the journal *NETCOM* since 1987.

Telecommunications underscores and renders more visible phenomena that concern not only the geographer but also the developer, city planner, or regional economist, such as regional disparities, relational patterns, the hierarchy of spaces and subspaces, urban centers, etc. A number of questions find elements of their answer in the study of telecommunications: the distribution of facilities, the design of networks, the analysis of traffic flows, developmental projects. The efforts of local and regional governments to equip themselves with teleports or zones of advanced telecommunications capabilities or to draw regional communications diagrams all show a heightened level of consciousness that is rather recent.

Telecommunications allows us to anticipate how geographic space will be used in the future. Modern city planning efforts take account of telecommunications in the organization of urban life. The local constraints on activities and work can be modified by the advent of an undifferentiated communication space.

If geographic analysis can shed light upon the policies pursued by operators at the scale of the European continent, it can also make other contributions: on the macro-spatial level (the introduction of the variables of heterogeneity of habitat in the modeling of the costs of the new network) and on the micro-spatial level (the pertinence of retail agencies in relation to a business clientele, specific geographic analysis of the introduction of products and services for a particular clientele according to different kinds of neighborhoods).

A new IGU Commission was put in place by the General Assembly of the International Geographical Union (Washington, August 1992). A central part of the Commission's task will be for its four year term up to 1996, to examine the spatial processes, patterns, and impacts of global change. The underlying theme of its current work, is to draw attention to the critical crossroads the world's information system has reached and to point out the alternative international, inter-regional, and inter-city industrial scenarios. The need can be seen in the unprecedented increase in the rate, scale, and type of simultaneous changes (ie. global, urban, industrial, etc.) These are dramatically altering the structure of the global geographic and economic system and causing profound and complex socio-economic changes at the sub-urban, urban, regional, and also national levels. The use of telecommunications networks to transfer employment between developing and industrialized countries is an indication of the kind of changes underway.

The forces of change in the information and business environments are now, in a way, non-spatial. Yet, their spatial expression has been and is continuing to be intensified because together these forces have led to an enormous increase in spatial interdependence over great distances. Therefore, from the perspective of spatial information systems (and as well with a spatial industrial systems perspective), the functional "neighborhood" of Washington may include Singapore or Delhi, Kiev or Geneva, as well as Buenos Aires, Sidney, Dakar, or Kuweit. As noted by F.E.I. Hamilton (1979): "The past and continuing passenger- and-freight transport revolution and the telecommunications- information revolution are bringing about unprecedented scales and intensities of interdependence of place (town, region, nation) upon place across international and intercontinental divides."[1]

The role of the 92.C3 IGU Commission: The Commission will continue and enlarge the work of the past 88.C18 IGU Commision. The IGU Executive Commitee chose to maintain a specific commission: without such a specific commission, general problems, theories, and questions linked to this analytic framework would not necessarily be undertaken. This choice appears more profitable for the development of geographic analysis in this still new field, as much at the level of the IGU as at the level of the different national committees. Thus, the goals of the new term may be summarized briefly as follows:

Leadership: the Commission can best fulfill its leadership role by initiating new approaches to old problems or by applying new thinking to methods and research goals which are both intellectually stimulating and of practical utility. Theory, method and relevance must be integrated. This does not mean that Commission members per se are or must expected always to be the avant garde of the field. Rather, they should work towards that end both individually and collectively, while simultaneously involving other scholars who represent the most stimulating and progressive sources available for telecommunication and communica-

---

[1]F.E.Ian Hamilton, "The IGU Commission and the Changing World Industrial System," Meeting of the IGU Commission on Industrial Systems, Rotterdam, 1979, 17 pages.

tion-related problems. This requires an examination of the spatial character, scales, and dynamics of structural changes resulting from the operation of a variety of processes, environmental impulses, and regulatory contexts. Such an analysis will reveal new stages in the development of a telecommunication and information "age" at international, national, regional and urban levels of analysis. Its leadership role should be recognized as 'technology transfer' in scientific, education, and practical policy-making experience by the avant garde to those who are less advanced in their approach to the problems associated with spatial information and telecommunications networks, wherever they may be in the world.[1] To fulfill its leadership role, therefore, the Commission must act as:

- A forum for international discussion through the medium of conferences. Often the most valuable contribution to the dissemination of knowledge and mutual understanding between researchers of different countries and continents is through the new international contacts which conferences afford individual participants. Direct contacts are also made possible by the exchange of the institutional addresses of the authors of papers. Delegates from the widest range of cultural, economic, political, technical and locational contexts with expertise on relevant themes should be able to exchange their views, ideas, models, data analysis and case studies. At least one meeting will be held each year at the international level, within the constraints of the financial resources available.[2]

- An agent in the dissemination of relevant knowledge. If the commission is to take a leadership role, it is critical to disseminate relevant knowledge in the field, of course. It is also a measure of the effectiveness of the Commission's function as a forum. Results achieved in conferences and through research by Commission members and their colleagues are being distributed to a widening international audience with increasing regularity. Although mainly geographers, this audience also includes regional scientists, economists, policy-makers,

---

[1]The members of the commission try to organised themselves with an internationaly decentrallized organization structured around a policy of active editorial intervention. This is possible by the exploitation of modern means of telecommunications as a means of liaison between the Commission's members (i.e. mainly: fax, electronic mail, teleconferencing, etc.).

[2]The Universities organizing the annual meeting of the last S9 Study group (1984-1988) and the C18 Commission were Montpellier, France (1985), Sevilla, Spain (1986), Paris (1987 and 1988), Sydney, Australia (1988), Geneva (1989), Bochum, Germany (1990), Goteborg, Sweden (1991)... And Washington DC, USA, in next August.

telecommunications engineers, etc. Until now, some national working groups have been active within the C18 Commission, such as Germany and France. In other countries where there are no formal national working groups, such as Brazil, Canada, Italy, Israel, Japan, Holland, Sweden, Great Britain, and the US, members of C18 were very active. Work seems only to be beginning in China, Hungary and Nigeria. The Commission's publications will enlarge its forum.[1]

Co-operation with other organizations or bodies. First, within the IGU, which may be better developed at the commission level. It was necessary at first to concentrate on our own field. Nevertheless, co-operation and contacts with other commissions and with universities was done by personal contacts. Cooperation must be improved with national and international governments and non-governmental agencies.[2] Cooperation and coordination must continue as well with telecommunications operators.[3]

Prescription. Policies should be recommended, when and where appropriate, that may make decision-makers (policy- makers, planners, firm managers, industrialists) more aware of changes in global communication systems. The goal should be to advise them upon likely impacts

---

[1] A number of publications have emanated from the Commission authors from 1988 to 1992, including collective books: Bakis H. (Ed.) Information et organisation spatiale, Paradigme, Caen, 1988, and Bakis H. (Ed.) Communications et territoires/Communications and territories, La Documentation Française, 1990, Brunn S.D., Leinbach T.R. (ed.), Collapsing Space and Time: Geographic Aspects of Communications and Information, Hurwin Hyman, London, 1991). See also 55 issues of an international "Communication Geography Newsletter"(Edited by H. Bakis, Executive Secretary since 1985); and 6 volumes of NETCOM (Networks and Communication Studies). The "Five Years Table" (of authors, topics, and places) is now published (NETCOM VI-1).

[2] Through exchanges of publications, consultancy, and conference support (meeting places)... Such contact has been made with the OECD (Athens 1987, the lectures of R. Abler and H. Bakis), the United Nations (Badhovedorp near Amsterdam 1989, lecture of H. Bakis), the European Science Foundation- NECTAR (Athens 1990), the International Telecommunications Union (Geneva 1989, lectures and contacts, conference facilities in the ITU Headquarters for our "concluding session"); the Internation Union of Political Sciences (co- organisation of our symposium in Paris, may 1993

[3] Such as Deutsche Bundespost (June 1990, contacts around the Commission Meeting at Bochum, videoconferences facilities), Telecom Australia (August 1988, contacts around the Commission Meeting; 1991 contacts by J. Langdale), France Telecom (August 1984, videoconference facilities; January 1988, sponsoring of a Commission Meeting "Communications and Territories"; 1985- 1992, sponsoring of the Commission's letter and NETCOM, by CNET, France Telecom's Research Center), and Swedish firms (Volvo, for example, June 1991, contacts around the Commission Meeting at Goteborg)

that will be subject to regional variations so that actions may be taken to preserve or enhance the economic and social well-being of their populations. This role should be fulfilled no matter how modest our counsel. As geographers or regional scientists, therefore, we have a major role to play in identifying these forces and in offering advice on policies designed to maximize their benefits and minimize their negative impacts.

Objectives

This subfield is part of a major research path for all of human geography. The other thematic commissions of the IGU must systematically treat telecommunications each time it touches upon their own domain (in industry, transportation, tourism, commerce, etc.) If not, they will fail to understand a fundamental contemporary mechanism. We must represent the interest in the emergence of this kind of analysis and constitute the nucleus of specialists on the other commissions. The different commissions must be encouraged to interest themselves, more than in the past, in the intersection between telecommunications and their particular area of concern. While enriching their analyses with this perspective, it is not desirable that generalized commissions abandon their wider frame of reference. On the contrary, it is necessary that these themes be progressively integrated into the work of other commissions of human geography. For this, we may organize common sessions with other commissions.

We provide the necessary focus upon these themes, which are not taken up in a systematic fashion anywhere else. Our role will thus be unique within the IGU as well as a fundamental laboratory to facilitate the work conducted by others. It is essential that there be a place in which analysis of the communication of information and telecommunications are the primary focus. This concerns three relevant areas to be specifically addressed by this commission, as explained below.

Work will thus be structured along these three principle axes.

Intercontinental relations and modern means of communications

As with the flow of materials, immaterial flows such as capital, electricity, and information require the construction of different facilities for local, regional, national, and international networks.[1] Immaterial flows cannot be accomplished without various facilities (billboards and posters for ad-

---

[1] Undersea cables, satellites, and worldwide networks; the global geo-economy, multinational businesses; information flow (voice telephony, telex, telecomputing).

vertising, electric cables, etc.) and especially technical networks that are entirely physical (telephone lines, undersea cables, television antennas, fiber optic cables for cable television, antennas and receivers for citizen's band radio, earth stations for satellite reception, etc.). Even telecommunications between delivery vehicles (mobile telephony) is impossible without facilities (the installation of a reception/emission device and its antennae), an infrastructure (the Hertzian band) and a network (a series of relays and transmission equipment that may include satellites).

The geographic study of these facilities, and of the flows they support, permit us in particular to better understand intercontinental relations: the study of the installed base of hardware, of linkages, of data transmission rates. This study leads as well to a better understanding of the role of telecommunications in the function of non-governmental agencies as well as large multinational companies. The relational and economic life of the planet can become more and more global, as one may observe in the functioning of the large multinational companies.

We are beginning today a new dynamic: the conservation of non-deregulated services (especially the telephone) concerns competitive operators (in data transmission, radio communication, etc.). This opens new perspectives for the geographic coverage of territories by networks. A sudden liberalization that leaves all open to market forces would lead to the service of only profitable corridors at the national level (Paris-Lyon rather than Bordeaux-Brest in France) or the international (in Europe the London-Amsterdam- Frankfurt-Milan axis, in the United States the northeastern megalopolis). Will certain countries participate in the distribution of international or trans-European message flows, for example? Or will they be short circuited, which is to say bypassed?

In Europe, with such a hypothesis, one can imagine that the principal telecommunications axes will be built to conform with the lines of European territorial power and that the unequal development of regions will be thus virtually irreversible, at least insofar as making it possible to provide services at prices and technological trustworthiness comparable to other networks, notably satellite. The structures and dynamics of European space reveals the backbone of the megalopolis, its extension in a Southerly direction, long lasting effects with historic origins, the under-development of peripheral areas and the orbit of developments founded upon "high tech" (Montpellier, Toulouse, Glasgow, Copenhagen). New trans-European relationships appear around the Mediterranean (the growing center of Madrid-Barcelona, and its liaison with Lisbon, Lyon, Marseille and the "megalopolis"). On the other hand, the Atlantic coast is left abandoned: a string of related difficulties slice one part of France from another.[1]

Development and communication networks

To achieve greatest impact, the work of the Commission[2] must be directed at specific sets of related issues. Meetings will be primarily concerned with the initial definition of the spatial dynamics of communication networks and systems and the role of information and telecommunications as agents of change and the impacts they may have (on both firms and states) at different stages of development. The industrial countries have been studied more often because of their concentration of high technology equipment, information technologies, and electronic communications networks.

It is necessary to extend research in the geography of telecommunications beyond the industrialized countries. Industrialized countries have been the best represented among the members of our commission and, as a consequence, there has been more work done in this area. This has been a source of concern because participation in the work of the C18 commission does not reflect the global character of the IGU as well as it should. However, work has been conducted on the countries of Africa, Asia, and Latin America and when one looks at the record of the work of the group it is clear that these areas have not been neglected. Thus, a number of works have focused on Argentina and Brazil, Nigeria, the Congo, Ivory Coast, Malaysia, Singapore and China. It is, however, regrettable that more of the countries of North Africa, Black Africa, Asia, and Eastern Europe have not been better represented in the work of the C18 Commission (1988-1992). It is anticipated that this will change for the next period 1992—1996.

It is no longer necessary to demonstrate the importance of the new techniques of communication and information for the economic development of the different countries of the Union, and it is vital to study their geographic implications, particularly those concerned with regions. If the Executive Committee responds favorably the future IGU commission will enlarge its effort in this direction. We hope that the different National Committees of the IGU will provide access for us to the geog-

---

[1]See the document of P. Thinon on the model of R. Brunet (1988) reproduced in Informations RECLUS, No. 15, p. 7, GIP RECLUS, Montpellier.
[2]Telecommunications facilities and development in the countries of Africa, Asia, and Latin America; regional development and facilities; the particular case of Eastern and Central European countries

raphers of their countries in those countries where this has not been the case up to now.

The study of this theme will include three aspects:

- Telecommunications facilities and development in the countries of Africa, Asia, and Latin America.

- Regional development and communications network facilities. The importance of information flows in regional and spatial development and in particular of postal linkages in the case of developing countries. The existing functional lines between different localities of a region situated north of Lagos (Ogun State, Nigeria) was studied by focusing upon the movement of mail (10). The study demonstrated the usefulness of this method in defining functional regions, and identified six centers having a particularly active role in the region studied. The respective influence of secondary centers is also highlighted. The author is able to extract conclusions that have consequences for regional development.

- The case of the countries of Central and Eastern Europe merits special attention. The foundations of this research have been laid by the German members under the leadership of Pr. Hottes (Konrach Meeting, 21-22 February 1992).

The new differentiation of space by telecommunications networks

The territories in networks and the silent revolution of immaterial networks

Beside the distribution of materials[1] (the transportation of objects and people) our current era is characterized by networks for immaterial circulation (information, services) far more than in previous time periods. For more than forty years, the world economy is characterized by a growing process of integration concerning as much the exchange of goods as the movement of people, capital, and information. This circulation between cities, regions, countries, and continents is an essential dimension of that which we call the "Information Society" and that consists of the veritable creation of territorial networks. The organization in networks is inseparable from social life and this organization obviously

---

[1] The study of this theme includes (at least four our Commission) four aspects: Telecommunications and centralization (teleports, high technology centers); New spatial dynamics, differentiation and information networks (cities, regions, businesses); Urban hierarchy and new communications technologies; Social geography and the development of modern telecommunications (analyses on the neighborhood level, both middle class and underprivileged).

has a spatial component. Such an organization often rests on the circulation of information, which always plays a vital role. Thus, since most ancient times and throughout the Middle Ages a wide array of physical infrastructures have existed, notably for irrigation (Egyptian society, the Asian mode of production), transportation (Phoenician ports; Roman roads, paths, and relays by caravan for the spice trade), as well as networks for the circulation of information (the postal network of the Persian empire described by the historian Herodotus).

It is necessary to observe that it is not the network structure that is new, since it was implicit in these social networks. Today, it is the role taken by technical networks that has changed. By means of these technical networks, which telecommunications plays a role alongside rapid transportation, the ecology of geographic space is organized, characterized by the introduction of new elements that give these "new networks" aspects that are indeed original: speed, volume, direct connections, and connections in real time. The flow of immaterial networks thus contributes to a clearer comprehension of the complexity of the relationship between different geographic spaces.

Some indices lead to the observation that a new approach to territorial organization has begun to emerge, characterized by the popularization of the network organizational structure. Such organization existed prior to the telephone or the airplane, but its popularization has become possible by the combined effect of the improvement of rapid transportation linked with telecommunications. An example is the territorial coverage of bureaucracies or businesses. Linear space loses its practical importance when it is reorganized into relational space which is discontinuous and cut into zones whose limits depend on the relative costs of transportation and telecommunications. The pricing policies of telecommunications operators plays an important role and is of major concern for public services.

The policies pursued by network operators are linked with these problems.

Telecommunications plays a double role:
- The response to a need by making an instrument available that is adapted to meeting them that at the same time contributes to economic and social development.
- The reorientation of the conditions by which activities are spatially distributed. The spatial distribution of the population, the different socio-professional categories, the economic actors or the active population, as well as their volume or density determine the distribution of

facilities and the amount of traffic on a telecommunications network. This influence was already noteworthy from the early days of telephone networks when private companies located their transmission facilities, central switches, and terminal equipment with the unique concern of turning a profit on their investment. This influence may become important again if deregulation is carried to extreme degrees in certain countries. It is also important to analyze the question of the new differentiation of space by telecommunications networks.

That communications plays a strategic role is understood more and more by elected municipal officials and regional administrators. And telecommunications, which took some time to be accepted as a legitimate thematic approach in geography, now finds itself integrated as an essential dimension of regional development.

Places of low population density

In these areas, telecommunications networks can contribute to the support of the population with well-adapted services. They can furnish considerable help in tele-diagnostics, for example by providing the ability to distinguish between simple chest pains and the initial stages of serious heart trouble. Other applications are worthy of analysis such as tele-teaching. These are all the more crucial for countries spread over vast areas for which teledistribution can help provide certain services to widely dispersed populations.

Cities

Telecommunications techniques can improve the functioning of urban and municipal services. We have to be sure of a fact: cities concentrate now around halh the people living on this planet. It is the first time in the Earth history. So the problem is: how to let them live as well as possible? It will be impossible if the networks are not perfectly functioning. And, among all networks, the telecommunications networks are quite special ... They permit the perfection (or so) in the functioning of all urban networks.

Information and communications systems founded upon new technologies are superimposed upon classic forms of centralization and the differentiation of geographic spaces founded notably on the classic organization of space (urban and regional structures, notably). All means may substitute for others, as they may also be complimentary. The forum as a site where all paths converge no longer exists, but one may wonder if telecommunications networks are not able to provide at least a partial substitute (access to central services). The relationship between telecommunications and the city concerns especially urban organization and growth. One opinion on the subject is worth citing, which dates from 1895: "three new factors seem destined to exercise a powerful influence on the problems of the city. They are the trolley, the bicycle and the telephone. It is impossible to predict at this point what will be their influence upon the distribution of the population. But it is certain that this influence will add from five to fifteen miles to the radius of all large cities". Among the influences are the extension of suburbs, linked to the development of mass transit, the morphology of the urban infrastructure, the construction of municipalities prepared for home automation or pre-wired for cable television, the development of neighborhoods, cabling, civil engineering, services. The improvement of services, thanks to telecommunications, can facilitate the management of urban complexity. In France, following the Schreiner Report to Minister of PTT (1990), an organization called the "Observatoire des Télécommunications dans la Ville" (The Observer of Telecommunications in the City) was created in January 1991 to better understand the needs of local governments.

Cities are the nodes of the network on the local level (social and spatial interaction: the Greek agora, the Roman forum, the marketplace) and on the inter-urban scale (exchanges, mobility). The industrialized countries have gone progressively from a situation characterized by a deficit of infrastructures to a situation characterized by a deficit in the services suited for them. But with this the domain known and mastered by the engineers is left behind. We pass from technical understanding to a need for knowledge of society and at this level one finds the incisive remark: "We can do. But what?" In a city one lives, moves about, works, meets others. Cities thus serve different functions, a number of which can profit by telecommunications services. Some cities, however, have ambitions of improving their ranking relative to other cities by the reconversion of old industries. In France, Lorraine is a good example. The ambitions of cities can also be expressed at the level of the European Community. The Mayor of Metz, serving then also as Minister of Post and Telecommunications, can declare that "from a disabled region we have succeeded at building a center of excellence in telecommunications."

The evolution of geographical space

If telecommunications follows the lines of organizational power in a physical territory and accompanies the development of a neighborhood or an industrial zone it can go beyond this and play a role in the evolution of geographic space. Its influence is directly exercised on the structure of space and on patterns of social relations. It plays an important role in regional planning and, in particular, makes possible a more satisfactory distribution of activities. The disparities in both physical facilities and consumption may diminish as a consequence. Governments are aware of its ability in territorial development to liberate rural regions and assure the future of urban life by redistributing activities. The problem is to know how telecommunications exercises its influence.

Obviously, one cannot believe that telecommunications exercises an all-powerful structural influence. The implementation of an infrastructure is crucial for the policy of spatial development but cannot replace it. Telecommunications has most often been taken into account in locational decisions when a particular site is weak, or in the case in which a business's profitability is significantly effected because communications costs figure prominently in its production costs. Telecommunications can favor the development of new spatial organization models for businesses built around new markets. Thus, data transmission, already used for internal communications of companies with multiple business locations, permits an improvement in productivity, without however leading automatically to a scattering of sites over a wide territory. In particular, the "paper factories" that treat information such as administrative offices, banks, insurance companies, typing or translation services, may find in telecommunications the means by which they can be relocated to different sites or even different countries that offer cheaper land or office space or less expensive labor that has a mastery of the working language, meaning either French or English.

To increase the value of a location by exploiting telecommunications those responsible must be vigilant. Advantages must not be lost, for example, in the selection of a wiring plan or by the schedule decided upon for its implementation. It is important to observe that facilities for low rate data transmission often turn out to be sufficient to meet the needs of an isolated enterprise. On the other hand, the development of a zone of activity rests more on an intensive usage of a highly capable network and on the shared utilization of services, leading to the logic behind a high technology industrial zone, teleports, and zones of advanced telecommunications capabilities. A feasibility study must in each precise case define a role for telecommunications to play in a larger policy for territorial development. Urban policies can guide relocating businesses and businesses operating in multiple locations to priority sites.

The influence of telecommunications on the organization of space appears especially in two key areas: the city and the business. The city can be considered a physical support of a system of social interaction. The terms agora or forum, when they are used to designate modern urban centers, bear witness to this. Telecommunications is an essential dimension of social and spatial interaction.

Conclusions

Telecommunication can be the best and/or the worst of things. It can facilitate centralization as well as decentralization. It continues to be vital that geographers clarify for decision-makers the power of these tendencies and the conditions that lead to success in territorial development. This is the fundamental ambition of our commission, which will identify, discuss, validate, and publish what may be known on these questions.

In doing this, we hope to contribute to the improvement of the conditions of work and life (in urban spaces notably) and more generally to the economic and cultural development of humanity.

Bibliography

ANTONELLI C. (ed.) (1988), New Information Technology and Industrial Change: the Italian Case, Kluwer Academic Publishers, Dordrecht Borston London

BAKIS Henry (1984), Géographie des télécommunications, Que sais-je?, Presses Universitaires de France, Paris

BAKIS Henry (1987), "Géopolitique de l'information", Que sais- je?, Presses Universitaires de France, Paris

BAKIS Henry (1988), "Entreprise, espace, télécommunications. Nouvelles technologies de l'information et organisation de l'espace économique", Collection Transports et communications, Paradigme, Caen

BAKIS Henry (1991), "Telecomunicaciones espacio y tiempo", in Carmen Gomez Mont (ed.), Nuevas tecnologias de comunicacion, Editorial Trillas, Mexico, 1991

BAKIS Henry (1992), "Géographie des réseaux de communication et de télécommunications: bibliographie (1980-1992)". NETCOM, vol. 6, n.⁻ 2, avril, pp. 309-395 -see also: BAKIS H., "Tables quinquennales de NETCOM (1987-1991)", NETCOM 6-1, pp. 219-242

BAKIS Henry (Ed.) (1988), "Information et organisation spatiale", Collection Transports et communications, Paradigme, Caen

BAKIS Henry (Ed.) (1990), Communications et territoires/ Communications and territories, Collection de l'IDATE, La Documentation française, Paris

BAKIS Henry (Ed.) (1993), "Géographie des réseaux de télécommunication" (Actes de la table-ronde tenue en Sorbonne, juin 1992), Bulletin de l'Assocation de Géographes Français, n.⁻ 1.

BAKIS Henry, HOTTES Karlheinz, WEBER Hans-Ulrich (eds.) (1991), "Telecommunications and Emerging Spatial and Economic Organisation", in NETCOM, 5-2, pp. 327-498

BRUNN Stanley D., LEINBACH Thomas R. (eds.), Collapsing Space and Time: Geographic Aspects of Communications and Information, Hurwin Hyman, London, 1991

ESTABROOKS Maurice F. & LAMARCHE Rodolphe H., (eds.) (1987), "Telecommunications: a strategic perspective on regional, economic and business development", Institut Canadien de recherche sur le développement régional, Moncton

HALL P., NEWTON P., BROTCHIE J., BATTY M. (eds.) (1991), "Cities of the 21st Century: New Technologies and Spatial Systems", Longman Cheshire, Halsted Press. John Wiley & Sons New York.

HEPWORTH Mark E. (1989), "Geography of the information economy", Belhaven Press, London

KELLERMAN Aharon *Géography of telecommunication* Belhaven Press, London, 1993.

SPRIANO Giorgio (Ed.) (1987), "Telecomunicazioni e territorio", Cooperativa di cultura Lorenzo Milani, Torino

2 Interdependence and Autonomy in International Telecommunications

Aharon Kellerman

Interdependence and autonomy patterns in international telecommunications may be examined along at least three dimensions: (1) at the national level - organization and ownership patterns of telecommunications systems; (2) at the international level - the international system for accounting settlements among national telecommunications agencies; and (3) the dependence of international telecommunications traffic on other international movements, notably those of commodities, people, and capital.

National patterns of organization and ownership of telecommunications systems

The organization and ownership of telephone services has probably turned into the most important and "hottest" aspect of the contemporary telecommunications industry. Major problems are questions such as: should telecommunications services be provided as a governmental public utility service or should they rather function as a business utility service, privately or publicly owned? Should competition be introduced into the provision of telecommunications services? At first sight it seems as if these questions have economic, political and social ramifications, but no geographical ones. However, there are at least four ways in which the ownership and organization of telecommunications services have geographical aspects and ramifications.

First, and "traditionally," the ownership and structure of telecommunications services are determined on a national basis, so that differences in organizational patterns actually amount to variations among nations. Second, and despite the previous point, contemporary conditions in the telecommunications business do not let countries enjoy full autonomy in structuring and restructuring their telecommunications services, though formally they are still autonomous. Once telecommunications services have become a technologically dynamic industry with rapidly emerging and diffusing innovations, and once the provision of such services has to be fast, efficient and profitable, foreign transitions and resulting imitations, cannot be avoided (see also Robinson, 1991).

Third, the impacts of telecommunications services on service industries and manufacturing at large, may create new global maps of the importance and specializations of countries and cities, based, among other things, on differences in the organization and ownership of telecommunications services. Fourth, once various options for the structure and ownership of telecommunications utility companies become feasible, companies' capital may be invested in foreign telecommunications companies, thus creating new interdependencies.

Two characteristics typified telecommunications services until the mid-1980s: they were considered "natural monopoly", and with only two permanent exceptions (U.S. and Canada), they were operated by national governments as an integral part of PTTs. Natural monopolies related to the unique character of the supply of utilities at large, including gas, water, electricity, and telephone services. These utilities require connections by pipelines and cables to each served point, and competition among various networks, could amount to physical, and in some cases also financial chaos. The role of economies of scale is, therefore, crucial for utilities which have to reach every building. However, whereas various utilities were often supplied by a private monopolistic company, telephone services were considered a government service. They were somehow similar to public transportation, where route-networks, stops and terminals have to be structured and maintained, competition is usually absent, and the service provider charges users for each ride. Like in most public transportation services, profitability was not required in telephone services, and when capital surpluses acumulated, they were transferred to the general PTT budget or to the national budget.

The technological transformations of the telecommunications industry permitted several changes in the double-character of telephone services, namely its being a natural monopoly, and its being offered as a governmental service. First, it has become possible for competing companies to offer telecommunications services, at least long-distance ones. Second, newly invented technologies permitted two new options of service provision, namely using the existing system for new services (mainly fax and data transmission), and offering services without cable-neworking (mainly cellular telephones). Third, telecommunications has become a service that requires heavy investments on the supply side, and it has further turned into a crucial input on the demand side, whether in form of producer services, manufacturing or households. Fourth, and at a later stage, contemporary telecommunications has become by its very nature a global industry, so that foreign influences and investments were called for.

These new dimensions of telecommunications have brought about, within less than a decade, a structural change in the ownership and organization of telephone services, so that several modes have now become possible.

Table 1: *Various ownership options for telecommunications services*

PTT	Belgium†; Singapore†
Telecommunications administration	Germany
Government-owned company	France; Senegal; Zambia
Shared ownership by government and private capital	Israel; Hong Kong; Portugal; Nigeria; Argentina
Private domestic ownership without competition	Canada
Private foreign ownership without competition	Mexico; Hong Kong§
Competing private, domestic companies	USA§; UK§; Japan§; Australia§ New Zealand
Competing private, domestic and foreign companies	

§ For long-distance and international calls only.
† Change was expected in 1992.

These options run from the most restrictive and traditional form, namely PTTs, through various other forms of governmental ownership, to private ownership and competition. The technological sophistication of contemporary telecommunications systems and the complex interelationships among service agencies may sometimes introduce competition even if unwanted, through various kinds of bypassing, notably in international telecommunications. Thus, lines may be leased and then resold on a call-by-call basis, with several calls transmitted simultaneously through a single line, or calls may be placed to a domestic number which is connected to a computerized excahnge in another country offering cheaper rates.

The changes in ownership patterns are not necessarily related to a nation's economic development. Thus, France and Germany prefer more restrictive and public ownership modes, whereas Argentina and Mexico permitted private or foreign ownership, respectively. It may further be noted that Western European nations, with the exception of the U.K., prefer more conservative forms of organization, while developed countries in other parts of the world demonstrate more openness for private ownership and competition. The reorganization of telecommunications systems is still in process in many countries, so that it is difficult to present a definite international comparison at this point in time.

The various options in Table 1 reflect three aspects simultaneously: economic liberalization; functional deregulation; and power distribution. Economic liberalization, on its part, relates to three dimensions of ownership and organization of telecommunications services, namely the possible permission of competition, private ownership, and diversification of capital sources. In these three areas of economic liberalization, as well as in functional deregulation and power distribution, countries differ from each other. Functional deregulation, refers to the telecommunications services which companies may operate, and under which conditions. This applies to both the types of offered services (voice telephony, fax, data transmission, video services, cellular telephony), as well as to their geographical range (local, long-distance, international). Liberalization and deregulation usually go hand in hand, though a high level of change in one of the two does not automatically call for such a level in the other. Power distribution is also interwoven with liberalization and deregulation. The power of telecommunications provision may rest in government or in business. Telecommunications may thus be considered a public service or it could rather turn into a source for profitability.

The various ownership patterns presented in Table 1 emerged during the 1980s and they continue to undergo transformation in the 1990s. It is important to focus on leading industrialized countries in order to find out which countries led the change, why it affected the telecommunications industry on a global scale, and how did the various ownership patterns shape up. Given this emphasis the discussion will not go into all the country-specific details, and these may be found or referenced elsewhere (e.g., Snow, 1988).

The transformation in the ownership patterns of telecommunications services was led by the U.S., and this seems peculiar at a first glance, when it is recalled that the U.S. and Canada were historically different in that telecommunications services in these two countries were privately owned since their inception. Thus, any change in the American private system should not have affected other countries which traditionally have preferred a completely different ownership-path, namely PTTs. The global shaking of telecommunications systems ignited by changes in the U.S. is related to the increasing role of telecommunications in the emerging service economies, notably their international components, which on their part were related to the vast technological breakthroughs in telecommunications. Organizational changes in telecommunications in the U.S., the country which has led the evolution of service economies since the 1960s (Kellerman, 1985), have meant that the U.S. has become more competitive in its service economy, a challenge which could not be left unmet by other leading countries. Thus, the transformations of telecommunications organizational patterns are, at least in part, related to the evolution of the global economy. It is clear, therefore, that the U.S. leadership in telecommunications innovations has not been restricted to technology, but it applies to ownership and organization patterns, as well.

Invented in the U.S., the telephone received a similar attitude as its predecessor, the telegraph, namely that the Congress did not show an interest in buying the patent, so that it was left for private ownership and development. The development of the telephone system by the Bell Company, or A.T.&T., was aided by the expansion of the U.S. in the late nineteenth century, a factor which was well-perceived by Theodore Vail who headed the company at that time. When the Bell patent expired in 1893, the company was able to compete efficiently, especially once it adopted direct-dialing in the 1920s (Abler, 1991; Dordick, 1990).

In 1934 the Federal Communications Commission (FCC) was established and charged with the mandate to monitor and control the U.S. telecommunications system. The deregulation of the U.S. telecommunications system has gone hand in hand with technological developments which were challenged by customers and entrepreneurs. The 1950s witnessed the deregulation of private microwave transmission, known as the Above 890 decision, followed by the permission given in 1969 to MCI to establish commercial microwave transmission lines (Langdale, 1983; Phillips, 1991). Attempts by the federal government since the 1940s to challenge the monopoly of A.T.&T. on the grounds of excessive customer charges failed. The emergence of computers in the 1960s was accompanied by demands for computer communications presented by IBM. These were not met by A.T.&T., and eventually brought about, in 1982, the divestiture of A.T.&T. into seven regional Bell companies ("the Baby Bells" or RBOCs), in charge of local communications, and a national A.T.&T. dealing with long-distance and international calls in a competitive market. A.T.&T. was permitted in return to enter the computer business (Toffler, 1990).

Two countries were fast in coping with the American challenge of rapidly declining prices, coupled with higher qualities and a larger variety of telecommunications services. The U.K. and Japan had their systems privatized and opened to competition in 1984-85. There were beginnings for this process in the early 1980s, at least in the U.K., and there were several factors behind it. However, the very privatization and deregulation processes in these two countries, as well as their pace, were influenced, at least in part, by deregulation in the U.S., thus aiming at safeguarding their competitiveness in global financial markets, operating in London and Tokyo respectively. Another reason for the U.K. move was the British desire to serve as the international telecommunications hub for Western Europe (Langdale, 1989).

The British romance with privatization and deregulation may be traced back to July 21, 1980, when the then Secretary of State for Industry, Sir Keith Joseph, informed Parliament on the intention to liberalize telecommunications services (Beesley, 1992, p. 223). This policy declaration led a year later to the British Telecommunications Bill, which separated telecommunications from postal services, and which gave the Secretary of State the powers of licencing independent operators, which, on their part, could either use (lease) lines from British Telecom (BT) or could provide their own networks. In 1984 BT was privatized and in 1985 a second PTO (Public Telecommunications Operator), Mercury, started operation, thus creating a duopoly in the British system.

In Japan, the Diet (Parliamant) passed two laws in 1984, which privatized, as of 1985, Nippon Telegraph and and Telephone (NTT), and deregulated the provision of telecommunications services, so that three companies started competition (Akhavan- Majid, 1990). These steps resulted from pressures by the U.S. as well as by Japanese big business for liberalized markets. The Japanese system attempts to assure national economic growth and the provision of social needs, side by side with profitability of the carriers. Thus, external subsidies, rather than cross-subsidies are provided for desired yet unprofitable services (Glynn, 1992).

The French and German approaches to change in the telecommunications system have been completely different than the American, British, and Japanese ones. In France, the development of the telecommunications system until the early 1970s lagged considerably behind that of other industrialized countries. France was able to enjoy an annual economic growth rate of 6% from 1955 to 1970 concentrated in the primary and secondary sectors, and in specific tertiary activities concentrated in Paris (Saunders et al., 1983, pp. 87-88). In the mid-1970s the French government realized that further economic growth will occur in the tertiary sector and that regional dispersion of industrial production is desired, and that both trends are telecommunications-dependent (Nora and Minc, 1980). Thus, a major, and probably unprecedented, governmental effort was directed towards closing the telecommunications gap and towards the modernization of the system. Only as of the beginning of 1991, the PTT structure was reformed, so that France Telecom, a state-owned company was established (Staple, 1991). However, an advanced telecommunications system and an advanced service economy functioning in a highly regulated environment may call for low flexibility in the provision of sophisticated services (The Economist, 1991).

Germany too had its telecommunications system anchored in its PTT (Deutsches Bundespost, DBP) until 1989, when a separate monopolistic telecommunications administration was established (Schmidt, 1991). The high level of services and the special concessions granted to financial institutions delayed the pressures for reform presented by high-tech industries as well as by political parties until after liberalization was introduced in the U.K. The new system has left only 10% of the market open to competition, mainly leased lines and cellular telephony. Though the new organizational system has turned out to be complex, further reform has been slowed down by the integration of the old and lagging East German system into the German Telekom (Schmidt, 1991).

One cannot conclude this very partial review of major changes and trends in ownership patterns without mentioning the Mexican experience. In 1990 Telemex was privastized by selling the company to domestic and foreign investors (American and French). The deal called for generous tax conditions, assuming an annual increase of 12% in the number of exchange lines (The Economist, 1991; Staple, 1991).

International accounting for telecommunications

The currently prevailing international accounting settlements for telecommunications services have been challenged by the changes in both technology and ownership patterns, which both resulted in lower calling prices and in more varied calling options. The purpose of the international accounting system for telecommunications is to settle the

costs of provision of a service that originated in one country and termi-
nates in another. The transmission of calls from any telephone subscriber in one country until that country's international gateways,
whether through cables, radio stations or satellite antennas, is the sole
responsibility of the domestic carrier. International cables usually constitute joint enterprises, and satellite services are leased or bought from
Intelsat or other companies. However, the domestic company serving
the call sender has to pay for the transmission of the call from the gate-
way of the receiving country to the called subscriber. This portion of
international calls is the object of the international telecommunications
settlement arrangements.

Until 1944 one could recognize three systems of arrangements, representing three powers, namely the British Empire and later the
Commonwealth dominated by Cable & Wireless, the West European
nations functioning through their PTTs, and the U.S. where most of the
service was provided by A.T.&T. and regulated, as of 1934, by FCC.
The British attempted to divert as much traffic as possible through
London, the hub of their global system. The Europeans negotiated fixed
bilateral agreements, while the Americans, notably following the establishment of RCA as the radio service provision company after World
War I, attempted to minimize the costly use of the British system (Ergas
and Paterson, 1991).

The universal system which was developed in 1944, and which generally prevails until now, is based on a distance-based fixed charge, usually
per minute call, which is usually equally divided between the sending
and receiving parties. The charge may be defined in U.S. dollars or in
SDRs (Special Drawing Rights; a currency basket established by the
International Monetary Fund). This arrangement was successfully negotiated by A.T.&T. and FCC at the time for three reasons: the changing
geopolitical balance from a British dominance to an American one; the
nationalization of international telecommunications services in most
Commonwealth countries; and the modifications in radio- telephony
and the later construction of maritime cables required the use of the
shortest transmission routes (Ergas and Paterson, 1991).

The settlment proved itself as a convenient one until the telecommunications revolution as of the 1970s. It was simple, universal, permitted
a geographically-efficient service as well as investments in infrastructure,
and above all, it assumed equal players in the telecommunications game
(Ergas and Paterson, 1991). However, technological improvements and

later on the introduction of competition have lowered call tariffs in some countries, notably in the U.S., so that payment deficits have emerged.

The annual payment deficit of the U.S. reached $2.4 billion in 1989, growing at an annual rate of 22.6% (Stanley, 1991). The U.S. was in surplus with only 17 of its 188 correspondent countries in 1987, with a total net outflow of calls equivalent to almost one-third of the U.S. international traffic (Cheong and Mullins, 1991). The deficit was attributed to several factors: 1—significant disparities in prices and pricing policies for service in the United States as compared to service in other countries; 2—an international settlement procedure that is unresponsive to changing demand and supply conditions in the industry, which impedes remedial steps; 3—differences in regulatory environments, goals, and initiatives in the United States and other countries; and 4—differences in incentives and market conditions in which entities provide international communications service in different countries. Other factors, such as per capita income differences and fluctuating exchange rates, also contribute to the deficit (Stanley, 1991, p. 412).

The relative importance of each of these factors is still questionable. It was noted that the U.K. and Japan also adopted a competitive system, but they did not suffer deficits in the 1980s, whereas Australia and Canada which did not permit competition in the 1980s did present deficits. The U.S. deficit was, thus, attributed to prolonged surpluses in demand (Cheong and Mullins, 1991), maybe because of the American tendency to make more use of the telephone. Also, statistical regression analyses using U.S. and Australian payment balance data with other countries as dependent variables and GDP of those countries as independent ones proved useful ($R^2 = .55$) (Ergas and Paterson, 1991; Cheong and Mullins, 1991). Thus, while countries with an annual per capita GDP below $5,000 accounted in 1987 for only 18% of Australia's two-way traffic, they received 55% of outpayments. Such countries generated 39% of A.T.&T.'s traffic, but received 62% of the payments (Ergas and Paterson, 1991). However, there are wealthy countries with high calling tariffs, such as Germany, which ranks very high on the U.S. list of deficit countries.

The existing settlement system does not permit full use of the telecommunications infrastructure, and it punishes the cheaper, innovative and more efficient side. Furthermore, it encourages the development of high-demand routes at the expense of more modest ones. On the other hand, it controls the system in developing countries, so that surplus-demand for international telecommunications is regulated by high prices, and international telecommunications also becomes a source for foreign exchange for them (Ergas and Paterson, 1991). Current pressures by countries which introduced competiton will probably bring about some change which will reflect declining costs as well as the emergence of competitive markets viewing the provision of telecommunications services as a business rather than a public good. Thus, the ITU International Telegraph and Telephone Consultive Committee (CCITT) which handles international accounting settlements, has begun consultations in this regard, though no decisions are expected before 1993 (Staple, 1991).

International telecommunications and other international movements

We identified some connection between the organizational patterns of telecommunications which are formally autonomous, but which are influenced by transitions in other countries, on the one hand, and international accounting settlements, on the other. The international traffic of information is further dependent, however, on other international movements to and from each country, namely on the movements of people, commodities, and capital. This dependency may be tested for three aspects: (1) annual growth rates in traffic at large; (2) geographical variations in traffic volumes by destination countries in any given year; and (3) variations along time in traffic to specific countries. Detailed longitudinal studies using this international movement model have been pursued for the U.S. (Kellerman, 1992a; 1992b), and for Israel (Kellerman and Cohen, 1992). Partial examinations were conducted for several other countries (Kellerman, 1990), for The Netherlands (Rietveld and Janssen, 1990), and were proposed for Portugal (Gaspar and Jensen-Butler, 1990).

The average annual growth rate for American international telecommunications 1962-1989 was 25.6%. Regressing the annual growth rates 1962-1988 against the growth rates of the two-way movements of capital, people, and commodities yielded low results ($R^2=.32$). The best results were received for the period 1965- 1979 ($R^2=.76$). This finding was interpreted as reflecting a technological factor. The period before 1965 (when satellites were introduced) was typified by low supply, whereas the period 1965-1979 was typified by growth in both supply and demand, through the introduction of new transmission and dialing technologies, resulting in lower calling prices and improved service qualities. In the 1980s supply exceeded demand again, especially as of the mid-1980s, when it was estimated that each of the U.S. major carrier had the capacity to transmit the whole U.S. demand for international services (Staple and Mullins, 1989).

The most important variable in the explanation of growth was foreign visitors to the U.S., representing a blend of social and economic ties with the U.S. For Israel, annual growth rates for the period 1952=1988 were analyzed, with the two-way movements of people and commodities serving as independent variables. The best explanation was achieved for the period 1975-1987, when exports and imports were lagged two years after telecommunications ($R^2=.88$). Here too the period of most intensive technological improvement in telecommunications infrastructure was best explained by the model.

Variations in traffic volumes to most frequently called countries in each year separately were also well explained by the international movement model. In the U.S. the levels of explanations were higher than $R^2=.96$ for every year 1961-1989. The most important variable was outgoing tourism from the U.S., and the general order of explanation by variables in descending order was people, capital, and commodities. This attests once again to the impact of households, or social calls, which stem form visits to foreign countries, blended with the impact of business visits. The increasing importance of global capital markets is expressed in the more important role of capital exchanges compared to those of commodities (Kellerman, 1992a; 1992b). Similar analyses for Israel, yielded high results as of 1957, though here exports were generally found to be the crucial explanatory variable (Kellerman and Cohen, 1992). In The Netherlands a similarly high explanation by exports was found for 1983 (Rietveld and Janssen, 1990). In partial analyses for 1985 and 1986 for France, West Germany, Italy, Netherlands, Switzerland, and the U.K. high results were obtained for all countries except for Germany, given the unique nature of the geographical distribution of its international telephone calls. In all countries, except for the U.K., it was for exports or imports to serve as the most important variable, rather than tourism (Kellerman, 1990). The wide use of the telephone in the U.S. and its being an immigration country may explain the predominance of social variables there. British data, on the other hand, require further analysis before decisive conclusions can be made.

The use of the international movement model for explanations of trends in the changing number of calls to specific countries has proven more doubtful. Results were mixed in both the U.S. and Israel, namely the obtained levels of explanation were different from country to country, as well as the leading variable, reflecting the changing nature of relations with foreign countries. The mean R^2 coefficient for analyses of eleven countries most frequently called from the U.S. over the years was 0.74. The coefficients were high for France and Italy where the leading variable was outgoing tourism to these two popular countries. They were further high for Switzerland with American financial investments as the leading variable, or for Israel with exports leading. On the other hand, the explanation was low for the U.K. with its complex ties with the U.S., as well as for Venezuela (Kellerman, 1992b).

For Israel similar trends could be observed. Thus, the leading variable for calls to Germany for the period 1951-1963 was tourism from there, and low explanatory results were obtained for the U.K., France, Netherlands, and Italy. For the period 1973-1988 it was for exports and imports to provide the best explanation for the annual variation of calls to Switzerland, while the size of the Jewish community led the explanations for the U.S. and France.

Conclusion

We showed three dimensions of autonomy and interdependence of telecommunications at the international level: ownnership patterns for telecommunications services; accounting settlements; and interrelationships with other international exchanges. These three dimensions of autonomy and interdependence of international telecommunications presented here attempted to show that whereas national telecommunications systems are still formally autonomous, international interdependencies in them are growing. It was argued that technological improvements increased the dependence of international telecommunications on other international movements. As such, international telecommunications have turned into an indispensable component of the emerging global economy and community. However, the interwoven movements of information, people, commodities, and capital have brough about increasing inward pressures in many countries towards the establishment of more flexible, competitive and business-oriented international telecommunications systems and services. As more and more countries have adopted these changes, international calls have been repeatedly made to reform the existing accounting settlement procedures.

Table 1 demonstrated that the transitions in ownership patterns are still short of the most sweeping change, namely permitting foreign telephone companies to compete with domestic ones. Such competitive regimes are common in the international airline industry. One should bear in mind, however, some basic differences between the two services. First, buying an airline ticket commits the passenger to a single use of that airline's service, whereas shopping around for each telephone call could cancel out the advantage of telecommunications as an instant service. Second, airlines are considered a form of transportation, while telecommunications is looked upon as a utility, and thus as a basic element for national survival. However, given the recent histories of the airline and telecommunications industries, it might well be that arrangements will be made for foreign competition in international calls, whereas domestic calling will be provided by domestic carriers only, with or without competition, and with or without limited ownership of foreign capital.

References

Abler, R.F. (1991), "Hardware, software, and brainware: mapping and understanding telecommunications technologies", in Brunn, S.D. and Leinbach, T.R. (eds.), *Collapsing Space and Time: Geographic Aspects of Communication and Information*. London: Harper Collins Academic, pp. 31-48.

Akhavan-Majid, R. (1990), "Telecommunications policymaking in Japan: the 1980s and beyond", *Telecommunications Policy* 14, 159- 168.

Beesley, M.E. (1992), *Privatization, Regulation and Deregulation*. London: Routledge.

Cheong, K. and Mullins, M. (1991), "International telephone service imbalances: accounting rates and regulatory policy", *Telecommunications Policy* 15, 107-118.

Dordick, H.S. (1990), "The origins of universal service: history as a determinant of telecommunications policy", *Telecommunications Policy* 14, 223-231.

The Economist (1991), October, 5.

Ergas, H. and Paterson, P. (1991), "International telecommunications settlement arrangements: an unsustainable inheritance?", *Telecommunications Policy* 15, 29-48.

Gaspar, J. and Jensen-Butler, C. (1990), "Telecommunications and the location of Portugal in global information space", in Bakis, H. (ed.), *Communications and Territories*. Paris: La Documentation Francaise, pp. 165-176.

Glynn, S. (1992), "Japan's success in telecommunications regulation: a unique regulatory mix", *Telecommunications Policy* 16, 5-12.

Kellerman, A. (1985), "The evolution of service economies: a geographical perspective", *The Professional Geographer* 37, 133- 143.

Kellerman, A. (1990), "International telecommunications around the world: a flow analysis", *Telecommunications Policy* 14, 461- 475.

Kellerman, A. (1992a), U.S. International Telecommunications 1961-1989: Temporal and Spatial Aspects by Various Modes of Measurement. International Center for Telecommunications Management (ICTM) Research Paper 8. Omaha: University of Nebraska.

Kellerman, A. (1992b), "U.S. international telecommunications 1961-1988: an international movement model", *Telecommunications Policy* 16 (forthcoming).

Kellerman, A. and Cohen, A. (1992), "International telecommunications as international movement: the case of Israel, 1951-1988", *Telecommunications Policy* 16, 156-166.

Langdale, J.V. (1983), "Competition in the United States' long- distance telecommunications industry", *Regional Studies* 17, 393- 409.

Langdale, J.V. (1989), "The geography of international business telecommunications: the role of leased networks", *Annals of the Association of American Geographers* 79, 501-522.

Nora, S. and Minc, a. (1980), *The Computerization of Society.* Cambridge, MA: MIT Press.

Phillips, A. (1991), "Changing markets and institutional inertia: a review of U.S. telecommunications policy", *Telecommunications Policy* 15, 49-61.

Rietveld, P. and Janssen, L. (1990), "Telephone calls and spatial interactions: the case of the Netherlands", *Netcom* 4, 132-144.

Robinson, P. (1991), "The international dimension of telecommunications policy issues", *Telecommunications Policy* 15, 95-100.

Saunders, R.J., Warford, J.J., and Wellenius, B. (1983), *Telecommunications and Economic Development.* Baltimore: The Johns Hopkins University Press.

Schmidt, S.K. (1991), "Taking the long road to liberalization: telecommunications reform in the Federal Republic of Germany", *Telecommunications Policy* 15, 209-222.

Snow M.S. (1988), "Telecommunications literature: a critical review of the economic, technological and public policy issues", *Telecommunications Policy* 12, 153-183.

Stanley, K.B. (1991), "Balance of payments, deficits, and subsidies in international communications services: a new challenge to regulation", *Administrative Law Review* 43, 411-438.

Staple, G.C. (ed.), (1991), *The Global Telecommunications Traffic Report - 1991.* London: International Institute of Communications.

Staple, G.C. and Mullins, M. (1989a), "Telecom traffic statistics-MiTT matter: improving economic forecasting and regulatory policy", *Telecommunications Policy* 13, 105-128.

Toffler, A. (1990), *Power Shift.* New York: Bantam Books.

3 Exploring the Potential of Telecommunications: Perspectives from the European Periphery

Seamus Grimes

Exploitation of new information and communications technologies are at the heart of contemporary economic restructuring, which has been conceptualised in terms of a new model of flexible specialisation. There is, however, considerable disagreement about the nature of these changes, and while the analysis of spatial outcomes to date has been inconclusive, some authors are predicting increased agglomeration of economic activities in urban areas, partcularly in the context of the European single market. Analysis of telecommunications usage in Ireland, one of Europe's most peripheral regions, reveals considerable concentration in the most urbanised East region, despite EC programmes to diffuse the new technology into more peripheral areas.

Exploring the potential of telecommunications: perspectives from the European periphery

This paper explores how policy makers can help peripheral regions exploit the potential for economic development arising from the new information and communication technologies. In order to do this, the role of these technologies in the current phase of economic restructuring is examined. Insights are sought from the current debate about flexible specialisation, which some authors believe presents optimistic prospects for a new phase in regional development. Experience from successful regions, where flexible specialisation is characterised by a networking culture among small and medium sized enterprises, may present a framework for a successful strategy for promoting economic development in peripheral regions. The case of Ireland is examined in some detail, to see how the emerging pattern of telecommunications usage, partcularly in relation to telematics, compares with European Commission and national government policy objectives in this area.

Flexible specialisation theory

One of the most interesting conceptualisations of contemporary economic restructuring is the work of Piore and Sabel (1983, 1984), which presents a model of flexible production or specialisation emerging from the Fordist period of mass production. Hirst and Zeitlin (1989) point to two converging developments underlying this new model; first, interdependent networks of small and medium sized enterprises (SMEs) subcontracting to one another and sharing common services within industrial districts; and second, large multinational companies (MNCs) decentralising into lower federations of operating units and asociated subcontractors in search of more specialised products and more flexible production methods. The enabling technologies which are facilitating this economic restructuring are transport and communication, production and process organisation, with information technology (IT) playing a pivotal role. Flexible specialisation theorists point to regions such as Emilia Romagna and Baden-Wurrtemberg as examples of what is referred to as the 'post-Fordist' model of development.

It should be noted at the outset that this conceptualisation has been heavily criticised on many counts, including its tendency to make broad generalisations from very specific circumstances in particular regions. Amin and Robins (1991) have led a sustained attack on this theory for lacking a political economy perspective and thus underestimating the effects of globalisation and the control by MNCs of economic decision-making. They are adamant that evidence of fragmentation in production units must not be interpreted as fragmentation of control, and they suggest that from a spatial perspective, the periphery still resembles the so-called old Fordist branch plant economy. They question whether the local economy can be regarded as a significant cátegory any longer, since in their view it can only be seen as a node within a global economic network. As with many such discussions in the social sciences, however, varying viewpoints tend to be tinged somewhat by ideological considerations and some of the fundamental philosophical aspects have been referred to in a recent exchange (Lovering, 1991). This debate, however, provides a very useful framework for investigating the potential for exploiting the new technologies in peripheral regions.

Other geographers have been much less critical of the 'post Fordist' model of flexible specialisation and have suggested that both the decline of vertically-integrated corportate structures and the premium being attached to networks of firms could provide the basis for a new era in regional development (Gillespie and Goddard, 1990). This new model of development is associated with small units of production and services, with each being information-intensive both internally and also in relation to external networks (Sweeney, 1987). Among the possible outcomes of this type of development are greater possibilities for indigenous development and stronger horizontal integration between firms within a region. While Amin and Robins (1991) do not dispute these possible outcomes, they stress the need for policies which would promote cooperation and trust between firms and between capital and labour, in order to bring them about.

Among the characteristic features of flexible specialisation is the emphasis placed on knowledge based skills and the application of communication technologies, increasing the ability of firms to respond to emerging sophisticated affluent markets with their frequent shifts in consumer tastes (Sweeney, 1987). Referring to the Third Italy, where much of the empirical evidence for these new patterns is found, Amin (1989) wonders whether this flexibility is more to do with an ability to survive. He suggests that other factors, such as the exploitation of family labour, tax evasion and low overhead costs, are underlying the capacity to respond to new market signals.

Amin and Robins (1991) find the general theory of post Fordist industrial spaces to be unacceptable, since it is inclined to idealise flexible specialisation and to demonise Fordism and mass production. They would suggest that capitalist industry has always combined flexibility with inflexibility and that rather than witnessing a simple trend towards greater flexibility, there are new permutations of each. They also suggest that the dynamics of the restructuring process of the current period are both contradictory and divergent, with powerful countervailing and competing tendencies towards transnational networks on the one hand, and tendencies towards local agglomeration in industrial districts on the other. Amin and Robins (1991) question whether fragmentation and local agglomeration is an inexorable trend, particularly if it involves greater product differentiation rather than the breakup of mass markets.

Malecki's (1991) analysis of the implications of technological change on the economic development of peripheral regions makes grim reading, since he concludes that the process of technological innovation, which is the essence of economic development, is being centralised in urban agglomerations to a greater extent than for some time. In his view the synergy of amenities, accessibility and agglomeration factors found in large urban regions cannot fully be substituted in small regions, and despite the numerous policy efforts to disperse innovative technology activities, they display a persistent tendency towards agglomeration. One of the major factors which works against peripheral areas is the attraction of urban agglomerations to professional people and especially to dual-career couples. So, while Malecki (1991) sees the emergence of flexible production and inter-firm linkages as significantly changing the way in which economic activity takes place, the persistent geographical outcome is for economic activities to agglomerate in large urban regions.

Much of the conceptualisation of contemporary economic change focusses primarily on manufacturing activity and the role of the services sector, which is the main source of employment growth in recent times, tends to be neglected. The work of Illeris (1989) in a European context, therefore, is important in restoring some balance, but its conclusions for the future of peripheral regions, while being somewhat inconclusive, are by no means optimistic. His findings suggest increasing probability for regional concentration of service activities in Europe and among the factors contributing to this pattern are the increased significance of qualified labour, privatisation and deregulation. Illeris (1989) holds out some hope for regional development policy supporting service activities in less favoured regions (LFRs). Howells (1988) also concludes that the major structural, organisational and technological trends in the European Community (EC) services will have a centralising effect, although there are few constraints for dispersal at the sub-regional level. So, despite the new developments in information and communication technologies (ICTs) which could allow new forms of service organisation that are potentially not constrained by distance, in reality the various constraints appear to be restricting the spread and indigenous development of technological innovations in services.

Information technology

Information and communication technology, sometimes referred to as the 'permissive technology', is at the heart of contemporary economic restructuring, facilitating change in the nature and organisation of economic activity. IT is the key element in the transition from the industrial to what is termed the 'information economy', bringing new dimensions to innovation and opportunities for new economic activities.

In the new economic circumstances, information is the strategic resource, which when linked with the potential of computer networks or 'telematics', has the potential to transform economic activity (Arnbak, 1990). Among the applications of IT are Just-in-Time (JIT) organisation of goods from supplier' warehouses to buyers and consumers and

Electronic Data Interchange (EDI) or 'paperless trading'. The new ICTs facilitate the exploitation of economies of scope as opposed to economies of scale, allowing production of different designs at the same cost as identical products under mass production (Gillespie et al., 1989). The new technologies also allow for increasing organisational flexibility with different functions being optimally located and effective control being maintained at a central location.

The new ICTs are for the most part dominated by large organisations, particularly multinational companies, and are found predominantly in urban core areas. Yet it has been claimed that IT will bring about a fundamental transformation of spatial relationships between core and periphery at both national and international scales (Gillespie et al.,1989). This new flexibility presents both opportunities and threats for the periphery and for small firms. The domination of the new ICTs by multinationals presents the danger of 'telecolonialism', whereby peripheral areas could be relegated to a subordinate niche role, such as the location for 'back office' activities of insurance companies, a trend which has already begun in Ireland and elsewhere (Gillespie et al, 1989; Grimes, 1992c). Additional dangers include the the possibility of supplier companies for MNCs being 'locked into' their computer mediated control, when they insist on the use of applications like EDI and JIT. A greater danger is that small firms in the periphery could be 'locked out' of such markets, by being denied access to the propietory networks of MNCs (Gillespie and Goddard, 1990). It would appear to be more likely that larger, more competitive operators will capture the market potential of the periphery, than for small firms in the periphery to gain market share in core areas.

Networking SMEs

Increasing attention is being given by organisation theorists, geographers and regional economists to the concept of developing a networking culture among small and medium sized companies in peripheral regions (Johannisson, 1987; Camagni, 1991). Networking is an important form of flexible organisation which can serve the need for balance between conditions of local production and international competition. SMEs can benefit from competence embedded in other firms and information channels can be created for inter-firm cooperation in areas such as R+D and marketing, thereby reducing transaction costs. Through networks, costs and risks are spread between members, allowing for strong specialisation and innovativeness within each of the small enterprises, and leaving room for a high degree of flexibility in the event of required changes in production. Such regional and national networks can create the basis of competitive advantage, providing SMEs with economies of scale and strength of numbers to enable them compete in world markets.

Information flow has been identified as a major problem affecting SMEs in the periphery and acting as a major barrier to the diffusion of the new ICTs (Sweeney, 1987). This issue was identified in the Swedish DEMOTEL project, whose objective was to improve buyer-supplier interaction, and it was clear that it was poorly understood by policy makers (Carlson, 1990). Peripheral regions suffer from information impoverishment, with plants having few useful technical contacts locally. It is necessary, therefore, to improve the stock of knowledge of local entrepreneurs, and to increase the flow of information relating to new technological developments, techniques and markets. A priority here is the need to increase the effectiveness of decision-making by reducing the cycle time between the demand and supply of information required for decision-making. Malecki's (1991) view is that while IT may be able to substitute for the absence of intensified levels of personal contacts which characterise the more creative regions, it is not clear that the sorts of relatively routine business information needed by small firms can be provided outside the infrastructure of core regions. It would appear that few actors in regional development have the skills or expertise to educate the market about telecommunications applications, not to mention creating a networking culture (Morgan, 1990).

There is considerable Nordic experience, however, in fostering networks among small firms, which provides useful recommendations for regional policy. Networks of competence have been created sharing specialised skills and helping small companies face the challenge of the deepening integration of their small open economies. Industrial markets are increasingly characterised by a complex set of linkages reflecting mutual interdependencies between firms. These growing interdependencies, whereby each member of a network depends on the performance of other firms results from the need to coordinate JIT deliveries. Examples in the Nordic countries are to be found of cooperative agreements between firms for joint research institutes, data banks and marketing organisations (Christensen et al, 1990). Swedish researchers also stress the complementarity and trust that develops between firms through such networks, despite the normal power relations. Over time solidarity is increased, with innovations resulting from interaction based on the free flow of information. On-line computer systems connecting firms are becoming more common, facilitating such interaction. The state has a key role to play as a catalyst in developing SME networks, and a networking grant may be necessary because of the considerable time period necessary to build up networks.

While some authors show considerable enthusiasm for prospects which they see arising from networking SMEs, other researchers have introduced a cautionary note to the discussion. Wiberg (1989), examining the Swedish experience, is positive about cooperation between small plants who are affected by high costs, low competitiveness and low levels of management competence. He wonders, however, whether a regional organisation of small plants in sparsely populated areas can reach acceptable profitability or efficiency. In Denmark, one of the many technological regional development programmes, supported by the European Regional Development Fund, while proving to be an important support for SMEs in relation to the diffusion of IT, did not succeed in creating business networks, new products or new markets (Cronberg et al, 1991). Also in the Northern region of England, while survey work revealed a much greater appreciation in the SME sector of the potential of telecommunications in 1988 compared with 1985, there was much more limited success with attempts to establish collaborative networking between independent firms (Gillespie and Goddard, 1990). Part of the difficulty lay in devising inter-organisational networks that met the potential users' real, rather than hypothetical needs.

Ireland

Having outlined some of the current thinking in relation to economic restructuring and the prospects for peripheral regions, attention is now turned to the case of Ireland, one of the most peripheral regions in the European Community. Ireland's development model in recent decades has been strongly influenced by an industrial policy with an emphasis on attracting inward investment. Being one of the smallest and most open economies in Europe, Ireland is strongly characterised by dualism, with a branch plant economy consisting of major overseas investment in high technology sectors such as electronics and pharmaceuticals, and a rather weak indigenous sector predominantly concentrated in agriculture and food processing activities (Grimes, 1992a). Overseas industries account for 75% of manufactured exports and employ 41.3% of the workforce in manufacturing. The small indigenous sector accounts for only 5% of manufactured exports and employ 27.5% of industrial workers (Grimes, 1992b). With only 150 Irish companies having a turnover of IR£5m, the primary focus of industrial policy is to build indigenous companies of sufficient quality, scale and strength to win and sustain profitable positions in international markets (Review of Industrial Performance, 1990).

As one of the European Community's most peripheral regions, Ireland is now facing the daunting prospects of trading and competing within the single market. The process of European Monetary Union is also quite advanced which will place considerable pressure on Ireland's economy to fall in line with the wealthier European regions. At the European level, policy making is mainly focussed on European integration, and for example, in telecommunications policy, the emphasis is on liberalisation and deregulation in order to reduce the cost of interaction and to counter market fragmentation. Under EC regulations, all Community telecommunications authorities must face open competition for the provision of advanced services outside telephony, and while some benefits can be expected from competition, there are strong fears that private sector companies may ignore the least attractive sections of the marketplace, such as the rural periphery (Morgan, 1990). At the same time European policy makers, and indeed the poorer regions of Europe are very concerned about the strong likelihood of a trend towards increased concentration of investment in the core regions resulting from these policy measures. It is in this context that the prospects for peripheral regions like Ireland in the European single market must be assessed. Attempts are being made at the EC level to bring about greater social and economic cohesion between Europe's different regions, but the rate of convergence during the past twenty years or so has been very disappointing (Kennedy, 1992).

The strategic role of telecommunications in economic development has been given considerable recognition by policy makers in Ireland. Both the Industrial Development Authority and Telecom Eireann (the national telecommunications authority) have ensured that more than IRÎ1bn was invested in telecommunications infrastructure during the early 1980s. Structural Funds from Europe have played an important role in this investment, but it has also involved Telecom Eireann becoming significantly indebted. As a result of this investment Ireland is now equipped with one of the most advanced networks in Europe, with the level of digitalisiation being second only to France (Grimes, 1992c). After the completion of the Channel Tunnel, Ireland will be significantly disadvantaged in terms of its distance from European markets, and policy makers are accutely aware of the need to obtain as much competitive advantage as possible from the use of advanced telecommunications services. Modernising the telecommunications network was a major priority in order to make Ireland an attractive location for inward investment; helping indigenous companies to become more competitive was also important but appears to be a secondary policy consideration.

Because of the new competitive environment emerging in the telecommunications sector in Europe, access to data on the evolving pattern of telecommunications usage is very restricted, and little or no empirical analysis of this pattern has been carried out. Yet it is possible to give a brief outline of the main developments. The philosophy of Telecom Eireann is to provide advanced services according to the level of demand and thus Ireland is not to the fore in relation to ISDN. The small size of the market results in a slow growth rate for advanced services, and much of the network company's attention to date has been geared towards the internal networking needs of its larger customers, who are mainly overseas and Irish companies employing 500 or more people, and having a number of sites either within the country or internationally, and also government departments and the larger semi-state utilities.

One of the most significant private networks to be established in recent years was the Government Telecommunications Network (GTN), which links government offices nationwide (Grimes, 1992c) . The GTN is effectively an important infrastructural link between the centre of the state in Dublin and fifteen provincial centres in the western periphery. The driving force behind the state's significant investment in this network is a programme for decentralising government offices to counteract the inordinate concentration of the services sector in the main metropolitan centre. In 1991 the East region's share of the national service sector was 50%, although it contained only 38% of the country's population. Dublin and the East region have attracted an increasing share of the national workforce, and especially of the better paid professional, administrative and technical jobs. It has been shown that even large urban centres outside Dublin are perceived by the private sector as offering relatively poor environments for new service firms (Bannon and Ward, 1985). While the number of jobs which have been relocated as a result of the public service decentralisation programme has been quite modest to date, the programme is continuing, and even modest contributions can play a significant role in provincial centres. A more pertinent question relates to the long term effects on regional autonomy of this type of 'electronic' decentralisation, if it does not involve the dispersal of decision-making processes (Qvortrup, 1989).

As in other advanced economies one of the biggest users of telecommunications infrastructure in Ireland is the services sector, and particularly financial insititutions. While there is likely to be some negative consequences of increasing usage of IT by these institutions for peripheral regions within the country, such as the closure of rural branch offices, Ireland has been exploiting its modernised telecomunications infrastructure very effectively within an international context. One of the biggest government initiatives in this respect has been the International Financial Services Centre, known as the 'Customs House Dock Development' in Dublin. This centre is a special tax zone with 10% corporation tax, which is aimed at attracting major international financial institutions who will engage in internationally traded financial services. Already the centre has developed a specialisation in captive insurance, whereby multinational companies set up a subsidiary to look after their own internal insurance requirements. Apart from low corporation tax and considerably lower costs relative to London, a plentiful supply of well trained graduates together with sophisticated telecommunications infrastructure have been important selling points.

While there is only a small number of Irish-owned companies exploiting advanced telecommunications services from a peripheral location and competing effectively in international markets, the trend in recent years has been for large overseas companies to locate back office operations in relatively remote locations in Ireland. A number of American insurance companies have transferred some of their data processing operations to small centres along the western periphery of Ireland. This trend towards off-shore software and data processing is substantially driven by growing staff shortages, and the increasing availability of trained computer staff in Ireland is a big attraction. Differences in time zones allow insurance companies based in the United States to add five hours to their working day, by using leased lines from their operations in Ireland during their mainframe downtime period. The cost factor is also very important and US companies obtain savings of up to 25% on their equivalent costs in the home market. The main disadvantage with this type of development is the generally low level of skills involved and the fact that low wage regions in the Carribean and the Middle East are likely to provide greater savings for such operations.

The regional pattern

Table 1 gives some indication of the evolving pattern of telecommunications usage in Ireland in recent years. It shows a regional breakdown of both analogue and digital leased lines and also a breakdown of Eirpac connections, which is the public packet-switched data network, allowing access to global databases and other transaction services such as EDI. The charges for Eirpac, which were reduced recently by 40% are among the lowest in the EC for this type of sophisticated service, and the number of customers increased during the past year by 35%, while usage of the service increased by 45% (Euristix, 1991). Another important development in telecommunications was the launching in 1990 of Dassnet, a digital and special services network, a Telecom Eireann managed network of leased digital circuits. This network has many of the promises of ISDN, pulling both voice and data services onto common lines. Few other countries have managed networks like Dassnet, and with recent reductions in tariff structures the digital charges will work out cheaper in some cases for more distant connections than the old analogue circuits. Among the major users of the packet-switched network is the Government Telecommunications Network, the National Lottery and the Electricity Supply Board. The network company has been surprised by the level of interest in Dassnet from outside the major urban centres. However, the demand for Dassnet has been slower than projected and its digital circuits remain outnumbered ten to one by private analogue connections.

As Table 1 shows Eirpac currently has 424 leased line and 2,304 dialup users. Irish companies with either parents or subsidiaries overseas, often cannot justify the cost of a dedicated leased line. Eirpac provides a more general solution by giving them the necessary connectivity together with access to other services, such as electronic mail. Eirpac is an implementation of a genuine global communications standard known as X.25, which consists of a number of nodes interconnected by high speed digital links. Users connect to their nearest node via a leased line or a dial-up connection. Once connected to a node, a user can talk to any other computer on the network or indeed to a computer on any X.25 network worlwide.

As in other countries the regional pattern of telecommunications within Ireland reveals a considerably concentrated structure both spatially and within large organisations. Clearly this pattern reflects the Irish urban network with a significant concentration in the East region, containing the principal metropolitan area of Dublin. Economic development within Ireland is highly concentrated, with the East region accounting for almost 40% of the population, 40% of Gross Regional Product and 34% of expenditure on R+D (Eolas, 1990). It is not sur-

Table 1 *Regional pattern of telecommunications usage 1989/92*

		Leased Lines				
Region		**Ana-logue**	**%**	**Digital**	**%**	**% of Pop-ulation**
East	'89	5938	(63.8)	78	(77.2)	
	'92	9384	(58.2)	855	(73.7)	38.3
Midwest	'89	621	(6.7)	1	(1.0)	
	'92	1783	(9.9)	76	(6.5)	8.8
South west	'89	425	(4.6)	3	(3.0)	
	'92	1766	(9.9)	78	(6.7)	15.1
South east	'89	790	(8.5)	3	(3.0)	
	'92	1147	(6.4)	32	(2.7)	10.8
West	'89	604	(6.5)	12	(11.8)	
	'92	1084	(6.0)	52	(4.5)	8.2
North east	'89	283	(3.0)			
	'92	1048	(5.8)	25	(2.1)	5.5
North west	'89	318	(3.4)	1	(1.0)	
	'92	902	(5.0)	23	(2.0)	7.2
Midlands	'89	318	(3.4)	3	(3.0)	
	'92	718	(4.0)	18	(1.5)	5.9
Totals	*'89*	*9297*	*(100.0)*	*101*	*(100.0)*	*100.0*
	'92	*17832*	*(100.0)*	*1159*	*(100.0)*	

prising, therefore, to find that 63.8% of all analogue leased lines in 1989 were in the East region, but the proportion had dropped to 58.2% only three years later. The East region accounted for a lower, though significant proportion of Eirpac connections, and while dial-up connections have become more dispersed outside the metropolitan core in recent years, X.25 and X.28 connections have become more concentrated. The lower concentration of Eirpac connections reflects, to some extent, the considerable spread of overseas branch plants throughout the country, particularly in the Midwest, West and Southwest regions.

Since the use of information technology in Ireland is still concentrated in large organisations, the challenge remains to diffuse this technology away from the main urban centres and down to small and medium sized enterprises. The most important EC initiative to date to bring this about has been the STAR programme (Special Telecommunications for the Advancement of Regions). The jointly funded EC/Irish government 100m Ecu programme was targetted at the particular development needs of advanced services. The programme assisted Telecom Eireann

Table 1 *Regional pattern of telecommunications usage 1989/92 (Cont'd)*

Region		X.25	%	Direct X.28	%	Dial-up X.28	%
East	89	129	(58.6)	25	(86.2)	888	(50.0)
	92	293	(69.1)	22	(88.0)	1042	(45.1)
Mid-west	89	34	(15.4)			243	(13.6)
	92	45	(10.6)			239	(10.3)
South-west	89	30	(13.6)	1	(3.4)	179	(10.0)
	92	40	(9.4)			267	(11.5)
South-east	89	6	(2.7)			100	(5.6)
	92	8	(1.9)			195	(8.4)
West	89	13	(5.9)	2	(6.9)	125	(7.0)
	92	18	(4.2)			175	(7.6)
North-east	89			1	(3.5)	74	(4.1)
	92	9	(2.1)	2	(8.0)	162	(7.0)
North-west	89	3	(1.4)			93	(5.2)
	92	8	(1.9)	1	(4.0)	109	(4.7)
Mid-lands	89	5	(2.3)			80	(4.5)
	92	3	(0.7)			119	(5.1)
Totals	*89*	*220*	*(100.0)*	*29*	*(100.0)*	*1782*	*(100.0)*
	92	*424*	*(100.0)*	*25*	*(100.0)*	*2308*	*(100.0)*

Source: Telecom Eireann

in meeting the challenge of continued network development, particualrly in areas like fibre-optic cabling and cellular radio. SMEs were the main target population of the programme, since such firms were unlikely to benefit from IT, if left to their own devices.

A major criticism of the STAR programme in Ireland was the bias towards infrastructure, which accounted for 80% of expenditure (Morgan, 1990). There has been little critical assessment of the STAR programme to date, although a further extension of the applications side of the programme, TELEMATIQUE, has been launched. One of the main dangers of the STAR approach, which involves speeding up the integration of Less Favoured Areas (LFAs) into telecommunications networks, is the easier access it could provide for external economic interests to the periphery, and who would have a competitive advantage over local interests (Gillespie and Robins, 1989). Under the STAR programme, however, a number of IT centres were established along the more peripheral western half of the country with the precise objective of diffusing IT skills to SMEs. While much of the EC literature dealing with IT programmes for less favoured areas places great emphasis on the goal of creating SME networks, it would appear that little strategic thought or planning has gone into the ways and means by which this might be achieved. The critical factor, of course, is to convince local entrepreneurs of the benefits of such networks.

Conclusion

The debate which has grown up around flexible specialisation theory as a coherent conceptualisation of contemporary economic restructuring provides a useful framework for considering the prospects of exploiting new information and communication technologies in peripheral regions. Applications of these technologies by means of computer networks provide the basis for benefiting from economies of scope and responding rapidly to market changes. While there is little dispute about the significance of these changes, there is considerable difference of opinion about how they will impact on the relationships between cores and peripheries. Multinational companies are the dominant actors in the emerging geography of computer networks and suppliers to these companies, partcularly if they are located in the periphery, could be either locked into or locked out of such private networks. Nevertheless, flexible specialisation theorists hold out considerable prospects for replicating a new model of development based on networking interdependent SMEs, and allowing economies of scale through sharing skills and services.

A major criticism of flexible specialisation theory is its tendency to generalise from particular regions with specific cultural and historical circumstances. It is too early to suggest the extent to which the new information and communication technologies can be used as a basis for enabling more peripheral regions to participate in the emerging model of flixible production. Generally, much of the literature dealing with the spatial dimension of economic restructuring is quite pessimistic about remotely located regions and emphasises the continuing concentration of economic activity in urban agglomerations. Analysis of the services sector, which traditionally has been more concentrated in core areas, is also rather gloomy about prospects for the periphery, stressing the impact of the professional workforce on trends towards agglomeration. Nevertheless research to date is somewhat inconclusive, and despite the tendency for many authors to lean towards a fatalistic determinism about future location patterns, exploitation of the new technologies provides considerable scope for policy makers to influence these patterns.

The emerging pattern of telecommunications usage in Ireland provides a useful case study of the empirical reality in one of Europe's most peripheral regions. Industrial policy to date has placed considerable emphasis on exploiting telecommunications for promoting economic development. The evolving pattern of usage in Ireland, however, must be analysed in the context of the larger picture of European telecommunications policy, with European integration and the functioning of the single market being the main focus of attention. The fears of peripheral regions like Ireland about the issue of increased economic concentration in the European core are being addressed to a small extent by reallocating funding away from the Common Agricultural Policy towards increased expenditure on structural funding. EC programmes in information technology for peripheral areas have contributed towards modernising infrastructure and increasing awareness in peripheral regions like Ireland. Nevertheless, overall policy at the EC level is lacking in coherence, and to some extent efforts at the local level may be in competition with macro scale policies with their emphasis on the market and on competition.

At the national level the main thrust of policy in relation to telecommunications is on increasing inward investment, and while indigenous industry in Ireland has benefitted considerably from significant investment in digitalising the network, the needs of this much weaker sector have been very much a secondary consideration. Thus Ireland's branch plant economy continues to be characterised by the older Fordist model of economic development, and policy makers to date have shown little sign of formulating an integrated strategy or developing an endogenous growth model. One could summarise the main achievements in the information technology area to date as being the development of a financial services centre in the most urbanised East region, and the attraction of a number of American owned back office operations to the remoter western half of the country. Exploitation of telecommunications in Ireland, therefore, remains solidly in the domain of larger organisations and diffusing the associated skills and services to networks of SMEs remains a major development challenge.

References

Amin, A., (1989) 'Flexible specialisation and small firms in Italy: myths and realities', *Antipode*, 21, 13-34

Amin, A. and Robins, K. (1991) 'These are not Marshallian times', in Camagni, R. (ed.) *Innovation networks: spatial perspectives*, Belhaven Press, London, 105-118

Arnbak, J.C. (1990) 'Telematics - aims and characteristics of a new technology'. In H.M. Soekkha et al (Eds) *Telematics - Transportation and Spatial Development,* VSP, Utrecht, 11-20

Bannon, M. and Ward, S. (1985) Introduction, in Bannon, M. and Ward, S. (Eds) *Services And The New Economy: Implications For National And Regional Development,* Regional Studies Association, Dublin

Camagni, R. (1991), (Ed) *Innovation networks; spatial perspectives,* Belhaven Press, London

Carlson, B. (1990) 'DEMOTEL: new communications applications using known technology'. Paper presented to the OECD/Government of Sweden seminar on 'The regional impact of advanced telecommunications services', Kiruna, Sweden

Christensen, P.R. et al (1990) 'Firms in networks: concepts, spatial impacts and policy implications'. In, Illeris, S. and Jakobsen, L. (Eds) *Networks and Regional Development,* NORD REFO, University Press, Copenhagen, 11-58

Cronberg, T., Duelund, P., Jensen, O.M. and Qvortrup, L. (1991) (Eds) *Danish Experiments - Social Constructions of Technology,* New Social Science Monographs, Copenhagen

Eolas (1990) *Irish Research and Development,* Eolas (The Irish Science and Technology Agency), Dublin

Euristix (1991) *The Impact Of Communications On Industry And Industrial Development: A Report By Euristix Ltd To The Industrial Policy Review Group,* Dublin

Gillespie, A.E. and Robbins, K. (1989) 'Spatial bias of new communications technologies'. *Journal of Communications,* 39 (3), 7-18

Gillespie, A.E., Goddard, J.B., Hepworth, M.E. and Williams, H. (1989) 'Information and communications technology and regional development: an information economy perspective', *Science, Technology and Industry Review,* No. 5, April 1989, OECD, Paris, 85-111

Gillespie, A.E. and Goddard, J.B. (1990) 'Telecom and what more? Maximising the potential contribution of telecommunications to regional economic development'. Paper presented to the OECD/Government of Sweden seminar on 'The regional impact of advanced telecommunications services', Kiruna, Sweden

Grimes, S. (1992a) 'Ireland: the challenge of development in the European periphery', *Geography,* 77(1), 22-32

Grimes, S. (1992b) 'Fostering indigenous entrepreneurship in the European periphery'. In, O CÌnneide, M.S. and Grimes, S., *Planning and Development of Marginal Regions,* Centre for Development Studies, University College Galway

Grimes, S. (1992c) 'Information technology and regional development: the Irish experience', *NETCOM* (Networks and

Communications Studies, International Geographical Union), 6 (1), 281-296

Hirst, P. and Zeitlin, J. (1989) 'Flexible manufacturing and the competitive failure of UK manufacturing', *Political Science Quarterly,* 60 (2), 164-78

Howells, J. (1988) *Economic, Technological and Locational Trends in European Services,* Avesbury, Aldershot

Illeris, S. (1989) *Services and regions in Europe,* Avesbury, Aldershot

Johannisson, B. (1987) 'Beyond process and structure: social exchange networks', *International Studies of Magangement and Organisation,* 17 (1), 3-23

Kennedy, K. (1992) 'Real convergence, the European Community and Ireland', Presidential Address to the Statistical and Social Inquiry Society of Ireland, 14 May 1992

Malecki, E.J. (1991) *Technology and Economic Development: the dynamics of local, regional, and national change,* Longman Scientific and Technical, New York

Morgan, K. (1990) *The regional impact of advanced telecommunications services:* Final report to the OECD on the Kiruna seminar, June 1990

Piore, M.J. and Sabel, C.F. (1983) 'Italian small business development: lessons for US industrial policy'. In, Zysman, J. and Tyson, L. (Eds) *American Industry in International Competition: Government Policies and Corporate strategies*, Cornell University Press, Ithaca NY, 391-421

Piore, M.J. and Sabel, C.F. (1984) *The Second Industrial Divide: Possibilities for Prosperity*, Basic Books, New York

Qvortrup, L. (1989) 'The Nordic telecottages', *Telecommunications Policy*, March 1989, 59-68

Review of Industrial Performance (1990), Department of Industry and Commerce, Dublin

Sweeney, G.P. (1987) *Innovation, Entrepreneurs and Regional Development*, Frances Pinter, London

Wiberg, U (1989) 'Information technology and the periphery'. In Gustaffson, G. (ed.) *Development in marginal areas*, Research Report 89 (3), University of Karlstad, Department of Geography, pp 147-155

4 Using Telecommunications and Information Technology in Planning an Information-Age City: Singapore

Kenneth E. Corey

In the human generation since Singapore's internal self governance began in 1959, the government and people of this city-state have planned and worked themselves from having Singapore be a pre-industrial city to being a post-industrial city. The primary resource of the Republic of Singapore is its 3,002,800 people. This includes 312,700 foreigners as temporary worker-residents. Singaporeans and permanent residents consist of the following, mostly immigrant communities: Chinese 77.7 percent; Malays 14.1 percent; Indians 7.1 percent; and others 1.1 percent (Balakrishnan, June 20, 1991: 17). In 1990, Singapore's gross national product per capita was US$11.160; this is one of the highest levels in Asia (The World Bank, 1992: 179); the latest preliminary figure for the 1991 gross national product per capita is S$22,867.1 (Ministry of Trade and Industry, 1992: xii).[1] Economically, Singapore's policies of export development have been based heavily on the investment of more than 700 or so foreign transnational corporations.

A culture of planning, management, political control and quality of life

Unlike any other large city of the Pacific Rim, Singapore's development has been characterized by comprehensive, state-led interventionist strategies and planned programs of implementation. Early in the post-colonial days of independence, Singapore's political leadership, as represented by Lee Kuan Yew and the People's Action Party (PAP), was compelled to plan and manage the city's development to a high degree. This was necessary for Singapore to survive, and later it was deemed necessary so as to prosper and to enhance the quality of life for the Singapore electorate.

---

[1] Gross national product (GNP) is a measure of a nation's output of goods and services. As of this writing, in mid-July 1992, the exchange rate is S$1.61 to US$1.00.

49

As a result of a generation of experimental learnings from these planning practices, Singapore's elected officials, their bureaucrats and the populace have evolved an interdependent culture of successful planning and management (Sandhu and Wheatley, 1989). This planning culture is continuously steered and stimulated by a mix of domestic political pronouncements and external regional and global economic and political forces. The role of the state has been, and continues to be, paramount in the development of a modern and competitive Singapore.

Fundamental to this culture has been the achievement of an improving and high quality of life. The perception of quality of life enhancement by the majority of the Singapore electorate has resulted in a political and social covenant between the PAP-dominated government and its multi-ethnic population.

Information technology in Singapore's development

Independent Singapore has long planned and strategized to draw on its geographical and historical strengths to achieve economic niches, both regionally and globally. Even at the height of its industrialization program in 1970, PAP leaders were looking to the future and calling for "science-based and technology oriented industries" (Goh, K.S., 1972: 275). They were preparing to strategically place the city-state in an advantageous position for a world economy that then was expected increasingly to rely more on services and relatively less on manufacturing. Stimulated by the unexpected economic downturn in Singapore of 1984-1985 (See Table 1), Singapore strategists issued the report of the Economic Committee, *The Singapore Economy: New Directions* (1986). Among many other proposals, the committee recommended an accelerated strategy for Singapore to diversify and transform its development portfolio from that of an offshore industrial production and assembly base for developed countries, to become a Southeast Asian regional headquarters for transnational corporations (TNC) and also to enhance local enterprises. This planned new niche, driven in part by research and development strategies, is intended to produce a modern and strengthened capacity for Singapore to export services and capital. One of the city-state's major policies for stimulating and sustaining this form of post-industrial growth is an IT program. Information technology as used here and in Singapore has become the generally accepted umbrella term for a rapidly expanding range of equipment, applications, services, and basic technologies. They fall into three primary categories: computers, telecommunications, and multimedia data, with literally hun-

Table 1: *Employment change and gross domestic product change
In Singapore, 1980-91**

Year	Employment Change (No. Employees)	GDP % Change
1980	37,200	9.7
1981	62,200	9.3
1982	41,500	6.3
1983	35,800	7.9
1984	-7,200	8.2
1985	-101,100	-1.6
1986	11,100	1.8
1987	66,000	9.4
1988	65,900	11.1
1989	72,100	9.2
1990	60,100	8.3
1991	64,000	6.7

Source: Economic Survey of Singapore 1980 Through 1991, Ministry of
Trade and Industry, Singapore.
*Gross domestic product (GDP) is a measure of a nation's output of goods
and services minus income from investments abroad.

dreds of subcategories. Increasingly, the three elements have become interdependent (Keen, 1991: 98).

For this paper, the emphasis is on information technology policy planning and implementation with particular attention to the critical and developmental roles of telecommunications infrastructure and computer-based innovations and applications. The multi-media communications conditions of IT in Singapore recently were documented and assessed by Professor Eddie C.Y. Kuo (Kuo, 1991); earlier, he and a colleague also published a communication policy analysis for Singapore (Kuo and Chen, 1983).

By the mid to late 1980s Singapore had developed the necessary information technology pre-conditions to enable it to move to the implementation of a national plan (National IT Plan Working Committee, 1985). This had been preceded by the Civil Service Computerization Program begun in 1981 (Goh, C. T., 1981); in this program Singapore's civil service was used to pilot and perfect computerization practices and standards and thereby gain sufficient initial experience to be able to provide technical assistance to Singapore IT companies and local software developers (IT Focus, March 1990: 2). That initiative had been preceded nearly a decade earlier by a call for Singapore to be transformed "into a regional centre for brain services and brain service industries" (Hon, 1972: 23).

Singapore's rich history as a world-class sea port and global crossroads city has provided it with a foundation upon which to build a strong IT strategy to guide its future development. Because of its background in trading and as an entrepot, Singapore long has been a service economy. By 1980, 60.7 percent of the Singapore workforce was in the service sector (Kuo and Chen, 1987). During the early post-colonial period, the PAP political leaders sought to diversify Singapore's economy by initiating an industrialization drive. This effort succeeded in developing a critically important manufacturing sector; in 1990 it accounted for 29 percent of the gross domestic product (GDP). This is Singapore's second largest economic sector just behind the financial and business services sector. As early as 1973, the information sector accounted for 24 percent of Singapore's GDP (Jussawalla and Cheah, 1983). From their empirical analysis, Jussawalla and Cheah concluded that Singapore was moving toward an information economy. By 1980, 34.07 percent of Singapore's workforce was classified to be in information occupations (Kuo and Chen, 1987). Based on these trends and based on a decade of achievements under the computerization initiative and the National IT Plan, it is reasonable to conclude that an IT strategy represents a sound basis for planning Singapore's future development for a post-industrial era (Toh and Low, July 3-6, 1989).

Singapore's national IT plan

In late 1984 a government working committee began to conceive an IT strategy for Singapore. Eighteen months later the committee's work resulted in a plan, consisting of seven elements: 1—continuing to upgrade information communication infrastructure; 2—developing IT and information communication personnel; 3—promoting an IT culture; 4—finding new applications for IT; 5—building a Singapore IT industry; 6—encouraging creativity and entrepreneurship in IT; and 7—implementing the IT plan by coordination of the previous six plan elements and by collaboration among Singapore's government agencies, statutory boards, authorities and institutions, and with the private sector, including both TNCs and local Singaporean firms (Straits Times, December 4, 1986; and Corey, 1991).

Evaluation of Singapore's IT planning

Recently, the government set as one of its most critical IT goals, becoming a world-class exporter and exploiter of IT products and services (Ministry of Trade and Industry, 1990: 76). Compare this goal to then Finance Minister Hon Sui Sen's 1972 goal cited above of having Singapore transformed "into a regional centre for brain services and brain service industries" (Hon, 1972: 23). These similar goals are separated by eighteen years, and a great deal of progress in recent years has been realized, especially through the various programs that have been stimulated by the 1986 National IT Plan. The next section of the paper illustrates some of the representative accomplishments of Singapore's decade-long IT initiatives, firstly as a result of the 1981 computerization program, and secondly as a result of the 1986 National IT Plan.

Up-grading telecommunications infrastructure.

In stimulating development in various sectors, Singapore elected officials consistently have placed high priority on investing in modern infrastructure. This is the case also with telecommunications and information technology. For example, Singapore's national and international telephone networks are planned to be fully digitized by 1994. With 35 telephone lines per one-hundred population, Singapore ranks twelfth in the world just ahead of Israel. Singaporean leaders have learned that such improvements help in creating an attractive climate for foreign direct investment. Thereby, a base for modern local innovation also is provided. They have transferred these lessons about the importance of telecommunications infrastructure into the IT sector also. Below, two recent infrastructure accomplishments are illustrated (Wee, June 7, 1990: 16; and Singapore Telecom, 1991: 21).

In late 1989, Singapore became the world's first country to have a nation-wide *Integrated Services Digital Network* (ISDN). ISDN is an inexpensive high-speed, high quality telecommunications network with the simultaneous capacity to carry voice, video and data communications. ISDN permits the expansion of many new telecommunications services, e.g., packet services and videophone booth service. All ISDN Singapore subscribers are connected to all other ISDN Singapore subscribers, and they can use various IT hardware configurations on the ISDN. Further, Singapore ISDN subscribers can connect with other ISDN subscribers overseas (e.g., Japan, France, Australia, the UK and the US). All of these ISDN services are available at one-seventh of the cost of conventional, separate-purpose redundant telephone lines (Yeo, 1989). In 1992 broadband ISDN service will go into trial; commercial service is planned for 1996-97. The broadband ISDN system can transmit information at 150 million bits per second compared to the 64,000 bits per second of the current ISDN system (EDB, June and December 1991).

Singapore Telecommunication Pte Ltd. (or Singapore Telecom) is the principal institutional actor responsible for keeping the city-state's telecommunications infrastructure modern and competitive. After nine years of research and development Singapore Telecom produced an advanced photo-videotex system called *Teleview*. Teleview is an interactive, computer-based information network with visual displays on monitors and television sets that combines the use of the telephone network to permit transactions and communications (Corey, 1991). Teleview's principal functions include: information retrieval, transactions with service providers, e.g., personal home banking, computing of loan and tax payments, the transmission and receipt of residential and business messages, news, personal games and home tutorial packages, e.g., on Singapore history. The ultimate goal of Teleview is to offer useful information services for virtually everyone (Straits Times, November 2, 1990: 24). Prime Minister Goh Chok Tong saw Teleview as a productivity tool, because it can drastically reduce the time and effort used by Singaporean households and firms to pay bills, to bank, to shop, and even to communicate and participate with government. Government officials believe that physical travel and queues can be replaced by using Teleview in home and in workplace (Goh, C. T., 1988). Teleview also has potential for export from Singapore to other countries. After two years of commercial operation Teleview has 10,000 subscribers. That exceeds the French Teletel and British Prestel systems in their first two years of operation respectively (Ng, 1992: 2).

As part of NCB's new IT 2000 initiative, introduced later in this paper, the future of Singapore's IT-related infrastructure will be built on, and with the NII, i.e., the National Information Infrastructure. The NII will enable the integration of Singapore's IT investments in telecommunications, broadcast capacities and computerization (Lim, 1992). A parallel effort is the liberalization of the Singapore telecommunications industry. In April 1992, the Telecommunication Authority of Singapore was re-constituted. It is a statutory board and it now performs two roles, (1) that or regulator, and (2) that of a "developer and promoter of the telecommunication and postal industry of Singapore" (Mah, 1992: 56). In turn, Singapore Telecom was corporatized and became a telecommunications operating and holding company. It has the exclusive right to provide, for fifteen years, such services and domestic and international telephone services and telex and telegram services.

Developing IT and information communication personnel.

In 1991, there were 1,524,300 employed persons in Singapore. Only 30,000 of these were unemployed; this is a 1.9 percent unemployment rate (Ministry of Trade and Industry, 1992: xii and 38).

If Singapore is to attain its aspirations of becoming an "intelligent island" that is fully networked both domestically and internationally (Ong, June 8, 1991: 13), then its IT workforce must be able to support these intentions. Early in the implementation of the national IT plan, explicit personnel-development efforts were incorporated into Singapore's IT strategy; this has covered the full range of existing and intended future IT human resources of Singapore (Singapore Federation of the Computer Industry, 1987).

In 1980 there were 850 IT professionals in Singapore; by the end of 1988 there were 8,300 IT professionals practicing in Singapore. By 1991 this workforce has grown to 13,000. Of these IT professionals, 65 percent do software development; 12.4 percent are IT managers; 5.5 percent are hardware professionals; and 4.8 percent do IT marketing. Thirty-six percent of these IT professionals are women. Over 85 percent of this IT workforce is Singaporean; nearly one-third hold IT degrees; 34 percent of the IT graduate degree holders have degrees from overseas.   By the year 2000, Singapore IT workforce needs are projected to be 30,000-35,000 professionals (IT Manpower Survey 1989, 1990).

In order to educate Singaporeans for employment in the IT sector of Singapore, both tertiary education and skills development programs are underway. The total 1988-to-1989 student population at the National University of Singapore and the Nanyang Technological Institute was increased 7.5 percent to 20,120 students. Together the two institutions produced 5,302 graduates; this was a 12 percent increase. Of the enrollees, 46.8 percent (9,421) were in science, engineering and computer technology; of the graduates, 43.3 percent (2,295) were in science and engineering. In 1991 Nanyang Technological Institute became a full-fledged university, i.e., the Nanyang Technological University, with a concomitant expansion of enrollment and the addition of new curricula in computer technology and commerce. Graduates of the commerce curriculum are to be educated for careers in information services such as finance, banking, insurance, industrial management and marketing (Ministry of Trade and Industry, 1990: 73-75). In 1990 an additional polytechnic was opened, bringing to four the number of polytechnic institutions in Singapore. A total of 19,367 full and part-time students received skills training in 1989 via the Institutes of the Vocational and Industrial Training Board, and the Economic Development Board Joint Industrial Training Centers and Institutes (Ministry of Trade and Industry, 1990: 73-76). Twenty-four commercial schools also function in support of Singapore's IT training needs.

In 1988, a massive in-service IT literacy program was initiated; it is called ITPOWER. Jointly developed by the National Computer Board and the National Productivity Board, ITPOWER is intended ultimately to benefit an estimated 200,000 office workers in Singapore. More than 30,000 such workers have been trained to date (IT Focus, June 1989: 6; and IT Singapore, May 1990: 14).

In order to develop a pool of Singaporean experts in information and telecommunications software technologies, a collaborative S$50 million joint institute between AT&T and the National Computer Board of Singapore began implementation in 1990. The new Information Communication Institute of Singapore (ICIS) addresses the need to have a personnel-development capacity for Singapore in the new discipline of "information communication;" this is the integration of computer and telecommunication technologies.

The focus of this new institute's courses is on networking software and enabling IT professionals to monitor worldwide innovations in this new field. These training programs are intended to be responsive to the information communication needs of Singapore industry. The students of the ICIS are university graduates with degrees in computer science, electrical engineering and related fields. The coursework draws on the technical experience of AT&T's Bell labs and AT&T hardware. Personnel from the ICIS will be used to enhance Singapore's many national and international network initiatives, such as TradeNet, LawNet and so on (IT Singapore, June 1990: 1 and 10).

These various IT and information communication training and education programs address the many levels of Singapore's diverse personnel needs. This results in a strategy that ranges from professional to clerical to managerial, as well as from pre-service, to in-service and continuous training. Such an IT personnel-development strategy is designed to enhance Singapore's competitiveness in the global IT and telecommunications environment. Many organizations contribute to this strategy. In addition to those noted above, other major IT institutional actors contributing to Singapore's IT post-graduate specialist training and personnel development include: the National University of Singapore's Department of Information Systems and Computer Science; Nanyang Technological University's School of Applied Science in software engineering; the Institute of Systems Science; the Japan-Singapore Institute of Software Technology; and the Centre for Computer Studies.

Promoting an IT Culture.

Singaporeans receive a constant stream of information and exhortations about the importance of IT to their job, to their education, and to their quality of life. Singapore's high-rise shopping centers have floors of hardware, software and other IT retail opportunities. School, the factory, the office, the newspaper, television and propaganda banners are some of the media by which IT is infused throughout Singapore's society and economy. There are many IT events available to the general public and to IT professionals alike. One of the largest such events is Singapore Informatics. This IT trade exhibition has been held each December since 1986. Informatics in 1991 attracted an estimated 133,000 visitors; this is up 5,000 from Informatics '90 (IT Singapore, December 1990: 1) Informatics '90 included 1,200 exhibitors; S$10 million in business transactions occurred as a result of the exhibition. A calendar of formal IT activities in Singapore covering only the period from late May through late July 1990 lists sixteen significant IT events, including the major Singapore 2000 - Global Technopolis exhibition (IT Singapore, May 1990a: 1). These and many other interventions, have gone a long way toward establishing an IT culture in Singapore. In turn, Singapore's reputation as an international information technology center also has been enhanced. At 79 computers per 1,000 persons, Singapore was ranked among the top ten nations in the world; it ranked ahead of Switzerland, Denmark and Sweden; Japan had 87 computers per 1,000 persons (IT Singapore, August 1990: 1).

IT applications.

Government, local businesses and foreign firms based in Singapore have developed numerous new uses for IT (Corey, 1991). Different means are employed by the Singapore government to stimulate new applications. In 1990 a National IT Awards program was implemented. By recognizing innovation in IT, these awards, through example, can stimulate others to develop additional new IT applications. The criteria for the awards also focus attention on Singapore's shift in policy from merely using IT to improve productivity to "the implementation of world class strategic IT applications," including the assessment of the impact of such uses (IT Focus, March 1990: 10). Additionally, in March 1990, the Singapore government sponsored a seven-day National IT Application Conference, the theme of which was "IT for Better Business." Over 1,300 conferees attended. The focus of the discussions was "on how Singapore can exploit information technology to help it become a developed country by the year 2000" (IT Focus, March 1990: 6).

For years, Singapore has been moving toward the goal of becoming a "cashless society." Automatic teller machines (ATM) have been ubiquitous for most of the 1980s. Experiments are underway in the use of point-of-sales (POS) systems and portable-terminal personal identification number (PIN) systems by fast-food retailers such as A&W Family Restaurants and Pizza Hut (IT Singapore, March 1990a: 15; and IT Singapore, April 1990: 3). In 1986 the Network for Electronic Transfer (Singapore) -- NETS was initiated. NETS users purchase services and goods with ATM cards issued by Singapore's major banks. There are an estimated 1.2 million ATM card holders; most of the 840 NETS outlets are in the major department stores, petrol stations and supermarkets. S$216 million in transactions were recorded in 1989. Plans are underway to extend NETS to many other small and medium-sized retailers; by 1995 there will be 5,000 outlets; they are expected to generate a transaction volume of S$1.5 billion by 1995. The NETS system permits instant debiting of the purchaser's bank account and instant crediting of the retailer's deposit account (IT Singapore, March 1990b: 15). Exhibits and experiments are underway for Singapore application of "smart cards," i.e., a plastic card that contains a microprocessor; this permits intelligence to be added to PINs and the storage of other information. One application being conceived for traffic-congested Singapore is the use of the smart card in a planned Electronic Road Pricing (ERP) system. An ERP would automatically debit a vehicle's pre-paid "electronic purse" for distance or time traveled on specific roads (IT Singapore, May 1990: 12).

With the addition of each new tool to Singapore's IT capacity, new applications become possible thus producing multipliers into the IT mix. For example, since the inauguration of Singapore's ISDN, Singapore Telecom and the Information Technology Institute are jointly developing ISDN office workstations and specific applications for users in financial and trading services. The earlier Singapore can bring IT innovations to fruition, the earlier its enterprises can begin the development of new services, products and markets (IT Singapore, May 1990: 6). As a consequence, niches might be created, thereby Singapore's comparative advantages are strengthened.

The government of Singapore seeks to extend increasingly-sophisticated IT uses more deeply into most sectors of its economy. At the 1990 National IT Applications Conference, strategic IT applications were discussed in seven different sectors, including: government, wholesale and distribution, legal services, health care services, manufacturing, construction and financial services (IT Focus, March 1990: 6). Examples of IT industry sector network systems include TradeNet, MediNet and LawNet. Under development also is a construction industry system called BuildNet that will be designed to service the data, regulations and permit and plan-approval needs of builders, architects and engineers.

TradeNet is a "nation-wide electronic data interchange (EDI) network which allows business and government users to exchange structured trade documents and information electronically." The system has 1,400 subscribers and processes 8,500 trade declarations daily (Tay, C., January 14, 1991). In 1988/89, 4.2 million documents were processed with TradeNet. "It is a strategic productivity tool for both the government and private sector and will contribute significantly to Singapore's international competitiveness" (Singapore Trade Development Board, 1989: 46). TradeNet earned the 1989 "Partners in Leadership" award of the U.S. Society of Information Management. The principal developers of TradeNet, the Trade Development Board and the National Computer Board, were the recipients of the award (IT Focus, October 1989: 1-2). This kind of international recognition is yet another measure of a major Singapore IT program success.

The company, *Singapore Network Services* (SNS) Pte Ltd offers, in addition to TradeNet, these network services to the business community: MediNet; LawNet, AutoNet (automation industry); BizNet (credit and business information registry); StarNet (air cargo); RealNet (property market); GraphNet (graphics data interchange); OrderLink (purchasing transactions); InfoLink (various government and private sector international data bases); and MaiLink (messages) among others. SNS is based in Singapore's Science Park (Tay, C., January 14 1991).

After a brief feasibility study period, the government of Singapore decided to proceed with the full development of MediNet. This is another nation-wide computer network; its purpose is to make Singapore's health-care services sector more effective and efficient.

"The twin objectives of MediNet are to reduce the cost and turn-around time for the preparation, transmission and processing of health information and to speed up access to more health information, thereby improving service to health-care recipients" (Tay, E. S., 1989: 61).

Among other components, MediNet will create a single agency for processing medical claims and payments, and in the process better serve patients, hospitals and insurance firms. Other components targeted for development include: smart cards with medical information on the patient; paperless clinics; and terminals throughout all operational areas of hospitals (IT Singapore, March 1990: 4).

LawNet is a network with access to a data base of Singapore statutes. Ultimately it is intended that a comprehensive integrated IT justice system will be developed for Singapore. Such a system will enable practicing lawyers, judges and the public to share in using linked legal libraries, registries, legal data bases overseas, as well as stored regulations and rules (IT Focus, March 1990: 5).

Singapore's construction industry is to receive greater influence from IT. This sector has been sluggish in recent years and it has been little impacted by computerization (IT Singapore, April 1990: 15). The Construction Industry Development Board (CIDB) recently established a Strategic Technology Unit to develop an IT program (i.e., BuildNet) for Singapore's construction sector. IT applications and incentives will be at the core of this strategy.

Other sectors of Singapore's economy also have been impacted by IT initiatives. The Stock Exchange of Singapore has begun the first "floorless" stock trading system in Southeast Asia. Singapore hotels are providing guests with new, more comprehensive IT services. Singapore Airlines is a major participant in an innovative international airline reservation system (i.e., ABACUS); it will significantly improve trans-Pacific travel between North America and the Western Pacific Rim. A comprehensive information system on land use, buildings and physical planning-related data was launched in late 1990; it is called ILUS, for Integrated Land Use System.

The above applications are exemplary of the numerous IT innovations currently underway. Because of the diversity and great number of new IT applications being multiplied in Singapore, it is not possible here to be comprehensive and exhaustive. However, it is evident that as Singapore continues to expand its capacity and influence in the financial services sector, value will be added, costs will be reduced and even more IT-driven functions can be added to the city-state's total capacity.

Singapore now is one of the world's leading financial capitals. The financial and business services sector has been Singapore's leading growth sector for 1989 through 1991. More than 400 internationally-oriented institutions are providing Singapore's financial services (IT Singapore, March 1990: 5). Singapore can be expected to build further on this foundation and to strive to extend its services and markets in the Southeast Asian region.

Building a Singapore IT industry.

The May 1990 survey of 138 Singapore-based suppliers revealed that 75 percent of the companies have existed for less than 10 years (National Computer Board, 1990: 2). Nearly two-thirds of these firms are locally owned; 15 percent of the companies have alliances with foreign-based firms; these links are both technical and marketing in nature and only 20 percent of Singapore IT companies are engaged in hardware manufacturing; other business activities include IT services such as marketing, distribution, consultancy, education and training; business application dominates Singapore IT technical capability with 63 percent of firms so engaged (National Computer Board, 1990: 3—7). Further, the

...sales of hardware in 1989 was more than (S)$1 billion while that of software and IT services amounted to (S)$424 million. Their growth rates were 40% and 35% respectively (*Ibid*, 14).

A fundamental measure of Singapore's IT strategy is the revenue it produces. By 1990, IT revenues were S$2.147.78 billion. This is more than an eight-fold increase over the 1982 IT industry revenues of S$258.95 million (IT Focus, December 1991: i). Another measure of IT accomplishment in trade-oriented Singapore is export. Singapore IT exports in 1990 were valued at S$657.24 million, or 30 percent of total IT revenue. The major export markets were the ASEAN (Association of Southeast Asian Nations) countries.

Yet another indicator of IT industry productivity is the extent to which computerization has occurred. The 1989 National Computer Board survey of 4,900 Singapore establishments revealed that "computer penetration has risen to 68 percent of all establishments employing 10 or more people" (IT Singapore, May 1990b: 1). The response rate to this study was 64 percent, or 3,139 establishments.

Table 2: *Examples of foreign it firms Establishing centers in Singapore 1989-91*

A T & T Bell Laboratories	Microelectronics Design Center
Aston-Tate Asian Development Center	R & D In Software Development
British Telecommunications	Northern Telecom Regional Headquarters
Digital Equipment Corporation	Far East Regional Finance, Network Office Automation Competency Center
Dupont Singapore Pte Ltd	Regional Data Center
Fuji Xerox Of Japan	Operation Headquarters
Hewlett Packard	Asian Peripherals Division Asian-Pacific Personal Computer Div.
Hitachi Data Systems	Regional Distribution Center
Lotus Development Corporation	Design And Production Center
Mastek Asia-Pacific Pte Ltd	
Mcdonnell Douglas Information Systems International Limited	Marketing And Support Activities In The Asean Region
Mentor Graphics	Pacific Rim HQT, Including R & D
Mobil Oil Singapore	Regional Data Center
NEC	Business Coordination Center Software Development Center
Nippon Telegraph & Telephone Corp.	
Prairietek Corporation Expansion 1991	
Prime Computer, Inc.	Research And Development Center
Rank Xerox Corporation R & D Center	
Reuters	Regional Headquarters
Santa Cruz Operation	Regional Office For Marketing, Technical Support And Development
Siemans Nixdorf Asia-Pacific	Regional Headquarters Expansion 1991
Sita (Societe Internationale De Telecommunications Aeronautiques)	
Swift (Society For Worldwide Interbank Financial Telecommunications)	Regional Service Center For Network Support
Toshiba Electronics Asia Ltd	Lsi Design Center
Universal Instruments Corporation	Technical Center

Source: IT Focus, IT Singapore, and EDB Singapore Investment News, 1989 to 1992 issues.

One of Singapore's principal development goals is to establish itself as a regional center for corporate operational headquarters, software research and development (R&D) and other business and financial services, i.e., regional support centers and regional data centers. Significant measures of progress toward the IT strategy are the quality and number of firms that establish such IT and related functions in Singapore. Since 1989, nine TNC software R&D centers, with 500 R&D engineers have been established, along with forty or more local IT companies have been created in Singapore. See Table 2. This selected listing is exemplary of the kinds of cumulative outcomes realized by the IT foreign promotion initiatives of Singapore's Economic Development Board and the National Computer Board.

Creativity and entrepreneurship in IT.

One of the objectives of Singapore's development strategy is to engage in innovative research and development (R&D). In 1989, 46 percent (64) of the 138 Singapore IT companies responding to the 1990 IT industry survey reported that a portion of their total revenues was spent on R&D (National Computer Board, 1990: 8). Over 38 percent of IT business activity in Singapore is in software development and/or R&D (National Computer Board, 1990: 6). Dr. Tay Eng Soon, Senior Minister of State for Education and Chairman of the Committee for National Computerization, recently recognized the growing significance of R&D to Singapore's development:

"Our country has reached a stage of development where R&D is seen as an essential factor in higher value-added economic activities" (IT Focus, December 1990: 2).

One of the most effective techniques used in Singapore to promote local IT innovation has been incentives. The *Small Enterprise Computerization Program* (SECP) is an example incentive opportunity that will take on growing importance as IT uses diffuse from large corporations to small and medium-sized firms. In the case of the legal sector, the National Computer Board estimated that more than 90 percent of Singapore's law firms are eligible for SECP incentives (IT Focus, October 1989: 5). Singapore construction firms may apply for benefits from the *Investment Allowance Scheme* of CIDB to acquire computer equipment. For many years the Economic Development Board has used various tax incentives to attract foreign investment in Singapore's manufacturing sector; now this is also the case for the IT environment (Corey, 1991).

Other incentives include: Initiative in New Technology (INTECH); Software Development Assistance Scheme (SDAS); Pioneer Status; Export of Services Incentive; and the Operational Headquarters Incentive (OHQ) (Leck, June 3, 1991).

A major center for R&D in science and technology, creativity and entrepreneurship in IT is the *Singapore Science Park*. It was created in 1981 to provide the physical infrastructure for R&D. The park offers IT innovators both incentives (i.e., Research and Development Assistance Scheme) and needed infrastructure. The 110-hectare Park site is near the National University of Singapore (NUS). In 1989 phase one of the park was full, with 50 local and foreign firms and organizations occupying the facilities. There is a waiting list of firms, and as a consequence more space is being added by phases. The park is now home to about 100 firms. It is managed and developed by Technology Parks Pte Ltd, which is a subsidiary of the Jurong Town Corporation. Technology Parks was established in 1990. The first phase of the park includes three IT-dedicated buildings. The park also hosts incubator efforts in IT and other technologies, as in bio-technology. In 1992, fifty-one percent of the park's tenants were IT firms. The park employs several thousand personnel, many of whom are engaged in research and development. It is the home for many joint projects between Science Park firms and other Singapore research institutions (e.g., National University of Singapore). In the Science Park Singapore has shown early success in stimulating a "spirit of entrepreneurship and innovation" (Mah, 1989: 78). The park is the eastern anchor for the planned southwestern technology corridor of Singapore.

Singapore's recent National IT Awards program does a great deal to call attention to creativity and entrepreneurship in IT. Periodical publications such as *IT Focus* and *IT Singapore* regularly feature successful IT firms and individuals as role models who might stimulate other Singapore actors to be innovative in IT development, application and marketing. Singapore has begun to relax some regulations and reduce some tariffs. These liberalizations and de-regulations also can serve to release creative new initiatives by Singapore IT planners and managers.

In early 1991, the National Science and Technology Board (NSTB) came into operation. The mandate of this statutory board is to promote, focus and coordinate R&D activities in science and technology to insure that Singapore is internationally competitive in manufacturing and services. NSTB's programs include funding, enhancing science and technology capacities, facilities and infrastructure. These activities include:

the Research & Development Assistance Scheme (RDAS); TechNet to serve the R&D community in Singapore and worldwide; and the execution of the National Technology Plan 1991 (National Science and Technology Board, 1992).

Coordination and collaboration of the IT plan.

The Singapore National Computer Board (NCB) is the lead coordinating agency responsible for implementing the projects and programs that are formulated as a result of the National IT Plan. Since the Plan was unveiled in late 1986, the NCB has coordinated many successful IT initiatives. One of the recent such examples was the design and execution of the National IT Application Conference. The NCB organized the conference with six other Singapore government agencies; these included: the Construction Industry Development Board, Economic Development Board, Ministry of Health, Ministry of Law, the Telecommunication Authority of Singapore, and Trade Development Board (IT Focus, December 1989: 12). In 1991, the NCB celebrated its tenth anniversary and its leadership in coordinating Singapore's national IT policy planning and program implementation. This long-term experience in policy coordination has been central to Singapore's many IT outcomes.

Sectoral agencies also play lead-actor roles in their respective IT industry sectors. The Telecommunication Authority of Singapore, now Singapore Telecom, long has initiated IT infrastructure research and development as well as program implementation and facilities maintenance and management. Recently, the Singapore Housing and Development Board (HDB) has taken IT to the construction industry. For all of HDB's new contracts, contractors with HDB are required to use personal computers in managing the project. This initiative is expected to bring costs savings, efficiencies, increase productivity and assist in modernizing the local construction industry (IT Singapore, April 1990: 1).

As Singapore continues to deepen its experience in implementing the National IT Plan, both government agencies and local small and medium size firms will be collaborating more effectively with and extending their services to IT partners overseas. Further, more sophisticated spin-offs and technology transfers will occur across different phases of service and product development. For example, NCB and NUS have entered into a partnership agreement to take "upstream" research findings from the university and have NCB's research unit, the Information Technology Institute (ITI):

"...incorporate these research ideas into its midstream technology innovations and eventually transfer the technology in downstream developments of commercial products and pioneering applications" (IT Focus, October 1989: 12).

These cases are illustrative of the kind of inter-agency coordinative and collaborative activities that have proven to be effective in promoting and realizing the strategies inherent in Singapore's National IT plan.

IT2000 -- master plan for the future

The National Computer Board was formed in 1981. NCB led the Civil Service Computerization Program, which was initiated in the early 1980s; this marked the early, or phase I of Singapore's IT implementation effort. The middle range, or phase II began implementation in December 1986 with the implementation of the National IT Plan assessed above. With the March 1992 publication of the IT2000 report, the third or future phase of Singapore's IT policy development and implementation has begun. By this and any other overall evaluation it must be concluded that significant progress and success in Singapore's IT development has been accomplished in phases I and II. Indeed, in phase III, the city-state is poised to become an electronically integrated metropolitan node in the global IT network. Few other places have reached this level of IT development.

Not content with past achievements, Singapore's government routinely scans the future so as to maintain a competitive edge (Government of Singapore, 1991). At the opening of Singapore Informatics '90 in December 1990, Dr. Tay Eng Soon, Senior Minister of State for Education and Chairman of the Committee on National Computerization, announced that Singapore's National Computer Board was developing a new IT master plan. After five years of operating from the 1986 National IT Plan, Singapore planners re-visited the question "what role will IT play in Singapore's future ... as we move towards the year 2000?" (Tay, E. S., December 13, 1990: 4). IT2000's purpose:

"... is to turn Singapore into an intelligent island in which IT will be fully exploited to improve business competitiveness and, more importantly, to enhance the quality of life of our citizens" (Tay, E. S., December 13, 1990: 4).

The IT2000 report, *A Vision of an Intelligent Island* was published in March 1992 (National Computer Board, 1992). This new general strategy draws on Singapore's many recent IT achievements, such as those noted above, and seeks to combine these with new IT developments and integrate the various IT services into an enhanced information-age living and working environment for Singaporean society. Technology corridors will form the basis of Singapore's future business, housing, recreational and locational development (Urban Redevelopment Authority, 1992: 21).

An IT2000 steering committee conducted studies into user needs and the IT potential of eleven industry sectors. These included: financial services, manufacturing, leisure and tourist services, construction and real estate, retail-wholesale-distribution, publishing and media, transportation, health care, education, information technology industry and the government sector (Asia Computer Weekly, March 4-10, 1991: 20).

This latest stage of IT planning was designed to move Singapore to developed country status by the year 2000. "IT2000 will lead to an integrated material network that will facilitate the information flow between public, government and business organizations" (IT Focus, March 1991: 1). The IT2000 initiative is interdependent with two other NCB initiatives: the National IT R&D Master Plan and the Global City Study (National Computer Board, 1991). Monitoring the evolution of these three future initiatives will form the basis of my future policy analyses and assessment of IT2000.

Parallel to Singapore Telecom's efforts to develop a contemporary and competitive telecommunications infrastructure, is NCB's IT2000 mandate to plan the National Information Infrastructure (NII). This effort is guided by a re-constituted National IT Committee (NITC). Highest-level direction is given to the NITC by representatives of the Ministry of Finance, Ministry of Communications, Ministry of Information and Arts, and Singapore Telecom, Singapore Broadcasting Corporation, chaired by the Senior Minister of State for Education and advised by the Deputy Prince Minister and Minister for Trade and Industry (Tay, 1992).

Questions and planning challenges facing Singapore's future

From the foregoing, one might be tempted to conclude that Singapore is an ideal city, both from the perspective that it has solved most of its earlier, post-colonial development problems, and because Singapore might represent a kind of information-age urban model for others to emulate. Such conclusions should not be reached simply and quickly.

The demographic issues of declining fertility and an increasingly aging population are being engaged by the political leaders (Goh, C.T., February 15, 1988) and planners of Singapore (Planning Department, 1985). Although it is commendable and impressive to see the extent to which Singapore's IT and other development strategies already have shown increases in productivity and creativity, Singapore's modern chronic labor shortage in some occupational sectors is not likely to be resolved by the mere substitution of technology for human resources. With an increasingly educated and more affluent population of younger, potentially mobile professionals, how much longer can elected officials continue to use top-down approaches as the principal style of governance? Will the new generation of leaders be able to successfully steer the Republic through the transition to younger political leaders? As the world experiences more "democracy movements," and increased ethnic aspirations and communal fragmentation, what are the implications for contemporary Singaporeans and the future of this planned new city of the Pacific Rim? And what might be the role of information technology in Singapore's future development?

As Singapore gets even deeper into, and more dependent on, its evolving IT strategy and the inherent openness and individual experimentation that comes with handling information, how does this square with practices of government-led show trails, media control and censorship, expulsion of opposition party leaders and other political tactics designed to maintain tight political control (Sussman, 1990)?

As other newly industrializing economies of the Pacific Rim seek to become more economically competitive, what are Singapore's future development niches and options beyond IT? As Singaporeans become more mobile through education and more questioning through new exposures to the world outside of Singapore, how might emigration be muted and addressed creatively? What are the implications for Singapore as Hong Kong, the other city-state in the region, becomes part of China in 1997? The above listing of questions and challenges is not intended to be comprehensive. Rather, it is meant to suggest that even amid Singapore's admirable development successes and its culture of political control, rational planning and management, challenges and opportunities are constantly offered. This necessitates continual innovation and the persistent formulation of new strategies to meet the new problems (Ong, June 8, 1991).

Singapore as a model

Singapore has been a laboratory for the practice of planning and management like no other large city on the Pacific Rim. Because of its successes, others may seek to replicate its development planning. Be forewarned. Singapore's truly unique location and space conditions have exempted it from such traditional planning and management problems as rural-urban interdependencies and primate city-secondary city linkages (Goldblum, 1990). The recent Growth Triangle strategy, that links the economic development of Singapore, with the Riau region of Indonesia and Johore in Malaysia, is an innovative way of extending Singapore's comparative economic strengths into other parts of Southeast Asia -- even without having a political territorial hinterland (Ministry of Trade and Industry, 1991: 61). Generally, however, Singapore's substantive needs and solutions are different and therefore are not directly transferable to other cities and countries.

However, much is to be learned by systematic comparative analyses toward the end of deriving development outcome lessons rather than process lessons. In Singapore, IT is both a means and an end. Planners of another metropolis may desire to attain Singapore's relatively high quality of life, but these planners may well want to avoid the top-down, low-citizen participation approaches that characterize Singapore's development planning.

Some of the proven development lessons and guidelines, that might be derived from Singapore's generic development and its IT programs implementation are listed in Table 3. With appropriate tailoring, these lessons may prove to be useful guidelines to cities, regions and countries elsewhere.

These lessons were derived both from the above assessment of Singapore's IT sector planning and implementation and from analysis of Singapore's other development sectors (Corey, 1987). In essence, these are most of the principal attributes that compose "the Singapore planning and development model."

Table 3: *Lessons and guidelines from Singapore planning and development*

1. Address and meet the *needs of the electorate.*
2. Assess *internal resources* and build on them, include human resources and geographical resources such as location and space in the development strategy; develop potential opportunities. Maximize available assets; e.g. build on singapore's rich legacy as a world port.
3. Insure development capacity with early and continual attention to *contemporary infrastructure*, the full range of *human resources* needed to support the

intended development, and effective *leadership and coordination.* These policy elements are fundamental to implementation success.

4. Assess the *external environment,* with the intention of knowing the market for services, goods and competitors; identify niches and competitive advantages.
5. Develop internal and external *investment and re-investment programs*
6. that enable the pursuit of likely development strategies based on analysis of the above. Domestic savings and foreign investment can combine to generate surplus for further wealth creation.
7. Based initially on pilot, seed support, development innovations in
8. Singapore ultimately seek *self-financing continuance* if they are to be effective and successful. Increasingly, public-private partnerships are assuming greater roles in this process.
9. Cultivate, inform and *educate* internal constituents and external markets.
10. Stimulate new and additional demand for services and products by means of explicit, innovative *programs of application,* especially those that grow from and directly serve the needs and unique characteristics of internal constituencies, thus enhancing their lives and reinforcing the significance of the adopted development strategy. These applications ideally should multiply and spawn new, advanced, value-added services that develop deep technical and human-resource capacities.
11. *Upgrade and enhance productive capacity,* i.e., develop IT industry as in the case of services and products, and monitor and evaluate that capacity against intended outcomes. A development trajectory should be toward higher value-added productive activities. Develop measurement indicators of such progress.
12. Employ *incentives* to steer development in intended directions. This is especially useful in seeking to stimulate innovative, advancements by means of research and development as part of a commercialization process.
13. *Control development* such that internal values and resources are conserved and external investors may both contribute to the development strategy and derive a worthwhile profit.
14. *Integrate* each component and intervention of the development strategy such that a coherent, comprehensive and self-reinforcing whole results; this should be the original intended outcome.
15. Manage the development process such that a *coordinated and effective division of labor* fully utilizes the substantive and procedural expertise of the relevant *organizations* and individual *actors* in appropriate *roles* who are required to realize the intended development outcomes. This coordination occurs before and throughout the implementation process and it involves full representation of all impacted major interests, including government and private interests, both external as well as internal. It occurs at the highest levels; leadership is critical. The governance structure must be simple, manageable and responsive.
16. Be *flexible.* If the strategy is not performing according to intent, then be prepared to make immediate corrections that will serve both short-term requirements as well as long-range aspirations.
17. *Long-term and sustained strategic action* can produce intended outcomes. Such commitment also demands systematic experimentation such that lessons

are derived and used in future actions. Quick fixes are not conducive to the pioneering of holistic development.

Conclusion

This evaluation of Singapore's IT plan implementation has revealed major accomplishment. So much so that Singapore is held up here as *an* exemplar of development in the globally interdependent information age. This assessment may be taken as positive, for indeed, Singapore's attainment of a relatively advanced level of development in the short period of a human generation, is truly remarkable. However, the purpose here has been elucidation. This appraisal should not be taken as advocacy. What is espoused here is the need for the realization of more operational and measured understandings of IT planning and IT policies as they might enhance city development elsewhere. From this generic knowledge and from the localized knowledge of each of our cities, we contributors to (1) future urban policies and (2) to the understanding of city change (Yeung, 1990) might become even more useful to our respective societies if we are able to synthesize these case-study lessons and to tailor and apply them locally.

Based on a recent comparative analysis of the information sectors of Singapore, Japan and the United States, Toh and Low have observed that information technologies require two-way, "relatively comparable sophistication and development between sender and receiver" (Toh and Low, July 3-6, 1989: 16). They conclude that IT strategies engender cooperation rather than competition. In the end. this may be the most important lesson both for Singapore's future and for the futures of other cities in this information age. The integrative potential of information technology in development planning and implementation needs more widespread experimentation and perfection at various scales (i.e., local, national and international) and in different political economies and cultures.

Singapore represents a single case study in the utilization of information technology in urban development. It is a noteworthy case because it is a leading-edge, empirical example of a metropolitan-scaled country and unique political economy that is within sight of becoming a fully-networked society (Sisodia, 1992). Singapore has idiosyncratic characteristics, but so does every other place. Thus, improved scholarship of contemporary urban and IT policy analysis and policy planning requires many more studies of such IT urban development cases so that generalizability and theory derivation are advanced (Kuo, Loh & Raman, 1990). At various levels of development and under varying political economies IT urban development and planning cases exist in Japan, France and the US, as well as other areas of the Pacific Rim, such as in Australia (Blakely & Stimson, 1993 forthcoming). What do we know from the experience of the technopolis in Japan and France or the multi-function polis in Australia? How do we effectively use information technology to plan our cities? (Jalabert & Thouzellier, 1990; Smilor, Kozmetsky and Gibson, 1988; and Tatsuno, 1986). How might we operationalize these IT planning and development lessons elsewhere? Urban development scholars and their students should address these questions and significantly increase research and evaluation into the role of information technology in the future development of cities worldwide (cf., Brunn & Leinbach, 1991).

Learning from others is not new. Such knowledge exploration by Japan over the last century has directly contributed to its early and contemporary global ascendancy (Deacon, 1982). Indeed, Singapore's rapid development is, in part, attributable to intentional knowledge transfer, with appropriate tailoring, from the experience of others (Corey, 1987 & 1991). Such approaches recently have been documented for cross-national urban policy making (Masser & Williams, 1986).

In the United States, greater realization has developed about the criticality of being competitive in the global economy. As the perception of loss of U.S. competitiveness becomes more pervasive, there is growing concern for the importance of industrial policy (Greenhouse, July 19, 1992: F5). Lessons from countries with extensive experience in planning and implementing industrial policies, such as Singapore, may even begin to receive greater interest from laissez faire-committed U.S. policy makers and planners. If such comparative research and practice are stimulated as a result of papers such as this evaluation of Singapore IT planning, then at least one of the main objectives of this paper will have been realized.

Acknowledgements

I am grateful to the following colleagues who facilitated the research that enabled the preparation and strengthening of this paper. These include: Ang Peng Hwa, Pearleen Chan, Chong Siak Ching, Steven Choo, Peter Ee, Foong Tze Foon, Michael K.H. Lie, John Keung, Ambassador Tommy Koh, Eddie C.Y. Kuo, Angela Leck, Leong Wai Leng, Lim Beok Hwa, Aharon Kellerman, Shyong Lim, Loh Chee Meng, Suresh Natarajan, Ooi Giok Ling, Hilary Quah, Victor Savage, Wong Soon Yean, T. K. Wong, Yeo Piah Choo and anonymous reviewers.

References

Asia Computer Weekly March 4-10, 1991: Committee to Steer IT2000 in Singapore, *Asia Computer Weekly*, p. 20.

Balakrishnan, N. June 20, 1991: "Single-minded," *Far Eastern Economic Review*, 152, 25, p. 17.

Blakely, E. & Stimson, R. (eds.) 1993: *The New City of the Pacific Rim*

Briggs, M. July 9, 1991: "The Multifunction Polis Concept: Implications for Regional Development Strategies," A paper prepared for the Twelfth Pacific Regional Science Conference Organization, Cairns, Australia, 12 pp.

Brunn, S.D. & Leinbach, T.R. (eds.) 1991: *Collapsing Space & Time: Geographical Aspects of Communication & Information*, HarperCollinsAcademic, London.

Castells, M. 1989: *The Informational City*, Basil Blackwell, Oxford.

Chief Statistician 1983: *Economic & Social Statistics Singapore 1960-1982*, Department of Statistics, Singapore.

Chief Statistician, 1986: *Yearbook of Statistics Singapore 1985-1986*, Department of Statistics, Singapore.

Corey, K.E. 1987: "Planning the Information Age Metropolis: The Case of Singapore," in L. Guelke & R. Preston (eds.), *Abstract Thoughts: Concrete Solutions*, Department of Geography Publication Series No. 29, University of Waterloo, Waterloo, Ontario, pp. 49-72.

Corey, K.E. 1991: "The Role of Information Technology in the Planning and Development of Singapore," in S.D. Brunn & T.R. Leinbach, *Collapsing Space and Time: Geographic Aspects of Communications and Information*, HarperCollinsAcademic, London, pp. 217-231.

Corey, K.E., Fletcher, R. & Moscove, B. 1993: "Singapore: The Planned New City of the Pacific Rim," in E.J. Blakely and r.J. Stimson, *The New city of the Pacific Rim*, (forthcoming).

Deacon, R. 1982: *Kempei Tai: The Japanese Secret Service Then and Now.* Charles E. Tuttle Company, Tokyo.

Economic Committee 1986: *The Singapore Economy: New Directions*, Ministry of Trade & Industry, Singapore.

EDB June 1991: *Singapore Investment News*, Economic Development Board, Singapore, p. 7.

EDB December 1991: *Singapore Investment News*, Economic Development Board, Singapore, p. 7.

Goh, C.T. 1981: "Towards Higher Achievement," *Budget Speech 1981*, Information Division, Ministry of Culture, Singapore.

Goh, C.T. 1988: "Window on New Information Age," *Speeches*, Information Division, Ministry of Communications and Information, Singapore, 12, 5, pp. 16-18.

Goh, C.T. February 15, 1988: *Agenda for Action, Goals and Challenges*, A Green Paper to Parliament, Singapore.

Goh, K.S. 1972: *The Economics of Modernization and Other Essays* Asia Pacific Press, Singapore, p. 275.

Goldblum, C. 1990: "The Singapore Paradigm: Urban Planning Material for Making a 'Dragon', in G.C. Lim & W. Chang, *Dynamic Transformation: Korea, NICs and Beyond*, Consortium on Development Studies, Urbana, Illinois, pp. 223-231.

Government of Singapore 1991: *Singapore: The Next Lap*, Times Editions Pte Ltd, Singapore.

Greenhouse, S. July 19, 1992: "The Calls for an Industrial Policy Grow Louder, *The New York Times*, p. F5.

74   *Kenneth E. Corey*

Hepworth, M.E. 1990: *Geography of the Information Economy*, The Guilford Press, New york.
Hon, S.S. 1972: *Singapore: Economic Pattern in the Seventies*, Ministry of Culture, Singapore.
Hottes, K. 1991: "The Impact of Modern Telematics on Singapore, Kuala Lumpur and Georgetown/Butterworth (Penang)," *NETCOM*, International Geographical Union Commission on Telecommunication and Communication, Issy-les-Moulineaux, France, 5, 2, pp. 330-348.
Hu, R. 1988: "IT's Economic Impact in Singapore," *Speeches*, 12, 6, pp. 41-45.
Information Division 1989: *Singapore 1989*, Ministry of Communications and Information, Singapore.
IT Focus June 1989: "IT Power Reveals Benefits," *IT Focus*, National Computer Board, Singapore, p. 6.
IT Focus October 1989: "Four Steps to Help Law Firms Adopt IT," *IT Focus*, National Computer Board, Singapore, p. 5.
IT Focus October 1989: "New R&D Pact Will Involve High End Imaging Project," *IT Focus*, National Computer Board, Singapore, p. 12.
IT Focus October 1989: "TradeNet Wins World Award," *IT Focus*, National Computer Board, Singapore, pp. 1-2.
IT Focus December 1989: "Conference to Discuss Strategic Use of IT for Businesses," *IT Focus*, National Computer Board, Singapore, p. 12.
IT Focus December 1989: "Informatics Gets Major Endorsement," *IT Focus*, National Computer Board, Singapore, p. ii.
IT Focus March 1990: "Landmark IT conference Sets Tone for 1990s," *IT Focus*, National Computer Board, Singapore, pp. 6-7.
IT Focus March 1990: "Legal Profession Takes Quantum Leap into IT," *IT Focus*, National Computer Board, Singapore, p. 5.
IT Focus March 1990: "NCB Shares It's Experiences," *IT Focus*, National Computer Board, Singapore, p. 2.
IT Focus March 1990: "Winners Who Use IT for Better Business Performance," *IT Focus*, National Computer Board, pp. 10-11.
IT Focus December 1990: "National R&D Body Formed," *IT Focus*, National Computer Board, Singapore, p. 2.
IT Focus March 1991: "IT2000: Blueprint for the Future," *IT Focus*, National Computer Board, Singapore, pp. 1-2.
IT Focus December: "New Milestone for IT Industry, *IT Focus*, National Computer Board, Singapore, pp. i-iv.
IT Manpower Survey 1989 1990: "IT Manpower Grows 10-Fold Since 1980," *IT Focus*, National Computer Board, Singapore, pp. 12-13.
IT Singapore March 1990: "IT Can Spawn More Financial Products and Services," *IT Singapore*, Newscom, Singapore, 2, 3, p. 5.
IT Singapore March 1990: "Wide Acceptance Necessary for IT in Health-care Services," *IT Singapore*, Newscom, Singapore, 2, 3, p. 4.
IT Singapore March 1990a: "A&W Upgrades with New POS System," *IT Singapore*, Newscom, Singapore, 2, 3, p. 15.
IT Singapore March 1990b: "SME Retailers Can Now Offer NETS Facility," *IT Singapore*, Newscom, Singapore, 2, 3, p. 15.
IT Singapore April 1990: CIDB Launches Construction Industry IT Programme," *IT Singapore*, Newscom, Singapore, 2, 4, p. 15.
IT Singapore April 1990: "PC Ruling for HDB Contractors," *IT Singapore*, Newscom, Singapore, 2, 4, pp. 1-2.
IT Singapore April 1990: "Pizza Hut Outlets First to Install Portable PIN Pads," *IT Singapore*, Newscom, Singapore, 2, 4, p. 3.

IT Singapore May 1990: "How Smart Card Can Benefit Local Companies," *IT Singapore*, Newscom, Singapore, 2, 5, p. 12.

IT Singapore May 1990: "ITI Singapore Telecom to Jointly Develop ISDN Applications," *IT Singapore*, Newscom, Singapore, 2, 5, p. 6.

IT Singapore May 1990: "Over 9,000 Workers Trained to Date," *IT Singapore*, Newscom, Singapore, 2, 5, p. 14.

IT Singapore May 1990a: "Showcase of Future Applications," *IT Singapore*, Newscom, Singapore, 2, 5, p.1.

IT Singapore May 1990b: "Survey Points to Rising IT Usage," *IT Singapore*, Newscom, Singapore, 2, 5, p. 1.

IT Singapore August 1990: "Singapore Ranks High in World Rankings," *IT Singapore*, Newscom, Singapore, 2, 8, p. 1.

IT Singapore June 1990: "Sector-wide Information Networks to be Integrated into One Major Infrastructure," and "ICIS to Offer Broad Range of Telecommunications Courses," *IT Singapore*, 2, 6, pp. 1 and 10.

IT Singapore December 1990: "Informatics '90 Achieves Record Participation," *IT Singapore*, Newscom, Singapore, 2, 12, p. 1.

IT Singapore March 1991: "$11b Worth of Computers and Peripherals Exported Last Year," *IT Singapore*, Newscom, Singapore, 3, 3, p. 6.

Jalabert, G. & Thouzellier, C. (eds.) 1990: *Villes et Technopoles: Nouvelle Industrialisation, Nouvelle Urbanization*, Colloque International, Presses Universitaries du Mirail, Toulouse, France.

Jussawalla, M. & Cheah, C.W. 1983: Towards an Information Economy: The Case of Singapore," *Information Economics and Policy*, 1, pp. 161-176.

Keen, P.G.W. 1991: *Every Manager's Guide to Information Technology*, Harvard Business School Press, Boston.

Kellerman, A. 1993: *Telecommunications and Geography*, Belhaven Press, London (forthcoming).

Kuo, E.C.Y. 1991: "Communication Research in Singapore: Themes, Gaps and Priorities" *Asian Journal of Communication*, 2,1: pp. 109-128.

Kuo, E.C.Y. & Chen, H.T. 1987: "Towards an Information Society: Changing Occupational Structure in Singapore," *Asian Survey*, XXVII, 3: 355-370.

Kuo, E.C.Y. & Chen, P.S.J. 1983: *Communication Policy and Planning in Singapore*, Kegan Paul International, London.

Kuo, E.C.Y., Loh, C.M. & Raman, K.S. (eds.) 1990: *Information Technology and Singapore Society: Trends, Policies and Applications*, Symposium Proceedings, Singapore University Press, Singapore.

Leck, A. June 3, 1991: Personal Correspondence.

Lim, K. April 4, 1992: "Computer Links for All in 15 Years," *Straits Times Weekly Overseas*, Edition, p. 1. Mah, B.T. 1989: "The Move Towards Automation," *Speeches*, Information Division, Ministry of Communications and Information, Singapore, 13, 5, pp. 76-79.

Mah, B.T. 1992: "A New Era in Telecommunications," *Speeches*, Ministry of Information and the Arts, singapore, 16, 2, pp. 56-60.

Masser, I. & Williams, R. (eds.) 1986: *Learning from Other Countries*, Geo Books, Norwich, UK.

Ministry of Trade and Industry 1991: *Economic Survey of Singapore 1990*, Ministry of Trade and Industry, Singapore.

Ministry of Trade and Industry 1992: *Economic Survey of Singapore 1991*, Ministry of Trade and Industry, Singapore.

National Computer Board 1990: *IT Industry Survey 1990*, National Computer Systems Pte Ltd, Singapore.

National Computer Board 1991: *1990/1991 Year Book*, National Computer Board, Singapore.

National Computer Board 1992: *A Vision of an Intelligent Island: IT2000 Report*, National Computer Board, Singapore.

National IT Plan Working Committee 1985: *National IT Plan: A Strategic Framework*, National Computer Board, Singapore.

National Science and Technology Board 1991: *National Technology Plan 1991: Windows of Opportunities*, National Science and Technology Board, Singapore.

Ng, W.J., June 23, 1992: "Time Now for Teleview?" *The Straits Times*, Innovation section: p. 2.

Ong, L. June 8, 1991: "A Peek into a Networked Singapore Society," *Straits Times Weekly Overseas Edition*, p. 13.

Sandhu, K.S. & Wheatley, P. 1989: *Management of Success: The Moulding of Modern Singapore*, Institute of Southeast Asian Studies, Singapore.

Savitch, H.V. 1988: *Post-Industrial Cities*, Princeton University Press, Princeton.

Singapore Federation of the Computer Industry 1987: *A Guide to Jobs and Careers: The Information Processing Industry in Singapore*, Singapore Federation of the Computer Industry, Singapore.

Singapore Telecom 1991: *Annual Report Financial Year 1990/91*, Singapore Telecom.

Singapore Trade Development Board 1989: *Singapore Trade Development Board Annual Report 1988/89*, Singapore Trade Development Board, Singapore.

Sisodia, R. S. 1992: "Singapore Invests in the Nation-Corporation," *Harvard Business Review*, May-June, 92311, pp. 40-50.

Smilor, R.W., Kozmetsky, G. & Gibson, D.V. (eds.) 1988: *Creating the Technopolis:Linking Technology Commercialization and Economic Development*, Ballinger Publishing Company, Cambridge, Massachusetts. Straits Times December 4, 1986: "Seven-prong Approach to National IT Plan," *Straits Times*, p. 14.

Straits Times November 3, 1990: "Dr. Yeo Launches $50m Teleview Info System," *Straits Times Weekly Overseas Edition*, p. 24.

Sussman, G. 1990: "Singapore's Great Leap: Information Technology in Context," *Artificial Intelligence Review*, 4, pp. 53-59.

Tatsuno, S. 1986: *The Technopolis Strategy: Japan, High Technology,and the Control of the Twenty-first Century*, Prentice Hall Press, New York.

Tay, C. January 14, 1991: Personal Correspondence, 6 pp.

Tay, E.S. 1989: "Better Management of Information Through MediNet," *Speeches*, Information Division, Ministry of Communications and Information, Singapore, 13, 6, pp. 60-63.

Tay, E.S. December 13, 1990: "Opening Speech," Singapore Informatics '90,National Computer Board, Singapore, 9 pp.

Tay, E.S. 1992: IT and the Evolution of the New Organization," *Speeches*, Ministry of Information and the Arts, Singapore, 16, 2, pp. 61-64.

Toh, M.H. & Low, L. July 3-6, 1989: "A Comparative Analysis of the Primary Information Sector in Singapore, Japan and the United States," A paper prepared for the Eleventh Pacific Regional Science Conference of the Regional Science Association, Singapore, 29 pp.

Urban Redevelopment Authority 1991: *Living the Next Lap: Towards A Tropical City of Excellence*, Urban Redevelopment Authority, Singapore.

Wee, K. W. June 7, 1990: *Towards 21st Century Singapore*, Ministry of Communications and Information, Singapore.

The World Bank 1989: *World Development Report 1990*, Oxford University Press.

The World Bank 1992: *World Development Report 1992*, Oxford University Press, New York.

Yeo, N.H. 1989: "The World's First Nation-wide ISDN," *Speeches*, Information Div., Ministry of Communications and Information, Singapore, 13, 6, pp. 22-25.

Yeung, Y.M. 1990: *Changing Cities of Pacific Asia: A Scholarly Interpretation*, The Chinese University Press, Hong Kong.

5 Missing Networks and European Telecom Systems

Peter Nijkamp and Jaap M. Vleugel

Transport and communications infrastructure has played a critical role in the history of Europe, not only many centuries ago but also in recent years. The European political and economic system has increasingly evolved from a set of relatively independent states into a collection of interacting economies connected by means of various types of network infrastructures.

Missing networks

Historically major transitions in the European economic system were always accompanied (or even induced) by major changes in transport and communications infrastructures. Four main transport and logistic revolutions in the history of western Europe have been distinguished, each of them characterized by the emergence, adoption and implementation of a new type of international infrastructure. These four revolutions are:

- The Hanseatic period (from the thirteenth to the sixteenth century), in which waterways (inland and coastal transport links) emerged as a new logistic system connecting cities along rivers and coastal areas;
- The 'golden' period (from the sixteenth century to the seventeenth century), characterized by a drastic improvement in sailing and sea transport and by the introduction of new banking systems, through which trade to the East Indies and West Indies was stimulated (with Lisbon, Antwerp and Amsterdam as major centres);
- The industrial revolution (from the middle of the nineteenth century), in which the invention of the steam engine generated new transport modes (sea transport, railways) which also created new market areas (e.g., North-America);
- The period from the seventies in our century, which is marked by informatization and flexibilization; in this framework JIT (just-in-time) systems and MRP (Material Requirements Planning) are evolving as

new management principles. The rapid developments in the area of new information technology have also led to the emergence of integral logistics. This may mark the beginning of a new era.

Economic development and infrastructure development go apparently hand in hand. Therefore, the European economy will remain critically dependent on well functioning networks as catalysts for future development. There is nowadays however a growing awareness that the current European infrastructure network is becoming outdated, without being replaced by modern facilities which would position the European economies at a competitive edge. There is not only a problem of missing links (i.e., Segments in a network), but even a more serious problem of missing networks as a whole. *Thus the notion of missing networks refers here to the absence of strategic layers or components of Europe's transport and communications infrastructure, be it material or immaterial in nature. Thus the term `missing networks' applies to the poor performance — in terms of convenience, speed, comfort, flexibility, reliability, costs, safety or social costs — of European infrastructure.*

Missing networks exist, because transportation systems are developed in a segmented way, each country seeking for its own solution for each transport mode without keeping an eye on the synergetic effects of a co-ordinated design and use of advanced infrastructures. Another reason for missing networks is the focus on hard ware and the neglect of soft ware and organizational aspects as well as financial and ecological implications. Cabotage, protection of national carriers, segmented European railway companies, and lack of multi-modal transport strategies are but a few examples of the emergence of missing networks. A European orientation of all transport modes is necessary to cope with the current problems of missing networks.

Europe on the move

In talking about missing networks, we have to be aware of the fact that the European economies have never been in a static situation, but always in a state of flux. Older infrastructures are constantly being replaced by more up-to-date networks to respond to new developments in the transport and communications sector.

In recent years a series of drastic changes can be observed in Europe's transport and communications. At the same time the fear is growing that our current networks are far from satisfactory in fulfilling the needs for the European infrastructure. Such changes concern *commodity* transport, *passenger* transport and *services/information* transport.

Far reaching changes in *commodity* transport include:

- the trend towards high value and low weight commodities (*dematerialization*), requiring flexible and varied transport modes.
- the tendency to produce more tailor-made goods in more diverse and smaller product series (*customization*), leading to a decrease in the role of bulk transport.
- an increasingly important role of new information technology and (both internal and external) logistics management (*informatization*), which places more emphasis on the coordination of physical transport (e.g., door-to-door transport).
- a world-wide orientation of modern transport, accompanied by the emergence of transnational transport companies (*globalization*), which also generates many new international trade patterns.
- the rise of combined transport of previously competitive modes (*integration*), leading to new demands for transhipment facilities (e.g., Road-rail or road-air).

In the area of *passenger* transport various megatrends are arising:
- a reduction in the growth of population (the '*grey revolution*'), leading to an aging society with much leisure time and hence a high geographical mobility.
- a tendency towards more, but smaller and alternative types of households (*individualization*), creating an additional demand for more mobility.
- an (expected) trend of gradually rising income levels per capita, accompanied by a higher female labour force participation and flexible working hours, the '*new economic progress*', leading to a rise in car ownership and car use (for both business and personal purposes).
- an ongoing rise in commuting distance and in urban sprawl (*suburbanization*), implying a rapid rise in motorization of our society.

Finally important developments in the field of *information/services* include the following:
- a trend toward integral logistic systems (the '*fourth logistic revolution*'), leading to the need for just-in-time (JIT) concepts, an increase in delivery frequencies and an increase in road haulage (based e.g. On preprogrammed routing).
- an increasingly important role of telecommunication and information in transport (*telematics*), leading to an intensification of physical and human interactions in space (telematics may act as both a generator of and a substitute for physical transport).

The conclusion which can be drawn from the above trends is evident: transport and communications become more intensive, not only locally/regionally, but also internationally. The potential offered by modern information technology and logistic systems will lead to a re-orientation of conventional transport systems. The need for reliability, flexibility and multi-modality in modern transport systems requires also modern infrastructure networks. An absence of such networks will hamper further balanced economic progress in Europe.

The new European economy

The world economy is in full dynamics, expecially in recent years. Traditional patterns of competition — within national borders — are being increasingly replaced by vigourous competition on a multi-national and even worldwide scale. "intra-country" competition is being replaced by "inter-trade-block" competition, since traditional boundaries disappear, as is the case in Europe and will be the case in other parts of the world. Countries within such trade-blocks are then part of an economic network. To maximize the competitiveness of such a network, and thereby maximize its socio-economic potential and performance, the quality of its infrastructure is of critical importance, as transport has become an important component of modern production processes, among others because of intensified division of tasks between firms (in different countries).

Because of this globalization and other factors (including the need for higher and sustained economic growth), transportation in Europe has grown enormously, especially in recent years. As the supply of infrastructure — for various reasons — followed this trend only in part, existing infrastructure bottlenecks have been accentuated. This is a very serious problem, since economic development and infrastructural development have always been strongly interlinked, as shown by hundreds of years of European history. The full benefits of the foreseen internal European market will only be reaped in case of (physical and non-physical) infrastructural adjustments in Europe. What is needed then, is European — and not national — thinking and action in infrastructural policy, based on knowledge of past successes and failures in infrastructural planning and of the future needs of the economy, the people living in Europe and their (increasingly threatened) (natural) environment.

In the past, infrastructure and its bottlenecks were normally dealt with in uni-modal terms: decision making focussing on only the mode in question and with specific links in uni-modal networks. Such uni-modal solutions have considerable limitations and the upgrading of specific problematic links gains only a little time as additional demand generated by the improvements follows additional supply. Consequently decision makers have begun to think in terms of the coupling effects of networks, both spatially and intermodally; individual transport infrastructure is part of a "network" of infrastructure. Proper decision making concerning the needs for new infrastructure and developing strategic solutions is likely then to increasingly have to rely on a more comprehensive systems approach, in which the quality of a hierarchy of different levels of harmonized transportation subsystems is the backbone.

The failure to recognize that individual transport infrastructure is part of a network, casts serious doubt on the ability of Europe to renew its transport infrastructure; as a result growing congestion, increasing waiting times and booming transport costs may severely worsen Europe's competitive position severely and may even force increasingly footloose firms to move to other parts of the world.

Missing economic development

As mentioned in section 3, Europe is in motion, politically, economically and spatially. In the past decades the European `space-economy' has featured a wide variety of socio-economic problems and bottlenecks at both the local/regional and the national/international level. The `old world' however, has in recent years shown surprising signs of economic and political revitalization. After several decades of desperate struggling for economic and political unification among the countries of the European community, the tide has changed. The magical year 1992 has been accepted throughout Europe as a decisive historical landmark in the evolution of Europe toward international competitiveness, economic and technological leadership at a global level, and internal cohesiveness and cooperation. It has become a widely accepted belief that a unification of the European economies is a *necessary* condition for economic survival of Europe in the medium and long term.

In the meantime, the socio-economic, socio-political and socio-political impact of 1992 is already immense, as can be seen from the current wave of international mergers and joint ventures. It has led to a complete reorientation of economic policies — both private and public — in Europe, followed by new initiatives in technology, finance, transport and science policy (e.g., Esprit, RACE, EUREKA, DRIVE). And it is conceivable that several non-member states (such as Austria, or Turkey) may apply for membership, whilst others (such as Switzerland, Sweden,

Finland, Norway and Hungary) look for special ways of avoiding exclusion from the economic benefits of the largest trade block in the world.

In various documents of the commission of the European Communities, especially in the so-called white paper (1985), a strong plea has been made for the completion of the single European market of all EC member countries from the viewpoint that the gains of an open and integrated market far outweigh the costs of semi-protected national markets. The failure of the original EEC treaty to realize a really common European market meant in practice support for national protectionism, despite the abolition of customs duties. The legalized common practice of non-tariff barriers has led to high opportunity costs. It is hoped that these *'costs of non-Europe'* can be avoided by creating a free internal EC market without frontier controls for goods, services and production factors. However, it is also recognized that a really free European market will only reap the fruits of an international integration if all social, economic, technology, environment, energy, transport and regional policies are harmonized and coordinated. The removal of many unnecessary and irrational obstacles — seen from a European angle — may herald a new era for the countries and regions in Europe.

The benefits of integration are already considerable if one only looks at *static* reallocation effects caused by relative price changes, but they may be much higher in the case of *dynamic* integration effects caused by shifts in the production structure itself, e.g. As a consequence of technological progress, institutional reforms or deregulation, improved international connections, or higher regional accessibility. The assessment of the potential gains of completing the internal market — or, alternatively, the costs of non-Europe — is of course far from easy, but may amount on an annual basis to at least 150 to 250 billion ECU's, with the highest benefits achieved in the micro-electronics industry, car industry, chemical industry, mechanical engineering and food industry.

These expected integration benefits will only come into being if Europe becomes an open and flexible network in which transport and communications infrastructure provides efficient connections between all regions and states in Europe. Consequently, the opportunity costs of missing networks are extremely high. There is plenty of evidence to show that productive investments and social overhead investments (notably infrastructure investments) need each other to arrive at a balanced economic development of nations. In general, the spin-off effects of new infrastructure investments are significant, provided they are tailor-made with respect to spatial-economic needs.

The crucial role of modern transport and communications

Transport and communications provide a stimulus for economic development (exchange of commodities, division of tasks, specialization etc.). According to the Cecchini report any additional economic growth is critically dependent on the physical exchange capacity of Europe.

Improvements in transport and communications systems are thus a critical success factor in generating highly significant dynamic integration effects. And there is an urgent need for such a strategic improvement. Even nowadays we see already that — from a geographical viewpoint — Europe is in fast motion. The action radius of commuting is structurally rising, the volume of commodities transported nationally and internationally is increasing, and airline activities for both passengers and commodities are booming. In a recent publication this mobility drift in Europe has been described as the 'Euro-mobile' phenomenon.

Transport policy favouring a free movement of persons and commodities in the EC is a sine qua non for a single market. The removal of existing barriers is of great importance for obtaining the highest dynamic integration benefits from a network economy.

In recent years transport in most European countries has exhibited clear signs of *devolution* leading to a less intensive involvement of central governments, although a European view would call for better coordination. This devolution appears to be a uniform phenomenon, although in various countries and cities it manifests itself in different forms, e.g., Deregulation, decentralization and privatization.

In this context, the first and most noticeable observation is that there is a striking parallel movement of transport infrastructure policies in most European countries in the past three decades: a period of expansion in the 1960's, a period of contraction in the 1970's and an era of selective expansion in the 1980's, in which the direction of selection is strongly governed by either market forces or by decentralization principles. Countries with a more liberal policy model and/or with severe deficits of the public budget are apparently the first ones to advocate privatization — in combination with deregulation — of transport policy, not only in the airlines sector and the freight sector, but also in the public transport sector. Among all these countries significant differences still exist, as the intensity of economic stagnation and of monetarist policies may drastically vary. In some countries local autonomy rather than privatization can be observed as a political ideology. Altogether, however, the hypothesis of a financially-driven devolution ideology is reasonably valid in many European countries.

A second observation to be made here is that European transport policy should not only be focused on an improvement of the intra-EC network infrastructure, but also increasingly on *external links* of this network. An open EC has the highest benefits for both the community itself and the world economy as a whole. Thus the improvement of cross-frontier routes is extremely important, such as the trans-European motorway, or the scandinavian links. In the future major links to east-European countries have to be envisaged. There is also a strong case here for cooperation between non-member countries which provide (transit) links between EC-members, such as switzerland, austria and yugoslavia. It goes without saying that a balanced transport policy is of critical relevance for regional equilibrium in the community. The current tendency toward major fast links is not by definition beneficial to all regions. Extensive evaluation research will be necessary here to provide policy-makers with adequate guidelines.

A third major observation is that the major stimulus for new advanced infrastructure policy is given by *information technology* (information, telecommunications and micro-electronics). Physical distribution is increasingly relying on informatics-related activities. That holds true for containerization, fast trains and airlines. Accessible and internationally coordinated information systems are becoming a major vehicle for the further improvement of the transportation and logistics network in the community. The International Transport Information System (INTIS) in the port of Rotterdam is a good example of this development. A necessary condition for the further penetration and success of such information systems is standardization, and this policy issue is one of the most crucial corner stones of the European transport policy. JIT principles and multi-modal logistic chains will never become fully operational without sufficient European standardization.

Shadow sides of the European transport scene

The transport system is in general the circulation system underlying the European economy. Unfortunately, no coherent view on the functioning of the European transport system has developed. Instead of a systemic view, in which the transport sector would be looked at from the viewpoint of coherence and positive synergetics, policy makers and planners have tended to develop segmented solutions to emerging bottlenecks by looking for specific local or modal solutions without due regard to the interwovenness of the transport system across different regions, sectors and modes. One of the main frictions in European transport policy is the absence of a strategic view on the 'wholeness' of the European transport system at all geographic levels.

Despite the increasing trend of JIT systems and related concepts, the actual practice of both commodity and passenger transport is disappointing and often frustrating. Severe traffic congestion phenomena at the urban or metropolitan level (e.g., Athens, Rome, Paris), unacceptable delays in medium and long distance transport during peak hours, unsatisfactory service levels of European railway systems and public transport in general, unreliable airline connections due to limited airport capacity, and the slow technical and institutional renewal of air traffic control in Europe; all these phenomena illustrate the difficult lesson facing the European transport sector. And there is no clear perspective for a drastic improvement of this situation. On the contrary, it is increasingly claimed that a free European market (beyond the year 1992) and a further deregulation of the European transport sector may lead to unacceptable accessibility conditions in major regions in Europe.

Another important factor will be environmental policy. In contrast to the deregulation trend regarding transport, environmental policy is critically dependent on regulations and interventions at both the supply and demand sides. In particular, technical restrictions are likely to be imposed, such as limited emission levels for motorcars or maybe even a selective prohibition of the use of certain transport modes. Recently, even a plea for a car-less city has been made.

Transport policy makers in most European countries find themselves in extremely complicated situations. A large number of interest groups, ranging from multi-national companies to local environmentalists are urging them to take action, often in quite different directions. On the one hand it has become obvious that the environment poses its limits on the volume, character and pace of the extension of transport infrastructure. On the other hand many business firms in western Europe are concerned about their competitiveness in a global context due to an inadequate infrastructure.

Inadequate infrastructure effects European business life in several ways. First, the relatively slow development of sophisticated telecommunication infrastructure in Europe may curtail the possibilities to offer new services. Moreover it may limit the possibilities to speed up international trade in a reliable way. Second, the restricted capacity of inland transport networks may cause higher production costs in Europe and affect global competitiveness.

For these reasons Europe must improve its transport and communications infrastructure to increase its competitive power, while at the same time sufficient care should be given to environmental considerations. This raises an extra difficulty, as due care is usually incompatible with swift action. Short term solutions, as advocated by some business-oriented interest groups, tend to rely heavily on a further massive extension of the European motorway system. This option may make sense in southern and eastern Europe, but for western Europe this option does not seem viable in the long run. Since supply tends to generate its own demand ('Say's Law), network extensions beyond the level of relieving unacceptable bottlenecks will create a new era of congestion at a higher level. Furthermore, this scenario will also be detrimental to a balanced spatial development of urban areas and the environment in western Europe.

A pentagon of concerns

Concern about transportation problems at the European level has increased in recent years. In the past such problems were normally signalled and treated at a local or national level, without due regard to the international context, to the impacts of local/national decisions on networks elsewhere.

In the netherlands, for instance, the strong growth of the road network — especially in the 1960's — coincided with a lack of new investment in rail infrastructure. The loss of a major client (coal transport), because of energy conversion from coal to oil and gas, forced the dutch national railways to rationalization. The closure of a large number of transhipment facilities worsened their competitive power. Since the national railways were not allowed to invest adequately in new infrastructure and rolling stock, they lost their competitive power in freight transport and to a lesser extent also in passenger transport. The strong growth of road transportation however, has led to serious environmental problems. These problems are partly due to growing congestion on the road network. Past solutions featured the extension of this network. This extension itself however, attracted extra demand, so that in a number of years this extra road capacity was seriously congested. Recently policy-makers have become aware of this phenomenon; complex problems are not dealt with any more by means of simple solutions.

As no individual network is able to satisfy current and future demands, uni-modal solutions must be rejected. Multi-modal network solutions come then to the fore, with a new spatial, i.e. European — dimension. Multi-modal solutions are part of a systems approach, of which the mutual influence and cooperation within and between networks are basic features. Combining the advantages of specific networks may then lead to synergetic effects for the whole transportation system and thereby for the economy as a whole.

This observation is once more important in the context of the European restructuring leading to an integrated euro-market of some 320 million consumers — the USA has 'only' 245 million consumers -, a truly European hemisphere with no political, economic or social borders between its member countries. Then Europe itself will be a network, but at the same time it will need an extremely well functioning transport and communications infrastructure network.

Since infrastructure networks influence both current and future economic developments, it is evident that — from a strategic viewpoint — such networks would have to be designed from a long-term European perspective. Good examples of pro-active planning in this context are the Japanese high-speed train, the *Shinkansen,* developed already in the 1960's in order to cope with accessibility problems in a densely populated country.

Besides the *regional attractiveness effect* of networks we should mention the *global coupling effect* of networks. This means that a qualification of networks should also take account of the fact that the quality of regional networks has both internal (intra-network) as well as external (inter-network) effects on transportation. For instance, the choice of the world's largest container shipment operator to use Rotterdam as its main port in Europe depends not only on the harbour facilities, but increasingly also on the quality of the European hinterland links from Rotterdam to West Germany — the terminal point of the major part of transhipments in rotterdam.

In the past, solutions to infrastructure problems were seen as having only one or two dimensions, viz., The hard ware (physical infrastructure) and the fin ware (funding) dimension. A number of failures in developing infrastructure projects points to the importance of dealing with these problems in a more sophisticated and comprehensive way. Proper solutions should take account of the following dimensions:

Table 1. *Pentagon with critical success factors*

Hard—ware	(e.g., Efficient technological standardisation)
Soft—ware	(e.g., Use of compatible information systems)
Org—ware	(e.g., Existence of effective management structures)
Fin—ware	(e.g., Access to private/public financial institutions)
Eco—ware	(e.g., Environment-friendly or regulated systems).

Note: transport and communication networks should not only be judged in view of physical infrastructure and funding problems. Instead, all of the above dimensions must be considered simultaneously.

These five critical success factors for appropriate network design and implementation can be represented as a *pentagon*. This pentagon-model will be used hereafter as a framework for judging European infrastructure network planning. It should be noted, that the pentagon model not only applies to links and uni-modal networks, but in particular to multi-modal network systems in which synergy is a sine qua non.

An illustration: European telecommunications

The development and use of telecommunications infrastructure has been evaluated in the light of the EC policy elaborated in its green paper on telecommunications. Following the main line of argument in this paper, we conclude that the most important cause of missing links in the field of telecommunications is the product of a chicken-egg problem, since *hard ware* and *services* are not introduced because of lack of demand, and demand is not revealed because of the lack of hard ware and services. With the execption of the french minitel and a few pilot projects, telecom in Europe is mainly used for basic services (telephone, datalinks and telefax), and more sophisticated services have not been introduced. One factor responsible for this is the lack of common European standards of hard ware. This underlies the current EC stimulation of research and development in this field (e.g., By means of programmes like ESPRIT, RACE etc.). The 'costs of non-Europe' because of market fragmentation are high, both at the supply side (low economies of scale etc.), As well as on the user side (higher transaction costs because of time loss, unnecessary travelling time, productivity loss etc.).

Trends

On the *demand side* there is an ongoing and rapidly increasing upward trend in the use of telecommunication services in business for data-transmission, telex, telefax and telephone purposes. There is also a similar trend in household usage. In the transport sector, however, telecommunications are only slowly being utilized — a missing network.

Missing networks in European telecommunications

The main problems in this field are the following:

At the *hard ware* level there is an extreme kind of diversification between EC-members. This is particularly evident in the differences in developing infrastructure (ISDN) and differences in transmission capacity etc.; incompatibility and lack of interconnection.

At the *org ware* level the main problems lie in the lack of standardization between national norms and standards for equipment, approvals etc., and — most important — in the way and pace in which European standardization is eventually achieved. Given the non-existence of a common European market in telecommunications, national priorities will then determine the kind of response to market needs. Another problem lies in the asymmetric way of price setting in telecommunication, determined by national considerations. For instance, high international telecom prices are often used to subsidize national users. Consequently, prices and costs are then more or less unrelated.

At the *soft ware* level a major problem lies in the absence of demand for sophisticated services using the telecom network. As long as this situation continues, suppliers of such services will not develop new applications.

Fin ware bottlenecks are also very important, since large investments are needed to develop a basic European telecommunications network.

Because of these problems, there is a real danger of a Europe 'a deux vitesses', with a clear division between those countries and/or regions having access to recent technology and those that have not. The socio-economic impacts of such developments are considerable, since existing differences in wealth and business opportunities will be accentuated.

Suggested improvements

To improve the current situation in European telecommunications the following suggestions can be formulated:

• The introduction of a base European telecom network including standard facilities, uniform rules and tariffs, and services. Local networks should be at least hard ware compatible with this base network. Management and ownership should be take the form of a public-private partnership in which governments, operators and users participate. Developing such a network will be very expensive, but will have

positive economic impacts both for the users as well as for the industry, the use of EC (development) funding is needed.
- A separation of responsibility between regulators (government; policy) and operators (implementation) (*org ware*) is needed.
- Avoidable barriers to entry should be minimized (*org ware*); the existence of monopolies should be avoided.
- Since delivery technologies are changing too fast, a sustainable basis for regulation is missing. Improving competition should then be the keyword (*org ware*).
- Telecom prices should be cost-related (*org ware*).
- Use the outcome of current Ens-applications (e.g., The European nervous-system) in transportation (EDI, ATMOS, FTM, single document etc.), Banking, environmental protection, health care, education (*org ware, hard ware, soft ware, eco ware and fin ware*) to develop European-wide applications.

Possible solutions include:
- The use of new *teleports* as a operational planning tool for connecting telecommunications with physical goods transport or passenger movements (cf. The Amsterdam teleport success story)
- The introduction of *new networks*:
  - •• Substitution of postal services by more efficient and faster express mail:
  - •• Express mail services are booming, but the lack of a true network and thereby inefficient competition leads to very high prices.
  - •• The combined use of *deregulation of national PTT services* and the *introduction of new standardized telecom services*. The French Minitel might be used as a basis for such an European network (*soft ware, org ware*). Experimentation with telecom zones in rural areas between two or three countries (*org ware*) is also an option in line with deregulation.
  - •• Where substitution is impossible in goods transportation, options include the use of *orbital fleet management* in relation to *electronic customs* (replacement of physical border controls by standardized electronic vehicle identification at the big European freight terminals, ports and airports).

Common problems: standardization in European transportation and communications policy

Lack of standardization is one of the main reasons for bottlenecks in transport networks. Technical standardization covers the areas of infrastructure, vehicle technology and cargo. Standardization has a number of dimensions, of which the technical one is nowadays in most cases not the most important one anymore. The *org ware* dimension is far more important, since standardization in European networks will only work if their design, development and management is of European nature. Joint European investments in uniform technology, components and subsystems, and experiments are the prime issue in this field.

Missing standardization in European networks

In *road transportation* the European network has a high degree of standardization. National standards for *infrastructure* are therefore no bottleneck for transportation. European standards for *international* transport exist; at this point there is no evident bottleneck. This is however not the case in the field of *domestic* transport. Harmonizing of national *standards for vehicle dimensions* is necessary because of the possibility that domestically used vehicles will also be used for international transport. The *environmental policy in the Alpine countries* may lead to standardization problems, since the favouring of combined transport forces the use of containers standardized to railway profiles. *Technical standardization of cargo* (containers, exchange bodies) is necessary, since the use of non-pallet compatible containers and exchange bodies is inefficient. This problem hinders especially the development of combined transport (road-rail).

In *inland shipping* there are only a few problems concerning standardization. There exists a European *infrastructure* network of rivers and harbours. Using a pusher tug with six carriers is only possible on the Dutch part of the Rhine under certain conditions, because of the *lack of width of parts of canals and rivers*. Efficient transport of containers (on deck) is not always possible because of *low bridges and the width of sluices*. If a wider container type becomes the standard one (the current tendency), the efficient use of decks would no longer be possible.

Rail transportation demonstrates a serious lack of standardization. Major problems exist in:
- differences in gauges (normal gauge, small gauge and wide gauge; see also section 8)
- differences in voltages, frequencies and supply type (overhead line, third rail)
- differences in signalling systems (hard ware and org ware), including norms for the use of foreign traction on domestic rails and on board (receiving) equipment, including lack of coordination
- differences in free profiles (prohibiting especially the development of international combined transportation

- differences in the carrying capacity of the infrastructure

A change of the current dimensions of containers might be fatal for the railways, since transportation efficiency would decline, while also severe org ware problems would arise. Interestingly enough, the railways themselves do apparently see standardization as of little importance, since a number of solutions is found to overcome these bottlenecks. The delay stemming from technical controls and customs when crossing borders is regarded as leading to a far greater loss of time. Full standardization of voltages, signalling and safety systems is very expensive and not part of the discussion as far as railway companies are concerned. The growing use of three-phase current motors in locomotives however, will make multi-voltage locomotion very easy, so the lack of standardization of voltages may be solved in due time.

In *air transportation* no bottlenecks exist in the field of standardization of *infrastructure* and *cargo*. The use of special air containers etc. is no hindrance in combined road-air transportation, whereas the opposite is through for (the very low developed) rail-air transport.

In *sea transport* standard containers are used. Changing these standards would however lead to great problems.

Combined transportation is faced with a great number of problems. Research into the necessity and problems of introducing new standard containers shows that this will hit sectors with long-term investment needs most severely (the shipping and rail sectors), both in terms of (lost) investments and less efficient transport.

Finally, in *telecommunications*, standardization issues are widespread, including both the networks and user hard ware and soft ware.

Suggested Improvements

The most important solution lies on the *org ware* level; the need for *a European vision on standardization*. This includes a strong need for public and private investments in standardization. The successful case of Eurofima in *financing* rolling stock all over Europe shows that financing and standardization may be achieved jointly and efficiently. The use of pilot projects should stimulate European standardization.

Technical standardization of *hard ware* and *soft ware* is needed in most sectors, given the need to achieve long term transport policy -increasing transport capacity, speed, reliability and safety, and reducing transport costs — and *environmental* policy aims — less accidents, more efficient transport etc. The use of three-phase current locomotives easily permits running on multi-current tracks.

The debate concerning changing cargo and vehicle standards should incorporate the efficiency and costs of transport, the costs of new investments and sunk costs, and the potentials for combined transportation. This means that that *standard dimensions for cargo should serve the transportation needs of all modes.* The Eureka-context might be considered as a useful scheme to implement the above mentioned projects.

Plans for action

Europe is in 'fast-motion.' Missing networks act as stumbling blocks for a rapid pace. The way in which Europe will actually move is uncertain, as strong forces of interest groups and bureaucracy are likely to act nationally, regionally and sectorally, since disappearing frontiers in the new emerging Europe will threaten their positions. This leads us to the heart of the problems, since a major part of current transportation problems is due to short-sighted self-interest of national politicians.

From the foregoing exposition it has become clear, that the transport system performs the same kind of function to the European economy as the blood circulation performs in the human body. There are however, also big differences between them, since the human body has a number of sophisticated control systems trained to cooperate with each other and is therefore able to achieve a high-level performance, whereas the 'European network body' lacks coherent materialization and coordination, since sometimes even basic transport functions do not exist (or perform very poorly), whilst major parts of this body compete with each other rather than complement each other.

It should be emphasized — particularly when considering policy choices — that transportation is a derived demand. Transportation is not an aim in itself, it serves 'higher' economic goals related to the requirements of a network economy. Access to economic activities and social facilities is the major service provided by infrastructure networks and — irrespective of the type of mode — this is the main goal of a European-oriented transport policy. This holds true for the two-tier system of a European-based transport system, viz. The local-regional network in metropolitan nodes and the long-distance network between major centres in Europe. Recent initiatives regarding trans-European networks are worth mentioning here, as they also take for granted a systems view on European infrastructure.

An important caveat for transportation planning is the fact that the most favoured solution to transportation problems (in the past) — viz. physical extension of networks (i.e., Investments in hardware) — has proven to be valid only for very short periods of time, since capacity extension will very soon show the same kind of congestion as other parts of the network. Three options seem to be useful to cope with this dilemma:

- Investments in *advanced modes of transport*, e.g., Transportation based on telematics infrastructure, open new opportunities to expand interactions without major extensions of other networks, but it remains to be seen for how long, given the predicted massive growth of transportation in the years to come. Large and focused investments in telematics and new information technology infrastructure is certainly necessary in order to reduce the problems of missing networks.
- It is increasingly necessary to *tackle the causes* of the growing demand for transportation facilities — e.g., Physical planning of residential areas, locational behaviour of firms and user charges — in stead of just extending networks at increasingly growing social (i.e. External) costs.
- *Improvement and/or establishment of multi-modal networks* is another meaningful option. This indicates both the need to think and act from a European perspective, when dealing with transportation problems and the need to give serious thought to all five dimensions of networks, i.e., Hard ware, soft ware, org ware, fin ware and eco ware. *Network quality* is the corner stone of this approach and must therefore be set high on the political agenda.

From the large number of *solutions* to the above mentioned frictions caused by missing networks the following directions are promising and viable for various transport modes.

To create a genuine European *railway* network for international connections requires stronger cooperation between the European railway companies (e.g., By means of mergers), international technical standardization, upgrading of cross-border lines and large investments in multimodal transhipment. To tackle the connection problems in public transport, the establishment of a coherent international public transport agency with a broad competence should be favoured.

To improve the quality of the European *road network* upgrading of existing or building of new cross-border motorways should be given high priority. Both the road safety and road capacity as well as environmental impacts may be improved by means of traffic guidance systems.

Investment in inland *waterways* (including sluices) and coastal transport systems is necessary to establish a European waterway network for mass transportation as well as for the growing container transport. The proposed and more or less environmentally-induced shift from road to rail transportation is likely to highlight strong capacity constraints in the railway network. Although water transportation has a lower environmental impact than road transportation, building new waterways however, has also a strong negative impact on the environment. An extension of the waterways network and a restructuring of existing facilities should however be considered as a useful option.

The major bottleneck in *air transportation* is definitely the lack of an integrated European air control system. Such a system may give capacity improvements of some 30 percent, thereby largely eliminating current - and extremely costly - air congestion.

In addition, *multi-modal* network solutions have to be favoured. Examples of multi-modal networks which could be established in Europe include the following:

- High speed trains as feeder lines between or for airports have a great potential;
- Combined terminals for transhipment between vessels, trucks, trains and airplanes are necessary for commodity transport;
- Transhipment of commodity transport between road and rail should be favoured.

In terms of *policy initiatives*, the following strategy for the various planning levels (regional, national and European) regarding all transport and communication modes is needed:

- A declaration of infrastructure development as a basic economic interest for Europe; such a status should, for instance, include access to the various fiscal and financial instruments of the EC for R&D and pilot projects in this field;
- The definition of a priority plan of base European networks (road, rail, air, waterways and telecom) in terms of network quality and performance (e.g., Maximum travel time, reliability of transportation etc.). Such a network would need sound links with lower level national and regional networks;
- A strategic policy analysis of how to implement such a network; for instance, coupling existing national networks is only a first step in this process, since nationalistic planning failures and thinking have strongly prevented a European network vision from emerging;
- The creation of efficient decision making procedures for European infrastructure (e.g. Coordination via a European Institute for Standardization. Growing constraints on infrastructure (e.g., Financial, environmental, technical, etc.) Have helped to create a climate in Europe which seriously affects its competitive position;

- A clear strategy on priorization of European infrastructure projects, including a sound transnational financing (e.g., On the basis of a European infrastructure bank associated with a coordinating body for European transport policy).

These initiatives are not adressed to the planning of infrastructure in the short term, but are focused on medium and long term projects, and contrast with the well-known short term demand-oriented planning failures of the past.

Based on the foregoing considerations and recommendations, the following *plans for action* to remove missing networks in Europe have to be implemented:

- To pursue a combined transport strategy for rail and road with several layers of networks, including a system of big European freight terminals linked by block trains on a higher level, and soft technology piggyback transport facilities on a lower level. This would ask for organizational and logistic innovations on a European level.
- To create an integrated European air traffic control system. In order to improve the capacity on the European sky traffic, corridors would have to be enlarged, air traffic control systems would have to be coordinated, and ground control technology will need improvement. In addition a coordination between the regional air traffic system and the rapid train network is needed.
- To create a genuine European railway network. The concept of common carriage has to be realized with a European public transport agency which owns the infrastructure and coordinates the activities. Investments are necessary in terminal capacity, transhipment facilities and logistic solutions.
- To improve the quality and use of the European road network. Road capacity can be significantly revised by implementing logistic systems.
- To invest in inland waterways and coastal transport systems. A European waterway network for mass transportation and containerized transport has to foresee multimodal solutions including rail and road transport.
- To invest in a standardized European telecom network. This network should have a common carriage character.
- To ensure a stronger market orientation in transport in Europe where infrastructure users have to pay the full social marginal cost and at the same time foresee a flexible regulation in order to guarantee coordinated European solutions. Institutions like a European institute for standardization in intra- and intermodal transport technology, a

European infrastructure bank and a coordinating body for European transport policy would help to realize the indicated solutions.

* In order to ensure a consistent and strategic European-oriented analysis and planning of infrastructure networks, intellectual talents in the area of transportation science would have to be brought together. This could be realized, for instance, in the form of a European infrastructure institute.

References

Adams, J., Transport Planning: Vision and Practice, Routledge and Kegan Paul, London, 1981

Barrett, S. & C. Fudge (eds.), *Policy and Action*, Methuen, London, 1981

Bruinsma, F.R. (et al.), *Employment Impacts of Infrastructure Investments, A Case Study for the Netherlands*, Researchmemorandum 1989-51, Free University, Amsterdam, 1989.

Cecchini, P., (et al.), *The European Challenge 1992, The Benefits of the Single Market*, Gower, Aldershot, 1989

Commission of the European Communities, *White Paper*, Brussels, 1985

Commission of the European Communities, *Council Resolution on the Trans-European Networks (presented by the Commission)*, COM (89) 643 final, Brussels, 18 Dec. 1989.

Council of Europe, *Conference on Regional Transport*, Cologne (FRG), 31/5-2/6-1989, *Working Documents and Conclusions, Studies and Text Series no. 13*, Strasbourg, 1989

Council of Ministers, *Major Trans-European Networks*, 21/22.XII.89 kis/AM/mn, Brussels, 1989

ERT, 1991, *Missing Networks, a European Challenge, Proposals for the renewal of Europe's infrastructure*, Brussels.

European I.T. Industry Round Table, *Contribution to Trans-European Systems (European Nervous System)*, Brussels, November 1989

Hall, P., *Moving Information: A Tale of four Technologies*, paper for Third International Workshop on Innovation, Technology Change, and Spatial Impacts (preliminary version not for citation), Cambridge, England, September 5, 1989

Marchetti, C., *On Transport in Europe: The Last 50 Years and the Next 20*, IIASA, invited paper on First Forum on Future European Transport, Munich, September 1987

Miles, I., *Telecommunications: Abolishing Space but Reinforcing Distance*, Science Policy Research Unit, University of Sussex, England, June 1989, paper prepared for the Third International Workshop on Innovation, Technology Change and Spatial Impacts, Selwyn College, Cambridge, England, September 3-5 1989

Nijkamp P., Reichman, S. & M. Wegener, *Euromobile*, Avebury, Aldershot, 1990

Padjen, J., *Transport Policy of Environmental Protection and its Evaluation*, paper presented at the workshop of NECTAR GROUP, Transport, Communication and Mobility (TCM), ESF, Athens, 17-20 Februari, 1990

PROGNOS (Cerwenka, P. et al.), Gemeinschaftsuntersuchung Güterverkehrsmarkt Europa, Zusammenfassungen und wichtige Ergebnisse in Schaubildern, Prognos AG, Basel, September 1988

Vickerman, R.W., *Regional Development Implications of the Channel Tunnel*, Eliot College, The University of Canterbury, Kent, England, paper prepared for Infotrans European Planning and Transportation Conference, Brussels 27/28 April 1989

Violland, M., *The Lessons to be Drawn for European Transport Policy from the Experience Acquired in the Process of Regulatory Reform*, W.8052m, Paper presented on Congres on Road Transport Deregulation, Experience, Evaluation, Research, OECD/INRETS, 2-4 November 1988

Zimmermann, H., *Die Regionale Dimension des Europäischen Binnenmarktes - Auswirkungen auf Regionsstruktur, förderativen Aufbau und regionsbezogene Politik*, Vortrag auf der Wissenschaftlichen Plenarsitzung 1989, Mannheim, Akademie für Raumforschung und Landesplanung, Nachrichten, Nr. 48, November 1989.

6 Submarine Cables in our Times – Competition between Seacables and Satellites

Karlheinz Hottes

The transcontinental transportation of men, goods, news and messages was bound to ships as the only possible conveyance (almost until the beginning of our century). Therefore the delivery of news and messages took a very long time and was — partly because of shipwrecking — not always safe. Economically relevant news, such as the departure of ships and freight documents arrived with the ship itself, other news (e.g. about crop prices) were too late for giving orders, based on such news.

After the discovery of electricity as an innovation for the modern signaltechnics it took until 1795, before Don Salva y Campillo[1] to transport electricity by circuits through water. In 1811 the German scientist Sömmering developed the first isolated subwater cable and sent the first telegraph signals through the River Isar at Munich. In 1843 Morse made his first test for subwater telegraphs through New York Port. 1845 E. Cornell laid the first durable cables also through the Hudson River between New York and Port Lee.

Sea cables in the 1950s

This submarine telephone development then was interrupted more or less until 1950 because of the wireless short and long wave radio connections. For long distance phoning by submarine cable there was a lack of suitable repeaters (= low frequency amplifiers).

About 1950 two guiding innovations have occurred in favour of the submarine phoning:[2]
- The invention of coaxial-cable with a grade of the carrier-frequency
- The innovation of a new amplifier, which could resist the pressure of 5,000 m water.

---

[1] 1) from Barcelona-University. - For the history of submarine cable traffic see also Zweig (1990), Kunert and Vierus. - Very useful for translations can be the special Thesaurus FIZ

[2] Compare f.i. Ashomeit and Nicholls (1988) p.1+2

Table: *Historical developments in sea cables*

1850	First submarine cable between Dover and Calais - fishermen destroyed it.
1851	40 km sea cable Sangatte-Dover; in use until 1875.(Thus we celebrate the 140-years-jubilee.)
1866	For 125 years there has been the first durable transatlantic cable connection;
1871	Since then India-Singapore-Java and Port Darwin are connected via combinated sea- and landcables to Europe;
1896	The cable Vigo/Spain-New York as the decisive part of the first German transatlantic cables came in use. All those cables were for telegraphy!
1902	Almost 90 years ago there was the first submarine telephone conversation between Sweden and Denmark.
1903	Between Cuxhaven and Helgoland (Germany)
1914	The longest telephone submarine cable at that time connected Boston with New York and Washington.

The coaxial-cable was tested between Florida and Cuba. 1956 the cable TAT 1 offered 36 telephone channels, 1976 TAT 6 made 4.000 telephone calls possible at the same time by the utilization of call-gaps.

Meanwhile the new satellite techniques had become a new crucial competitor to submarine cables.

Sea cables in the 1980s

In 1983[1] worldwide 189 sea cable-lines were in use plus two at times inactive cables around/between the south and north of Vietnam. The highest density (= 37%) of all sea cables can be found in Europe, next with 21.5% are Asia and the regional cable systems between the mediterranean intercontinental neighbours with roughly 16%. North-America with 7% subcontinental submarine cables comes far behind Africa, Australia. The Caribbean counters have all together 5%, Latin America none.

A scant 15% of all used cables in 1983 were allotted to intercontinental submarine cables:

Europe was dispatching and landing point in 12 cases, North America in 20, Latin America in 6, Asia without the above mentioned mediterranean in 5, Australia and the pacific area in 4, Africa in 2.

---

[1]For detailed descriptions of sable Lines: US Department of Commerce, Pal/Fournier and for glass-fiber cables around Europe Herdade (1990)

The frequency of traffic (= occupation of the cables) between Europe and North America is by far the highest, followed by North America-Asian traffic. That makes 69% of all submarine cable telephone traffic world- wide. If you add Europe to Asia, it makes up 87.5%!

According to the forecast for 1992([1]) there will be no decisive alteration. Only remarkable are the growing number of Europe/Asia east of Bangla Desh connections and the relative diminution of the Europe-Latin America connections. Whether it is the influence of economic difficulties in Latin American countries or the progressive switching over to satellites remains to be seen.

The increase of phone traffic[2] and the growing use of the network also outside of peak hours depends not only on the increase of phone-conversations. The explosion of facsimile, which has to be transmitted by means of the phone network and the over proportional quantity of data to be transported, have opened new wide fields of utilization. The role of telegraphy tends towards zero.

Comparison between submarine cables and satellites

Glass Fiber Cables

The most important innovation of the last ten years is the introduction of the glass fiber-technics into the submarine cable technology.([3]) The optical waves, conducted to such cable circles round the earth in fractions of a second. TAT 8 first long-distance inter- continental cable can transport up to 32,000 conversations at the same time apart from a mass of data, which can be rushed through during word intervals. Their higher investment costs[4] compared with coaxial cables are compensated by their extremely increased capacity. Coaxial cables now only are laid, where low frequencies or low growth rates are expected. Glass fiber cables normally can be operated without amplifiers. Because of their diameters from 25 to 30 mm they are lighter, more elastic and easier to be dug in. But the small diameter makes glass fiber cables more sensitive to biting of shark-fishes. In this case the cables have to be protected by a special cover.

---

[1] Compare Herdade (1990)
[2] Compare Ashgare and the reports of the following meetings of the World Plan Committee for the Development of Telecommunications
[3] For the early optical- fiber cable "Belgium 5" see Whittington, more generally Triehitta/Chen; Wright ; Davidziuk/Preston .
[4] Again Davidziuk /Preston as well-as Grenier and Ellis

Table: *Sea-cables - zonal quantities 1990*

Seacables Continental			**Mediterranean "Cabotage"**			
Connections	Quantity	%	out of it national	%	Islands	Coastal
Europe	71	37.2	31	41.4	24	7
Asia	41	21.5	32	42.7	26	6
Mediterr. Cabotage	31	16.2	1	1.3	-	1
North America	13	6.8	10	13.1	10	-
Africa	4	2.1	1	1.3	-	1
Australia	2	1.1	-	-	-	-
Carib. Cabotage	2	1.1	-	-	-	-
Sub-Total:	*164*	*86.0*	*75*	*99.8*	*60*	*15*

Seacables inter-continental	Quantity	%
EU-NA	8	4.2
EU-LA	2	1.0
EU-AF	1	0.5
EU-AF-LA	1	0.5
NA-CAR	6	3.1
NA-LA	3	1.6
NA-AS	3	1.6
NA-AUS=PAC-AUS	1	0.5
AS-AUS	1	0.5
PAC-AS	1	0.5
Grand Total:	*191*	*100.00*

EU = Europe
NA = North America
LA = Latin America
AF = Africa
CAR = Caribbean

AS = Asia
AUS = Australia
PAC = Pacific

Sources: US-Department of Commerce 1984 and own enquiries

Modern Cables in Comparison to Communication Satellites

Submarine cables were declared dead twice already — first with the introduction of the radio, second with the growing application of satellites in the 1970s[1] Meanwhile the submarine cable traffic has an amazing renaissance which has led to an efficient division of business between cables and satellites. The chances that sea cable traffic will gain more

---

[1]Also Kunisek-Holtz, O.V. , more generally : Clemmensen/Wallenstein

importance, are high as long as the disparities in world economy are still growing and thus the density of communication-flows will increase unproportionally.

First conclusion: With rapidly growing numbers of phoning, foxing and data-transportation (also processed data) sea cables stand better chances on such lineaments where big quantities have to be mastered. Satellite transportation is more profitable for the transmission of pictures (television, radiopicture-transmission) because conversation gaps do not have to be filled up.

Second conclusion: Sat-communications means less expenditure, if you have to serve areas/countries with a low density of population and economic resources. Then you can save money because you do not have to lay expensive continental cables with high cost maintenance.

Third conclusion: Coastal areas (also in developing countries as well as in big islands like Sumatra and Java) are connected by sea cables, if they lie near to an intercontinental submarine cable connection.

Fourth conclusion: Also for the national telephone service sea cables became more and more important in comparison with the radio. In 1983 seventy-five (= 39%) of all submarine cables served for such national connections. This concerns especially Island-States in the midst of industrial countries like Japan or Denmark as well as extended countries with a few important islands or archipelagos. Examples: USA/Hawaii, USA/Virgin Islands, France/Corsica, Italy/Sicily, Spain with the Baleares and the Canaries, the U.K. with Northern Ireland and the Channel Islands but also Malaysia's cable connection from Kuantan to Kuching/Sarawak. The 15 sea cables which are connecting mainland parts within a state, pass bays or ale very short test-lines as for example in Southern France.

Fifth conclusion: The co-existence of cable and satellite-use[1] of course improves the reliability of telecommunications operations. They can help each other, if one system has a breakdown.

---

[1] For INTELSAT- Organization see Clemmensen/Wallenstein

Table: *Contrast of advantages and disadvantages between submarine cable and satellite systems*

Submarine cable systems	Satellite systems
(A) Usage: mostly 25 years	*(D)* Maximum 10 years
(A) Shorter transmission distances and therefore shorter transmission time = higher efficiency	*(D)* Longer distances: satellites 36000 km over equatorial zone
(A) Independent from weather	*(D)* Dependent on weather (rain drops) in the transmitter/dispatcher area
(A) With intact insulation no magnetic disturbance	*(D)* Magnetic disturbance possible
(A) Even if narrowly laid sea cables do not disturb each other	*(D)* There are 191 private communication satellites around the equator. In future disturbances cannot be excluded
(A) Modern cable repair technology and maintenance allow reliable work	*(D)* Repair and maintenance normally are complicated
(A) Sea cable, which come out of use, do not impede	*(D)* Possibly dangerous orbit garbage
(A) Tapping hirdly possible	*(D)* Tapping not too difficult
(D) Higher risks by external facts: anchors, drag-nets, submarine boats, wrecks, near coast also storm damages, biting from sharks, pipes	*(A)* Extremly insensitive, if they are in their own orbit
(D) Endangered by earch and seaquakes also in oil mining areas	*(A)* Not concerning
(D) Sea cables: bound to few dispatch stations	*(A)* Satellites can be fed by many stations, thus they fit better for wide regions, sometimes with lower economy as f.i. Developing countries
(D) Television possible but not reliable enough in service	*(A)* Because reliable in service very good for television

Note: advantages *(A)* and disadvantages *(D)* of both systems

Improvement of lay- and control-technologies

Full electronically equipped cable-laying instruments[1] and the development of sophisticated ploughs are the main innovations in this field. They allow to lay the sensitive cables into ditches through non-compact sediments especially near coastal areas where are more risks of damages.

---

[1]Look Herdade (1989) for the application of remotely operated vehicles, Itano for one of the first ploughing operations and generally Nicholls (1988 and 1991)

Those ditches are filled up at once or washed full by currents. Other innovations are related to submarine maintenance and control[1] and also to the mechanical equipment on the layer-ships, fully electronic sensors are decisive in this context. The exploration of new feasible lines was accelerated and cheapened decisively by the use of radar.

Table: *Sea cables and their use by telephone-traffic*

Sea cable	Telephone traffic [x 1 mio. Charged min.]				Busy hours [in 1.000 erlangs]					
	1972	%	1979	%	1983	%	1987	%	1992	%
Eu-na	62.2	64.0	394.7	55.1	9.6	46.4	15.6	50.7	24.0	50.5
Eu-as 1	2.1	2.2	84.4	11.8	1.7	8.2	2.4	7.8	3.4	7.2
Eu-as 2	5.1	5.3	46.0	6.4	2.0	9.7	3.4	11.0	5.0	10.5
Eu-la	4.7	4.8	45.5	6.3	1.5	7.2	115	4.9	2.0	4.2
Eu-af	3.2	3.3	19.8	2.8	1.2	5.8	1.7	5.5	2.6	5.5
Na-as	19.2	19.8	120.9	16.9	4.4	21.3	5.6	18.1	917	20.4
Na-af	0.6	0.6	4.9	0.7	0.3	1.4	0.6	1.9	0;8	1.7
Total:	*97.1*	*100*	*716.2*	*100*	*20.7*	*100*	*30.8*	*100*	*47.5*	*100*

Note: information taken from different sources ; 1992 information is a forecast. *Abbreviations:* eu—Europe, na—North America, as—Asia, la—Latin America, af—Africa, as/i—Asia *west* of Bangla Desh—incl. B.D., As/2—Asia *east* of Bangla Desh

The more precise topographic preexploration mainly along steep deep-sea-reliefs diminish, the risks that sea cables may tear and waste of stock because of too much up and down. Sea charts are of course no innovation. But since 1970 a special working association is preparing sea cable warning maps and distributing them free of charge to fishermen, yachting clubs, pipeline- and dredging enterprises and others in order to avoid damages.[2]

Connection Problems on the Continent

The enormous capacity of glass fiber sea cables requires adequate capacity of equivalent land-cable systems.[3] Strong coordination is very necessary to avoid bottlenecks as with TAT 8, with which more than 30,000 calls can be transmitted, whereas initially only 4,000 were possible. TAT 9 again will double the capacity.

---

[1]Generally Spain , Nicholls (1988) , for computer-Systems Ricca/Muzi
[2]also Chisholm
[3]TAT 6/France as example ; Ferrieu; For TAT 8 compare Castells/Mouret

Investment - Financing - Profitability

Laying a new submarine cable stipulates high investment costs, especially if intercontinental cables have to be constructed.

Satellites are much cheaper but they — normally with less capacity — can be used for only 10 years (against 25 years).

Financing submarine cables is organized via a share- company which is as well the subsequent user-company. The number of share-investment is corresponding to the later shares of usufructs. In our case 50% are invested by American companies, 50% of European PTTs. Each side pays and/or is liable to fictitious limit point amidst the route. If there is a fork-point along the line, as it is the case for France and the UK, the limit point can move.

If only two countries are involved, normally there will only be two partners. If there are changes because of the present transfer of state's PTTs into private /semi-private enterprises, we will see to what extend governments will still participate in investment.

Up to now I could not get reliable information on profitability or the grade of utilization. This has to do with the fact that the cable companies rent packet- rights of use of other news-, order- and data- transmitting and data broker companies as for instance Reuters, Swift, Marc. Perhaps the PTTs are fearing that those licenses would try to reduce the rents, if they knew the concrete operation results. But if there wis no profitability, nobody would lay new sea cable line.

Sea cables and international law of sea

Also according to Art. 58 of United Nations Law of the Sea Convention all states still have the right to lay cables and pipelines within the so-called "economic zone". It seems to me that there are some new open points concerning the laying of cables on the seabed, which have to be clarified by the International Seabed Authority, created by the convention.

The submarine cable network in the 1990s

The map from 1989 shows less cable connections than the publication of the US Department of Commerce from 1983. Up to now i could not find the principles of this selection. Most of the coaxial cables might be shut down after being utilized for 25 years. Many shorter cables (especially in Japan) are not shown.

On the other hand the total figure of intercontinental cables from Europe and between America-Asia-Pacific has grown from 18 to 20! It attracts attention that glass fiber cables are in quite fast advance as well as for intercontinental, trans-channel and mediterranean cable line.

As far as I know, in 1989 nineteen glass fiber cables were in use or under construction or the financement concluded:

In the Pacific area:

HAW 4, San Francisco with connection to Hawaii- Guam-Tokyo; the TPC 4 Vancouver/San Francisco-Tokyo; the H-J-K Tokyo-Hong Kong-South Korea; the G-P-T Guam-South Taiwan/Manila; the HAW 5 San Francisco-Hawaii; the PAC-RIM East Auckland/Sydney via TASMAN 2; the PAC-RIM West Sydney-Guam- and via HAW 4 to Tokyo; the cable Manila-Singapore;

In the Atlantic area:

The TAT 8 Great Britain-New York, France-New York in use;[1] the TAT 9 Great Britain-New York, France-New York, Spain-New York;

In the Mediterranean area:

The MAT Estepona-Palma de Mallorca-Palermo; the EMOS South France-Corsica-Palermo-Greece-Turkey-Israel, Genova to Sardinia-Palermo to Greece to Turkey-Israel;

In the North Sea area:

Five glass fiber cables of which 1989 the tables Denmark-England and Belgium-England were in use.

Here with an efficient basic-net from Western Europe and the Mediterranean will function to North America already in 1992/93 and further ón via North America to the North and the South Pacific area. Up to now South and Latin America- Africa-Middle East, South and North Asia are not taken into consideration , as well as Eastern Europe. They will be excluded from satellite connections in the long run.

One host country Spain is fully integrated into this innovation and holds an eminent place as a mediator between the "old" world around the Mediterranean and America.

---

[1]For TAT8, compare Castells/Mouret.

Table: *Participation des divers pays au financement du câble TAT8*

Partenaires Europeens	(%)	Partenaires Americains	(%)
Allemagne	7.29497	Teleglobe	1.39889
Autriche	0.74074	AT&T	36.67328
Belgique	2.61243	TPCI	
Chypre	0.08598	FTCC	1.28307
Danemark	0.73413	HTC	0.19180
Espagne	0.19841	ITT Worldcom	3.09524
Finlande	0.30423	RCA Globcom	1.50132
France	9.80159	TRT	1.26984
Grèce	0.34392	WU	1.53439
Irlande	1.12434	MCII	3.06217
Italie	0.39683	*Total*	*100.0*
Luxembourg	0.33069		
Norvège	0.90608		
Pays-Bas	2.73810		
Portugal	0.39021		
Royaume-Uni	15.50926		
Suède	2.05026		
Suisse	3.59127		
Turquie	0.33730		
Yougoslavie	0.50926		
Sous-total	*50.0*		

Possible fields of research

From my point of view the following fields for geographical research could arise:

1) creation and current completion of a world-cable map, also for school atlases. The present youth obsessed with computer should become aware of the international exchange of data very early as well of the possibility to exchange data and results with overseas computer "freaks".[1]

2) the inclusion of applied marine geography and coastal regional geography into comprehensive research and planning along coastal areas has to be a "must"! The locations of submarine cables and dis- patching stations have to be considered especially. Such cables should not cross the main sea-routes and the entrances to the harbors. Therefore already now the dispatcher stations are situated in less populated coastal strips. Although such stations do not create many places of

---

[1] In the USA, these persons are knows as "hackers". *Ed.*

work, they are of local importance for some sophisticated speci- alists and unskilled guards.

3) comparative studies between international trade and global telecommunication.

4) special attention has to be directed to the sen- sible connection of the so called "third world" by submarine cables or satellite (radio). Here the progressive "telephonization" of far away regions apart from the capitals and active economic zones could be of interest.

5) comprehensive research on problems of deep-sea- mining and submarine cables in consideration of the law of deep sea within the context of political and economic geography.

References

List of abbreviations for references: FT—France Telecom Paris; MP—Messages des Postes et de Télecommunications, Paris; RF—Revue Français de Télecommunications, Paris; RIT—Revue Internationale Télecommunications; TJ—Telecommunications Journal; ZPF—Zeitschrift für das Post-und Fernmeldewesen, Starnberg; FIZ—Fachinformationszentrum Technik (1986) ZDE Dokumentation Elektrotechnik -Thesaurus Deutsch-Englisch , Frankfurt/Main

Asehmoneit, E. K. (1989) Fernübertragungen im Zeitraffer; in *Funkschau*, p.52-55, München

Ashgar, M. and Partners (1980), Work of the World Plan Committee for the development of telecommunications 1980 and the evolution of telephone traffic ; in *TJ* Vol-47 , P-557-571

Bender, H. (1981) Erfolgreiche Entwieklungshilfe im Fernmeldewesen dureh regionale Planungen ; in *ZPF*, p.42-45

Castells, G. and Mouret, J.C. (1988): TAT 8 ;in *FT*, Vol-67, P-36-43

Ckisholm, D.P.F. (1979) The International Cable Protection Committee in *TJ* Vol.46/1 p.29-32

Clemmensen, J.M. and Walleinstein, G.D. (1986) Innovation Paradox in Telecommunications in *TJ* Vol-53/12 p. 694 - 703

Davidziuk, B.M. and Preston, H.F. (1981) International Communications: Network developments and economics; in *TJ* Vol. 48/1, P. 19-31.

Ellis, L.W. (1977) Sinkende Kosten in der Fernmeldetechnik - Ist der technologische Fortschritt oder die Wirtschaftlichkeit großer Mengen die Ursashe? in *Elektrisches Nachrichtenwesen*, Vol-52 , p. 252-259

Ferrieu, R. (1977) :Le réseau français , relais du TAT 6 ; in *RF* p.44-49

Grenier, J. (ca-1986) :Satellites et câbles suus-marins: rivalité ou partage ? in *RF* p.49-54

Herdade, J.M.S. (1990) :The European Submarin Cable Network : A Fundamental Infrastructure for 1992 and beyond; *RIT* , p.59-65

Herdade, J.M.S. (1989) Application of ROV(Remotely operated Vehicle) in the Engineering and Maintenance of Submarine Cable Systems; in *RIT* , p.51-56

Kunert, A. (1962) Telegraphen - Seekabel ; Bd. 2 der *Gesehichte der deutschen Fernmeldekabel* , Köln

Kuniseh-Holtz, H. (1987) Wettlauf zwischen Himmel und Erde ; in *Manager-Magazin* 5, p- 174-178, O.V. (1990) :Kabel contra Satellit , *Funksehau* , p.24-30 , München

Nicholls, Ch. (1991) :*The Management of the Marine Aggregates Dredging Industry*; Paper given during the meeting of IGU-Commission on Marine Geography au Huelva - May 1991 Cardiff

Nicholls Ch.,(1988) :*Break in Communication* ; Diss. in Maritime Studies, Univ. of Wales , Cardiff

Pal, N.E.. and Fournier,M. (1983) Trans-Pacific Telecomwunieation Network Planning in *TJ* Vol-5o p.415-419

Ricca, R.. and Muzi, G..(1990): GECAV - a Computer System for tke Maintenance of Subuiarine Cables; in *British Tel. Engineering* Vol.8 P-73 - 79 London

Spain , D.G. 1986) Maintenance of Submritie Systems; in British *Telecommunications Engineering* Vol.-5 , p.165-169 , London

Trisehitta, P.R. and Chen, D.T.S. (1989) : Repeaterless Undersea Lightwave Systems; in *IEEE Communications* p.16-21

US Department of Commerce(1984):1984 *World's Submarine Telephone Cable Systems* Washington DC

Vierus D. 1989) Kabelleger aus aller Welt , Berlin

Whittington, R.(1986) UK-Belgium No. 5; in *British Tel. Engineering* Vol.5, p.133-137

Wright J.V. and Partners: Considerations for the Lifetime of Submarine Optical Cables; (1990) in *SPIE* Vol.1314 Fiber Optics p.116-122

Zweig, S. (1990) :Le premier mot traversa l'océan ;in FT Vol- 74, P-58-69

Itano, M.. (1977) :Burying work of the Japan-China submarine table; in *TJ* Vol.- 44 / VII D-323-327

Keil, P. (1971) Die Beteiligung der DPB un moilernen Feinspiechsetvebeln, in *ZPF*, p.188-197.

7   Towards Corporate Networks – A Conflict of Cultures

Henry Bakis and Yolande Combes

Technology cannot be seen exclusively in sociological terms, yet this dimension is by no means secondary.(1) Only by combining three approaches — the technical, economic and social — can we perceive in their totality the problems which network operators, confronted with the development of telecommunications in companies, will have to solve.[1]

Today corporate networks constitute a commercial and technological objective for telecommunications operators who face three challenges: technical, organizational and commercial [12]. The technical challenge is mastered by public operators (highly competent when it comes to equipment and networks). Public users are confronted by an organizational challenge due to a new environment (the appearance of a specified demand, exogenous constraints and a universal market). And the commercial challenge is due to deregulation, for even if they maintain services which are not deregulated (in particular the telephone), users have become competitors (transmission of data, radiocommunication, etc.) and this creates new relationships with their more demanding and experienced customers — those with big accounts. Public operators try to be competitive with their prices, quality, services and range of products.

The social sciences are in a position to contribute to this effort. They clarify the role of telecommunications in accompanying reorganizations (take-overs, mergers, externalization), or as a basic tool in the production of new capital gains (economy of ideas). They allow operators to better understand the internal functioning of firms and the articulation of their activities within a geographical space — an indispensable condition for defining, developing and proposing an adequate supply of networks, products and services. They describe the context and identify the causes of possible blockages in the utilization of telecommunications. This analysis enables us to evaluate the extent to which corporate culture influences the adoption of telecommunications.

---

[1] This paper was published in French in: *Annales des Télécommunications*, 1991-n.° 11-12

Today firms are faced with technological choices concerning the introduction, utilization or production of new information and communication systems. Without claiming to study such a vast subject, we will deal successively with two axes:

* The choice of telecommunication networks, products and services generally provides firms with the opportunity to develop new organizational frameworks. We will therefore firstly try to understand why, today, we talk of networks- companies. What structural changes does this new designation imply? What are the reasons motivating it? We will, within this framework, be led to analyze the types of relationships which firms establish with their environment, as well as the capital gains which an information-communication system can favour.

* We will then attempt to show why firms' choices regarding functioning, management culture and organization of work, form the mould in which information and communication technologies must be set before they in turn have an effect on the actors. We will study this action/reaction by looking at the different actors involved in this process of modernization.

The networks-company

The concepts of corporate communication, network-company, networks-firms, have become vulgarized since the 1980's [3,8,36,37]; we prefer that of "networks-company". In fact it seems judicious to use the plural, since in general companies do not have one network but several (social networks, production networks, transport networks, telecommunications networks). Furthermore, the unifying aspect of the use of the singular deforms the reality and gives a false vision of companies as being functional and organizational wholes.

The social sciences define the role of telecommunications as being a support for reorganization (take-overs, mergers, externalization). The notion of opening up to heterogeneity is fundamental; the concept of communication must incorporate it. In fact, firms do not know, a priori, who their customers and suppliers will be, or even what the limits to their respective relationships might be in years to come. Hence the importance of their choice (norms, networks) allowing for flexibility. It is a matter of being able to have access to as yet unknown sites.

The networks-company would be in the best position to manage horizontal transactions between firms in the same industrial sector. Communication exchange may thus become the area of the creation of information, the incentive for business.

The networks-company — accentuated externalization

The strategies of large firms seem to have been changing significantly over the past few years. Certain tend to rely on small and medium-sized businesses for a number of services and activities, notably for production and logistic organization — stock management, transport, etc. [30,37]. This in itself is not new and is a form of sub-contracting [3]. However, the scale on which it is carried out today is of particular interest to both the social sciences and telecommunications. The latter, while favouring this tendency, can in turn find in it new fields of application and a means of expanding its markets.

New telecommunication technologies (NTT) are becoming indispensable in areas like transport because they allow for the rationalization of this branch, and all the more so due to increasing externalization. We see the usefulness and necessity of NTT[1] in the organization and functioning of this economic sector [30]. Changing of trades, global organization, modification of structures (association of companies), evolution of different firms' position in relation to the sector (capital gains achieved through the use of these new tools), etc. The case of the transport industry illustrates the complete transformation of a firm's borders, with the chemicals industry providing a similar example (take-overs, mergers, externalization)[30].

Exchange relationships between firms are becoming complex. As N. Alter remarked: "the borders considered as being natural between main units, head-offices and delocalized units are falling away and leaving room for an organizational interlacing" (1). In this context, the economic relationship with the exact place of activity is not as fundamentally important as in the past. Certain firms have set up structures for cooperation with numerous other, spatially fragmented, firms, small businesses in particular. In this case, logistic coordination becomes essential for the efficient functioning of the whole (Figure 1).geographical system of location production

---

[1]*Note:* Do not confuse with Nippon Telephone and Telegraph.

Figure 1: *From the geographical location to the network firm*[1]

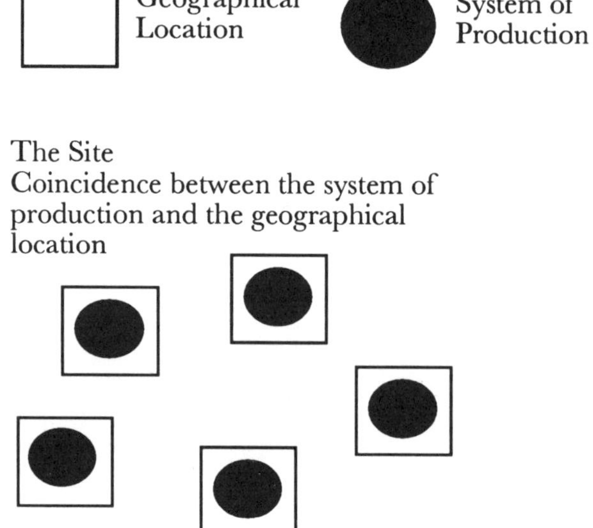

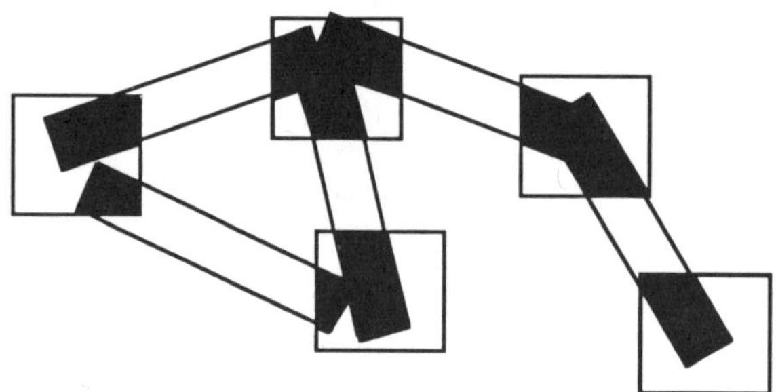

Nevertheless, this second case includes two fundamentally different situations which must also be distinguished, i.e.:

- the multi-unit company (several plants of the same firm participating in the same production process and spread across its territory — be this regional, national or international). In the case where needs are

---

[1]From G.Paché (1991), Netcom, 5-2, p.488. See also Gilles Paché et Claude Paraponaris *L'entreprise en réseau.* Presses Universitaires de France, 1993.

principally met from within, we can talk of an introverted networks-company.
* the extroverted networks-company which is organized as a pivot of scattered and substitutable competence.

We have represented this in Figure 2. Two types of logic are at work here:
* large firms attempt to create a closed space of transaction, superposing themselves onto other private networks, other zones of transition (competitors, for example);
* small and medium-sized companies, aware of the risk of unavoidable dependence, try to place themselves at the articulation of several networks-companies, in line with the sound management of risks which sub-contractors have been trying to promote for years, i.e. to avoid relying on a single contractor for the major part of their turnover [4]. This attempt is not, however, always successful since the balance of power is not generally in small businesses' favour, something which creates not only an economic problem, but also one of corporate development. It is the pivotal firm which has the privilege of organizing and managing the network; it is in control of all the activities and remains in direct contact with the final order. "Rather than controlling all the nodes of its network, it aims at controlling the network itself in which the nodes are interchangeable"[10]. Nevertheless, bad communication between the spaces of transaction engenders "insular sub-markets" [19].

The tendency towards making internal relations more complex on one hand, and externalizing numerous functions on the other, creates in firms an intrinsic need for telecommunication networks. The constitution of their relationship environment, of their particular territory, may thus depend largely on logistic networks: transport, but also telecommunications.

Thus, the case of IBM is indicative of the influence of telecommunication networks on the global organization of a firm[5]. We know that in the 1960's this computer manufacturer profoundly modified its worldwide organization [4]. From an American company with foreign subsidiaries it became a highly structured international firm, with the foreign subsidiaries being granted a large degree of autonomy (the parent-company set the global strategic options and the exact type of activity of each unit). A veritable international allocation of work took place at this stage in the field of production whilst until then factories had disposed of most of their products on their own local markets. The organization of manufacturing and research was henceforth to be carried out on an international scale. This break in IBM's organization accompanied the launching of a range of increasingly powerful computers with mutually compatible software (the Model 360) and with peripherals which could be connected to any system in the range. This project necessitated the recruiting of tens of thousands of employèes, the opening of five new plants from 1964 to 1967, and the extension of other plants. Yet the sixties was a decade characterized by the progressive vulgarization of computer networks in those firms which we can qualify as advanced edge users. We can conclude that the utilization of this means of telecommunication enabled IBM to control the world-wide dispersion of its units and to organize its production and its logistic circuits. Furthermore, the utilization of computer networks probably determined the multinational character of the organization of this firm as from the 1960's onwards.

The networks-company — economy of ideas

Information technologies are henceforth important prime movers for business growth [34]; in certain countries they exceed more traditional industrial activities, either in added value or sometimes even new employment opportunities. Modern economies do not however become service economies. On the contrary, a large part of the growth in services relates to a redeployment of manufacturing activities towards services. An OECD report [34] foresees the expansion of telecommunication networks in the economy and an improvement of information technology between industrial users and designers.

This model of the networks-company is opposed to the condensed company so dear to the Japanese, which produces ideas in a different fashion, i.e. the collection of information on the outside world followed by the reproduction and development of this initial resource. As we see, in both cases the growth in the role of ideas in the economy is becoming considerable. This factor, says J.Haëntjens "is slowly overtaking other production factors, namely the land (which is laid fallow), raw materials (of which the price is dropping), capital (which does not know where to be invested), or manpower (which is unemployed)" [20].

Although only sketched in outline, these problematics must interest us for their influence on the development of telecommunication techniques and corporate strategies. Even if, for the latter, capital gains due to the value of information or transactions are not always economically calculable (or easily identifiable in the present state of analytic accounting?).

Figure 2: *From the introverted to the extroverted network-firm*

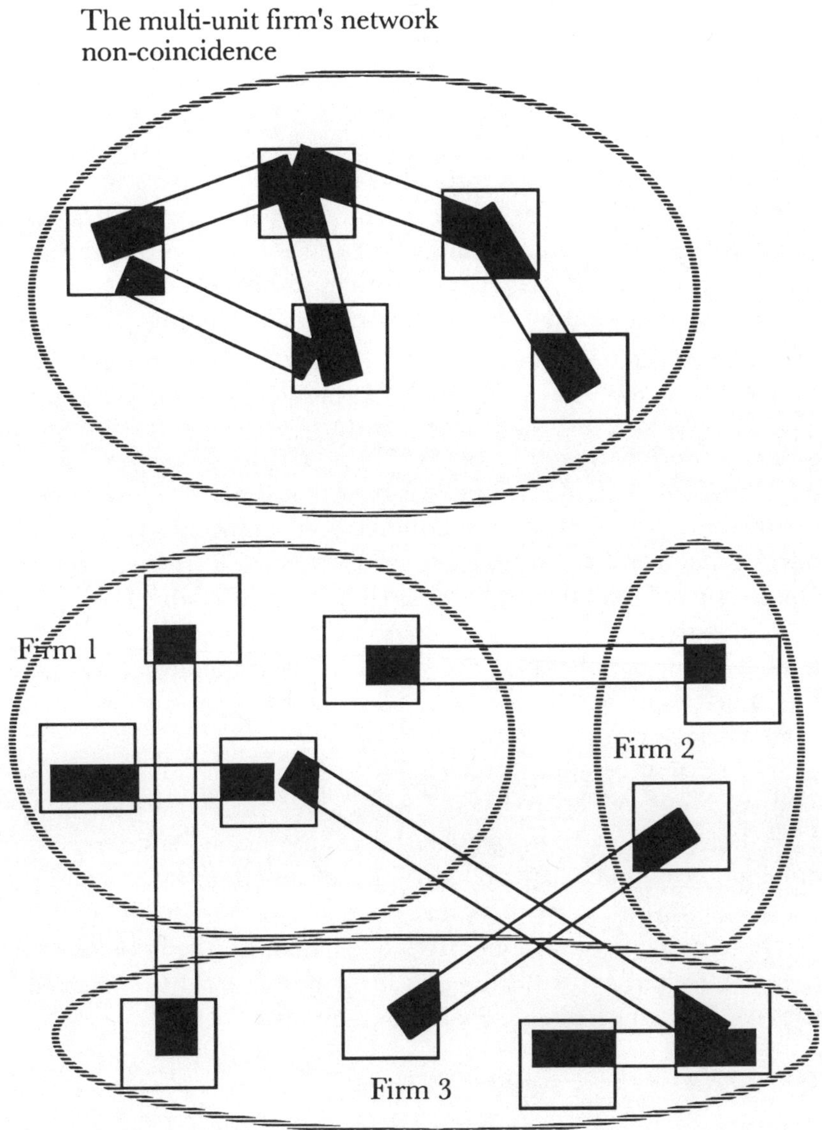

The research which we have been able to provoke, finance and follow,[1] shows that at present firms exteriorize certain activities and integrate others. Moreover, other researchers have reached similar conclusions. Like J. Haëntjens, we note that efficient firms tend to concentrate the main part of their activities on the immaterial, on methods and concepts, and buy or rent that which does not yield (equipment, premises, transport).

That is why telecommunications are often used to establish a competitive advantage. M.E. Porter [39] uses the term extended company for firms which design their information system and networks for penetrating new markets and which, in order to do so, innovate in matters of cooperation and relations by developing partner loyalty through contractual ties.

In the US, Mc Kesson [46] is a good example of this type of firm. This wholesaler-distributor based its strategy on the development of an on-line ordering system linked to 17,000 pharmacists and 2,500 hospitals. In this system, everything was based on the use of owner norms for the transmission of norms, communication protocols and labelling. The development of these services enabled the firm to gain, since 1975, 10 points of market shares and to increase its turnover by 424%, whilst its current expenses only grew by 86%. Yet, the competitive advantage offered by information and telecommunication technologies was limited in time since its competitors rapidly used the McKesson model to develop similar organizational systems.

Information economy is a new field of investigation for economists [33], and one which we do not intend going into here. We do however note that available monographs show there are no systematic and unambiguous links between added value, telecommunications and levels of technicality. The most technical does not automatically augur an increase in capital gains. Similarly, added value can only be certified at a precise moment in the history of a firm, and in order to maintain its advantage, it must constantly evolve and innovate.

Geographical weights — rigidity of the economic environment

Allowing regional firms and peripheral regions to play a more active role in the national economy is in keeping with objectives for national development. Although imagining that new communication techniques could contribute effectively towards this is not wrong, it would mean forgetting that the tools in themselves do not provide a new organization, nor a dif-

---

[1]Within the framework of the CNET-PAA invitation for tenders, launched in 1989.

ferent type of corporate management [11], nor, furthermore, a modification or even an inversion of the centre-periphery relations on a national scale, for example. Their effectiveness is conditioned by the existing political will of the dominant actors, i.e. the State for consequences on national development, head-offices in the case of firms. That is what the Committee for National Development of the VIIIth Plan noted in 1980 when it saw its hopes of 1976 diminishing.[1] "Past experience in the setting up of infrastructure networks and new services has shown that, unless there are deliberate policies to counteract its effects, the improvement of economic relations between economic poles of unequal importance and vitality more often than not sees an aggragvation of this inequality. It seems that to the technical profitability of the telematics tool is added a social logic of hierarchization of agents and economic spaces"[11]. It is interesting to note here that S. Maugeri's monograph clearly confirms this opinion.[2]

Even if certain peripheral actors can improve their positions thanks to the control of products, services and telecommunication networks, the introduction of these means does not necessarily lead to transparency, communication or decentralization of essential functions. As A. Rallet emphasized during a critical reading of B. Planque's work: "communication modes only constitute a permissive factor opening up new opportunities but not deciding on the direction they take... one travels in both directions on a motorway" [40]. If he admits that the very limited distribution of networks in firms does not yet (1988) allow for this question to be settled, he also reminds one that a communication technique does not decide on a model of corporate organization — be it spatial.

Thus, in the exploration of the national development — corporate organization relationship, the decisive factor is to be sought in the internal transformation of firms. One must question moreover whether the increase in information activities is accompanied by organizational transformations. P. Veltz's work stressed the importance of new organizational and management modes and the functional recomposition at work there [43].

There are cases where new telecommunication techniques allow for new situations on the business organization level. We saw this above

---

[1]"The very important effort undertaken concerning telecommunications and which the VIIth plan should confirm and amplify, will remove a non-negligible obstacle to a better distribution of our production machinery and should contribute towards facilitating the transfer to the provinces of central services, or even of the head-office of large firms or administrations" (Commissariat Général au Plan, 1976).
[2]Monograph on the Italian chemicals industry, 1991.

with the reorganization of IBM in the early 1960's, or with large industrial groups, and the accompanying externalization towards small and medium-sized firms, as G. Paché illustrated so well.

The hypothesis of a space constituted by multiple poles interlinked by networks is becoming technically credible. It is moreover partially put into practice in specific areas (encased and stacked), the network areas of different organizations, or which certain local collectivities try to put into practice (teleports, zones of advanced telecommunications).

Corporate organization and technological determinism

As stated, telecommunication techniques do not decide on a model of corporate organization as much on the global as on the internal level. They do not, in themselves, cause a different type of management. To understand the mechanisms between firms and technology, it is necessary to grasp their changing form, as the telecommunications scene and the business world have been moving simultaneously since the beginning of the 1980's.

Corporate communication is a field which has a large gap between that which technology allows and that which is implemented. Not that networks, products and services are ignored by the business world; on the contrary, the Telefax, the Minitel, Numéris, Transpac, PABX, Added Value Services (AVS), the linking of micro-computers to networks, etc., are well known. Firms well understand the potential usefulness of telecommunications for ensuring their functioning, organizing their functions and developing their activities.

But it is not enough to invest and to subscribe to networks in order to benefit from the new technologies. If new materials have to be acquired, the organizational problems linked to their implementation must also be overcome. Furthermore, the tools also have to be mastered. Large firms are in the best position to satisfy these conditions; yet they are confronted with a more difficult economic context where commercial strategies and greater competitivity are priorities and where the demand for quality is growing. Indeed, market constraints (competition, increase in the variety of supply, globalization) have different organizational implications for managing flexibility and complexity. Because of this firms must resort to new modes of functioning and management and must also adopt new processes of decision-making.[1]

---

[1] Rallet, A. Oral presentation corporate networks. CNET/DC Seminar, 30—31 January 1991 and 12—13 September 1991.

In other terms, firms are forced to change, and this change must pertain to its five basic components: capital, human resources, techniques, markets and management. This evolution must moreover operate in a reduced time-frame [13].

Who decides on telecommunications?

Four principal actors are likely to intervene:
- the operations management which may have specific needs;
- the information services management which bases its power on its knowledge of information tools (in large firms, computerization is the stepping stone to the use of new telecommunication technologies);
- the organization or logistics management, sometimes part of the human resources division;
- the general management which bears the strategic ambitions of the firm.

Each of these entities may be involved in decision-making. Responsibility for telecommunications is often not clear and is sometimes assumed by the general services (telephone in particular) of the information services or the finance division. Telecommunications are often considered as a cost factor (and so as an expenditure) and not an investment. Their full strategic significance is therefore not perceived. This situation is changing, with a new awareness, and it is no longer rare to see the creation of an information system division.

Three forms of technology management or decision-making can be distinguished:
- the Jacobin form exists when the general management involves itself to a large degree in the management of its technical means. It may consider these as strategic or may wish to strengthen its corporate image. We shall see below, in the case of Dolfy-Trans[1], how the general management relied on the information system division;
- baronnies exist when the feeling of belonging to a firm is weak. Each division or regional or local structure frees itself from central control and defines its own information and telecommunication strategy. The baron has specific applications developed in order to gain an advantage and see his influence grow. We find this form of decision-making in the monograph of a public sector firm [26,27] and, for the infor-

---

[1] A firm in the transport sector which has remained anonymous. The "Dolfy-Trans" case study, written and presented by a consultant, Mr. Acqué, at the France-Télécom CNET/DC Seminar "Télécommunications d'entreprise", 30-31 January 1991.

mation services division of a pharmaceuticals firm, in the Bax case [16,17]. We find a similar type of functioning in the case of recent mergers of different concerns within the same group. This is the case of the aeronautics firm studied by A.M. Laulan [25].

- logistic management is characterized by omnipresent control by the organization and logistics management. This division sets up, with the support of the general management, rules, modes and methods of management (instrument panel) and forms of network design which nobody can avoid. The Pierron case [22,23][1] can serve as an illustration. This form of management/decision-making may be adopted to reverse the barony form; a centralization process then takes place to change the preceding mode of management.

The distinction of management/decision-making into three main forms allows us to unveil the issues underlying choices in telecommunication technologies.

Social innovation — a question of social mobilization

The penetration into a given social fabric of a new technology gives rise to a creative action; this is not technical innovation but a form of social innovation. Depending on the attitudes adopted towards this action we find different modes of innovation. In this way we note: — either capillary diffusion: tools are installed without their specific functions being systematically defined (frequently the case with internal messaging), — or else voluntary diffusion: tools are integrated with well- defined aims, as is the case for specific services which develop the role of an interface.

The implementation of innovation rarely takes place according to a pre-established and controlled process, and a kind of cacophony reigns within firms during this phase of integrating a new technology. Any innovation calls for a capacity to mobilize human resources as a whole, yet, France is a country where in many cases this capacity still seems weak.[2] In this field, the difference between forms of sociability in use within the closed circle of elites, and the ordinary modes of management applied to the workforce favours neither the diffusion of innovation, nor the exchange of information and persons between these two spheres

---

[1]A firm in the agro-food sector which has remained anonymous. A Christine Jaeger case study presented at the seminar "Télécommunications d'entreprise" organized by the CNET and the Sales Division of France-Télécom, 30-31 January and 12- 13 September 1991.

[2]P.Y. Cossé. L'Etat stratège ("The strategist State"). *Le Monde* of 9 October 1991.

[44]. Furthermore, information services have for a long time operated in a vacuum, without taking into account the views of its users.

The case of Dolfy-Trans is an illustration of Jacobin management. In this transport subsidiary with 3,000 employees of which 1 000 are drivers, strategic modernization defined by the management committee in June 1986 consisted of launching a strategic plan in computerization and communication. An organization and planning manager, specifically recruited to that end, explained: "it is a matter of moving fast and striking hard, and not tergiversating due to a lack of consensus". He launched an ambitious EDI project, then a highly innovative solution in France, conducted with IBM who planned the installation in 1988 of 60 connected AS400's permitting communication between the agencies and with a 3090-200E as the server. The Edifact norm, then in its infancy, was to provide a common language for efficient communication. The information concerned all the details of the transport process: collecting, loading, transit, date and time of delivery. The sales division management and staff were sceptical about the project. Indeed, this strategy required two years of development, which can easily be understood in view of the equipment and language chosen. Furthermore, competitors had already developed applications on minitel, which often forced the salespeople to grant discount to their customers in order to win the market in spite of reservations such as "You are expensive and you offer less". The marketing people then demanded the development of a simplified service, while the computer specialists considered the minitel a false solution. Their reaction was not to question themselves, but on the contrary to recommend that all the marketing personnel undergo training on computerization, EDI, the running of the project and information systems. During 1989, delays followed delays and the project had still not materialized, so the general management decided to stop the project, to opt for a simpler solution... and to dismiss the information system manager.

The pharmaceuticals firm "Bax" [16] provides a similar example by way of the application of Numéris. This application however involved a part of the staff, for supplementary tasks.

From these examples we conclude that die-hard innovation is not always a good solution for firms. It is basically an old lesson in the history of information technologies: the setbacks suffered by the company Bull with the Gamma 60 were due to the excessive technical quality of the product — it made use of germanium diodes, a new invention. IBM acted differently in this respect: the race for technical progress was never an end in itself and the products strategy of this firm gave preference to the regular feeding of the market and a reliable after-sales service [4]. This strategy, implemented in particular between 1965 and 1975, aimed at transforming into a commercial asset a certain technical inferiority compared to its competitors.

Another major lesson: it is very difficult to bring to life an application when the designers are not in phase with the final users. The Jacobin method has proved to be ill- adapted to the introduction of new telecommunication technologies for it risks generating, more than the others, dissention between elite and employees. On the other hand, the logistic mode of management favours the human factor if it emanates from the human resources management. Technological choices are then subject to a process of experimentation which may take several forms: either capillary diffusion, or the testing of a choice, or the mobilization of the actors involved by the creation of a working group responsible for determining needs and for planning methods of setting up and generalizing the experiment.

This is how the agro-food firm Pierron which employs 3,000 persons introduced new communication technologies both for the development of applications on departmental systems and for internal messaging, from an IBM processor via Transpac, linking 620 active subscribers in 1990. Within this framework, the computer department was used as a advisor for technical choices. Michel Crozier recalls that "to make different practices possible, the required conditions must be created so that a different game can emerge"[18]. The process of experimentation, on condition that it is well understood by the actors, permits the establishment of new modes of cooperation. We note that innovation is carried less by computer specialists than by users looking for solutions to concrete problems and confronted by competitors on a daily basis [16].

Innovation — towards searching for new coherence

When it comes to innovation firms do not have a pre-defined policy; a certain indecision makes them waver between two movements: i—having a global strategic approach; ii—letting a technology infiltrate without trying to channel it.

The most common processes, and those which have the most chance of success, begin by calculated infiltration and continue by the definition of a network design; it is a concern for coherence which directs this second choice. There are several reasons for this process; we shall discuss two by way of examples.

As a first example: innovation management, temporal adjustment of different operations (production, distribution, commercialization), and quality management, supplant the increase in production which is today meeting its limits in a number of sectors. As far as organizational changes are concerned, we witness the introduction of a new kind of thinking, contrary to that usually employed. B. Coriat talks of "thinking in reverse"[15], and we also talk of "forward piloting". Communication and telecommunication techniques become indispensible means of liaison between commercial, productive and management entities, in so far as production responds to effective demand, contrary to the former situation where goods were first produced and then sold [6]. Interactivity and integration of operations and quality have thus become factors of competition [13]. The changes which these organizational upheavals imply are brought about gradually. For example, the firm Pierron, in its plants and its distribution, had separate applications developed by certain employees whom we will call "innovators", to use N. Alter's expression [2]. Thus, an application concerning distribution, initiated on IBM 8100 in 1982, was continued in 1983 under the DEC PDP1144 departmental system. Generalization in the 33 depots took place in the following two years. The manufacturing application was experimented at the start of 1984 on DEC PDP1144 and was rapidly generalized in seven plants. Each departmental system was linked by the X.25 network to the IBM DEC processor. It was only later that these applications were rethought, and a common application developed in 1989—90. At the same time the DEC PDP11 were linked to one another by X.25. This example indicates clearly the process integrating production and distribution thanks to the utilization of computer networks. Yet eight years were required before the evolution culminated in a systematically organized network.

The second example is that of the centralizing recovery, by the sales management, of an existing exchange network in a public sector firm. In this firm applications were developed which fall under the "baronnies" logic. The general management used electronic messaging to set up "logistic" management. This centralizing use of management also became known for other aspects:

- creation of internal control services (computer and telematics applications for local divisions)
- failure of horizontal communication applications
- putting into service of "compulsory" applications generated from above [27].

These two examples show that there is a tendency towards centralization and integration through networks. Nevertheless, the example of computer-aided production management developed by A. Hatcheul and J.C. Sardas [21] proves that one should be wary of looking for too much coherence. This type of network has a high density of formalization; by nature it prescribes a type of organization through the exchange it intends organizing. The cases studied show that the totalizing coherence of the model is reduced to the concrete scale of a sub-set. As C. Jaeger and A. Rallet stress "a network makes a firm flexible by means of rigidity and the firm risks succumbing to too much formalization of its rules. ... Networks pose a problem as soon as we represent them as the unifying totality which they are not"[24].

Success in social innovation is strategic in more than one respect. Firms which manage to integrate new telecommunication technologies without shocks have the ability to balance, within themselves, the different forces and logics which structure them. But this performance has all the odds against it, for there are numerous obstacles and good intentions do not suffice for avoiding them. The firms which are most likely to succeed practice a modernizing strategy which is, simultaneously, one of democratization and qualification, as H. Weber shows [45]. This is the case with Gervais-Danone which forms part of the BSN Group of which the president A. Riboud stated [41]: "the social control of NT is firstly by way of the modernization of social relations within the firm, and requires the lucid examination of the strengths and weaknesses of the firm facing its markets". He added: "modernize, yes, but without fleeing ahead, without wasting investments, without seeking technical prowess for its own sake, by informing employees and negotiating with their representatives, realizing a different division of tasks and responsibilities, training employees in the use of new communication technologies". And he concluded: "modernize, yes, but with the people". Yet, in 1991, within the framework of an invitation for tenders, a researcher noted in the aeronautics industry: "we may fear that management has forgotten to mobilize the social actors and has above all paid attention to technical and professional resources"[25].

Innovation and conflict of cultures

By corporate culture we can understand the result of multiple factors: managerial style, history, structures, products, organization of work, type of personnel, relation with the environment (State, customers, suppliers, markets, territories) etc.

Furthermore, within a particular firm, different sets of tasks exist (production, maintenance, sales, information systems, management...) implemented by personnel which constitute "working groups" each with its specific know-how and "culture".

Thus the introduction of telecommunications into a firm has effects at these two levels of corporate culture. Sometimes this cultural aspect is not at all taken into consideration by the technical project, but sometimes the "culture shock" relates to the contradiction between different ways of thinking (computer rationality versus the non explicit know-how in workshops). It follows that a technical system which is coherent at the global level may be inadequate at the working group level.

R. Sainsaulieu and P. Segestrin note that "if culture is the order of the day, it is largely because management has succeeded in seizing onto it as a relevant issue... Management faced with the complexity of systems chooses to favour the use of the symbolic or of ideology in the combination of productive resources" [42]. Since the 1970's slump, firms have entered into a phase of transformation. P. Chaskiel [14] remarks that ideology of human resources constitutes rationalisation factor for firms. Hence the cultural, and the "consensual", replace technology and hierarchy as prime-movers for transformations.

Consequently, the services which are developing the most in firms are those producing ideology. We see, for example, a firm like Bax regarding training as the place for learing the norms and values of the Group. In this type of firm, ideology becomes so strong that the structure develops around it. But is there not a gap between the speaches, the announcement effects, and reality?

New tools can, in effect, remain unused (can we not all remember newly-acquired equipment stacked away in a cupboard?). The users may prefer other modes of communication (take resistance to teleconferences — is the trip linked to that particular meeting only?). They may also prefer other tools which they know better or which give them other indirect satisfaction, and new tools may result in a purely technological satisfaction (art for art).

The studies which we have mentioned are dotted with significant examples:

• the masculin universe is strongly marked by an influence from the army, with the persistance of partitioning and the under-informing of executives. Thus, users favour the telefax because it allows them to retain a link with the written word, as well as conventional forms of socialization (meeting for a chat at the fax machine). This culture leads [25] to a rejection of new products (Temilex handles the automatic reception and transmission of telexes from a computer);

- technician's logic leads engineers to innovate technically without necessarily worrying about the market; hence the development of application software of little general use in other cases. The logic of personal promotion and the organization of a firm in "baronnies" leads executives to use new telecommunication technologies to realize noteworthy operations which increase their personal standing and that of their hierarchy. Thus, in this firm, numerous unused message systems were developed (for example telemanagement) [27].

These forms of resistance to managerial will illustrate the influence of executives' and the workforce's former culture on their practices. Another example goes even further. The employees of Dolfy-Trans found, in their traditional values, the strength to oppose a technological dream too distantly removed from their own culture. At the source of their collective identity were transit centres at dawn, motorways at night, truck drivers, and vehicles (the 38 ton). Many executives in this firm are former drivers. The computer specialist wanted to apply the concept of the extended firm and launch a highly advanced plan for computerization (EDI as from 1986). He had the support of the general management yet no idea of the corporate identity; his plan was doomed to failure from the start.

So, all innovation is not synonymous with progress, and cultural aspects play a definite role in the adoption of a novelty. So too, a firm like Bax excludes marginal behaviour at the origin of all innovation [16], for reference to the corporate image inhibits any "deviant" behaviour. And so, in the case where several firms merge into a single group, ties of identification remain in each original entity which clutches onto its own "culture" (e.g. the use of Mac or PC micro- computers). It is high time a new type of identity was created and a transversal culture found which could surpass particular cultures in the different merged firms.

"Culture shock" sometimes relates to the contradiction between different ways of thinking within a single firm, particularly in industrial firms. The workshop is changing (new technologies, professional versatility, tentative introduction of participative models) without production management being challenged. The internal functioning of firms is more oriented towards a search for improved management of interaction than in the past, and this leads to greater standardization. Yet, the integration of functions rigidifies certain mechanisms in the flow of information and communication [28,29]. At each decision-making level we find: autonomy, the capacity to formulate local objectives, the definition of variables for action, and the obligation to refer to partial indicators of results. These levels are hierarchically arranged in such a way that the autonomy is controlled by decision-making at the next level: the area of application of decisions, the temporal horizon, and the effects of diffusion [47]. This leads to a particular type of management design and calls for the adherance of employees to an organisation logic, to rationality and to the dominant values of the firm [17].

Working groups, in the way they are organized, are far more apt at maintaining skills and suggesting transformations. Modernistic management risks demotivating them; they have no more scope for expressing their refusal in the face of the new corporate logic. We then witness "paradoxal consent" from the workers; they espouse the interests of their firm whilst palliating the multiple dysfunctions caused by the new formal organization of work (resourcefulness for solving problems, mutual assistance). This unseen activity represents contestation of the logic of the technical system adopted by the firm. For the multiple interactions required in the execution of a task do not easily fit into the mould of homogeneity prescribed by the technical systems [25]. As F. Pavé [38] emphasizes, it is the theoretical perfection of computerized systems which make them socially inadapted. For him, "successful computerization is computerization which is diverted, colonized by the social actors who continually cheat with it". The computer specialist's culture, marked by the search for rational facts, proof and logical deduction, leads to a hyperfunctionalism and thus renders his social commitment difficult.

Conclusion

From this general view of corporate communication we can emphasize: i—that new managerial practices are establishing themselves; ii—that new links between firms can lead to a new exchange economy and to a redefinition of the scale of the different actors' territories.

These two tendencies provoke an increase in the need for telecommunications. The electronic control of semi-finished or finished products in the framework of inter-firm logistics must be ensured, and the deployment of new managerial practices allowed for. The means of telecommunication overlap the firm's organization and become indispensable for efficient overall functioning. This implies that customers will be more demanding than in the past in respect of deadlines for linking- up to networks, performance, and reliability.

Figure: *The two-way loop*

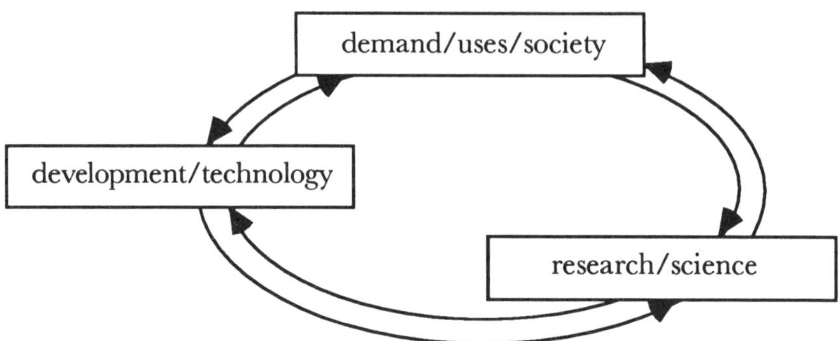

Furthermore, we must consider the game of the actors, whose role is fundamental for the success or failure of technically acceptable projects. Our conclusion is that there is no determinism as far as this is concerned, neither "social determinism" nor "technical determinism". The implementing of technical means is conditioned and reinterpreted by the particular social milieu of each firm. These means can even be purely and simply rejected by the users following strong resistance to a bad choice, or a progressive awareness of the basic unsuitability of the initial choices.

Therefore, the passage from designers to users is fundamental; it conditions the success of the applications. Putting the basic need — assurance of the product or service's usefulness — at the centre of the engineers'interests is essential.

It is thus from a sound understanding of the concrete processes at work, of the actual situation, and thus of a strong formalization of the need for information exchange, that the product and application software designers must depart. This is as true at a corporate level[1] as upstream at the manufacturer and network operator level — the passage under favourable conditions towards the customers in general, towards big accounts in particular.

Operators must thus always ensure the technical performance and ergonomic merits of their products, services or networks. They must, furthermore, ensure that the end users' needs remain of primary concern to the design engineers, something which, understandably, equally facilitates the sales engineers' task. There is here a basic deepening and systemization of the (two-way) loop, as seen below.

---

[1]Since each firm is an individual case it is advisable to promote the favouring of internal actors and the effective utilization of existing services.

With this point of view, a useful contribution can be made by the applied social sciences research on corporate communication — work situated on the border between sociology, economy, geography and management.

Bibliography

1—ALTER N. (1985), "Technologies nouvelles et travail: du doute à la recherche, in Boutinet JP, dir. Du discours à l'action, Les sciences sociales s'interrogent sur elles-mêmes 1985, pp. 159—164

2—ALTER N. (1989), Logique de l'entreprise informationnelle, *Revue Française de Gestion*, juill-ao.ñt

3—BAKIS H. (1975),"La sous-traitance dans l'industrie", *Annales de Géographie*, Paris, 1975, pp. 297—317

4—BAKIS H. (1977), *IBM Une multinationale régionale*, Presses Universitaires de Grenoble, Grenoble, 1977.

5—BAKIS H. (1987), "Telecommunications and the Global Firm", in HAMILTON F.E.I. (ed), *Industrial change in advanced economies*, Croom Helm, London, 1987, pp. 130—160

6—BAKIS H. (1988), *Entreprise, espace, télécommunications. Nouvelles technologies de l'information et organisation de l'espace économique*, Collection Transports et communications, Paradigme, Caen, 253 p.

7—BAKIS H. (Ed.) (1988), *Information et organisation spatiale*, Collection Transports et communications, Paradigme, Caen, 236 p.

8—BAKIS H. (1990), "La banalisation des territoires en réseaux", chapitre introductif, in -BAKIS H. (Ed.) (1990), *Communications et territoires/ Communications and territories*, Collection de l'IDATE, La Documentation française, Paris, pp. 15—31

9—BAKIS H. (1991), "Telecomunicaciones espacio y tiempo", in Carmen Gomez Mont (ed.), *Nuevas tecnologias de comunicacion*, Editorial Trillas, Mexico, 1991, pp. 49—60.

10— BARBANT JC, CHANUT P (1989), "les réseaux créateurs de richesses", in *Annales des Mines-Gérer et comprendre*, n° 15, pp. 16—27

11-BEGAG Azouz, CLAISSE G., MOREAU P. (1990), "L'espace des bits: utopies et réalités", Bakis ed., 1990, pp.187—217

12—BODIN P., éditorial, *La Lettre du SPES*, n° 19, "Des réseaux pour des entreprises"

13—CARRE D. & COMBÈS Y. (1991), "La messagerie grise", Culture technique

14—CHASKIEL P. (1991), "Mode des concepts, mode sans concepts. Vers une rationalisation par l'idéologique". Les cahiers du L.E.R.A.S.S., n° 23

15—CORIAT B.(1991), "Penser à l'envers", Bourgeois, Paris

16—CRAIPEAU S. et LE PELLETIER V. (1991), "Lorsque la stratégie du grain de sable et la conformité aux normes freinent l'inovation", *Ann. des Télécommunications*, vol. 44, 11—12

17—CRAIPEAU S. et LE PELLETIER V. (1991), "L'appropriation stratégique des télécommunications dans les entreprises", *IDATE*, Montpellier. Rapport pour le CNET.

18—CROZIER M. (1989), L'entreprise à l'écoute. Apprendre le management post-industriel. Inter Editions, Paris

19—CURIEN N. et GENSOLLEN M. (1989), The opening-up of networks... Paper 5th World conference on Transport research society, Yokohama

20—HAËNTJENS J., l'économie des idées, in *Le culte de l'entreprise*, Autrement n° 100

21—HATCHUEL A., SARDAS JC (1990), Métiers et réseaux: les paradigmes industriels de la gestion de production assistée par ordinateurs, in *Réseaux*, n° 41

22—JAEGER C. PETIT J.J., POUCHOL M., RALLET A., SEVERS M. (1986), La bureautique: technologie et changement dans l'entreprise. Etude pour le CNET

23—JAEGER C., RALLET A. (1990), *Les réseaux professionnels: réorganisation et stratégies d'entreprises*, tome I., synthèse. Etude pour le CNET

24—JAEGER C., RALLET A. (1990), Les réseaux professionnels: flexibilités ety rigidités... in *Réseaux*, n° 41

25—LAULAN A.M. (dir.) (1991), *Comment gérer la complexité? Le cas d'une industrie aéronautique en Aquitaine.* Univ. Bordeaux III, Rapport pour le CNET.

26—LE BOEUF C. et MUCCIELLI A. (1991), "Les deux dimensions des usages innovants des NTT dans une entreprise publique", *Ann. des Télécommunications*, vol. 44, 11—12

27—LE BOEUF C. et MUCCIELLI A. (1991), *Intégration des télécommunications dans la stratégie commerciale d'une entreprise publique*, Univ de Montpellier III, Rapport pour le CNET

28—LINHART D. (1990), "Quels changements dans l'entreprise", in *Réseaux*, n°41

29—LINHART D. (1991), *Le torticolis de l'autruche*, Seuil, Paris

30—MAUGERI S. (1991), *Les tribulations de l'EDI dans le transport routier des marchandises*, étude pour le CNET

31—MAUGERI S. (1991), "Marché du transport et besoins téléinformatiques: le cas italien", *NETCOM*, 5—1, pp. 205—266

32—MAUGERI S. (1991), *Pushed ou l'invention d'une invention... EDI dans le secteur chimique italien.* étude pour le CNET

33—MAYÈRE A. (1990), *Pour l'économie de l'informationn*, ed. du CNRS

34—OCDE (1989), *Technologies de l'information et les nouveaux domaines de croissance*, rapport 19, 221 p.

35—PACHÉ G. (1990), "L'entreprise éclatée, représentation économique de l'espace productif", Bakis ed., pp. 83—92

36—PACHÉ G. (1991), La firme réseau: mode ou modèle? in *Les cahiers du L.E.R.A.S.S.*, n° 23

37—PACHÉ G. (1991), "La PME dans la dynamique des firmes réseaux: aspects conceptuels, in NETCOM, 5—2, pp. 479—497

38— PAVÉ F. (1989), L'illustion informaticienne, L'Harmattan, 270 p.

39— PORTER M.E. (1980), Competive strategy, technique for analysing industries and competitors, New York, Free Press

40—RALLET A. (1987), "Les économistes devant les nouvelles technologies de transport et de traitement à distance de l'information", *NETCOM*, 1—1, janvier, pp. 88—102; et in Bakis (ed.) 1988, pp. 91—92

41—RIBOUD A. (1989) *Modernisation mode d'emploi*, rapport au Premier ministre, ed. 10—18

42—SAINSAULIEU R., SEGRESTIN D.(1986), "Vers une théorie sociologique de l'entreprise", in *Sociologie du travail*, N°1

43—VELTZ P. (1986), Information des industries manufacturières et intellectualisation de la production, in *Sociologie du travail*, pp. 545—566

44—VILETTE M. (1991), "Intégrer les multinationales", in *Annales Des Mines-Gérer et Comprendre*, juin, pp. 16—27

45— WEBER H. (1988), "Cultures patronales et types d'entreprises: esquisse d'une typologie du patronat, in *Sociologie du travail*, n°4

46—WISEMAN, *L'informatique stratégique, nouvel atout de la compétitivité*

47—ZARIFIAN P. (1990), Hiérarchisation, réseaux et systèmes de décision dans les grandes entreprises industrielles *Réseaux* n° 41

48—ROCHE Edward M. (1992), Managing information technology in multinational corporations., Macmillan Publishing Co-Maxwell Macmillan, New York/Toronto..., 450 p.

8 The Use of ICT at the Plant of ABB at Ludvika and at the Plant of Volvo at Skövde in Sweden – A Regional Perspective

Sten Lorentzon

A factor influencing the competitive ability of different places/regions is the possibilities of using information and communication technology (ICT).[1] New technological means, like electronic networks, make it easier to separate different production factors in time and space. This shapes new prerequisites to organize and locate activities. Thereby the use of ICT transforms social and economic organizations (jfr Claval 1990, Hagström 1990a, 1990b, 1991). As a consequence the division of labour can take place both within and between companies; in a geographical context varying from local to international level (Goddard 1990a, Törnqvist 1990a, Duong 1991). A key issue is the structure of communication systems. The ability to communicate and the position in networks based on ICT are important factors to consider at location of activities (Langdale 1989, Dicken 1990, Goddard 1990b, Porter 1990, Törnqvist 1990b, Langdale 1991). Thus the possibilities to communicate influence the attractiveness of different areas.

The importance of ICT has been strengthened by the development towards world-wide organizations. As the companies cross national boundaries additional problems of coordination and control arise. Other organizational structures are formed that are more sophisticated than the traditional hierarchical organization. The tendency is an increasing demand of reporting links, e.g between area and product segment of the company. In this context global coordination is one means to gain competitive advantage (Dicken 1990, Porter 1990).

The technological and organizational changes also influence the geographical pattern. Some trends can be delineated. There is an increasing international division of R & D activities and routine operations. It is even possible to separate R from D (Hagström 1990a). Another trend

---

[1] This study has been supported by the Swedish Transport Research Board.

is the concentration of economic power, which leads to the shaping of core regions (Shachar and Öberg 1990). However, the use of ICT may open up new opportunities facilitating both centralization and decentralization (Goddard 1990b, Törnqvist 1990b). The organization and location of economic power seem e.g to be influenced in at least two different ways. One of them is that important decisions move from the bottom to the top of organizations. The other change is related to the stream of many routine decisions in the opposite direction (Forsström and Lorentzon 1991).

These tendencies indicate geographical changes that significantly can change the location of activities. The development towards a more integrated international economy with the transnational companies (TNC's) as more important actors focuses the interest at organizational changes of TNC's. These changes influence the work opportunities at different places. Prerequisites for the changes are the possibilities to communicate.

The development towards a more informative society also means that attention should be paid to the possibilities to produce knowledge and to communicate within new networks (Andersson, Strömquist 1988). It is an issue of different types of linkages depending on activity. The exchange of informal information e.g needs face-to-face contacts.

In this paper two surveys of the communications are presented; one from the plant of ABB at Ludvika and the other from the plant of Volvo at Skövde. Since the merger of ASEA (Sweden) and BBC (Switzerland) in 1988 the plant at Ludvika is included in the production systems of ABB. The plant at Skövde is by the alliance between Volvo (Sweden) and Renault (France) in 1990 integrated to the production systems of the two companies. The surveys give examples of the information flows from these two places integrated to the production systems of the TNCs. The purpose of the study is to support an analysis of how the competitiveness of different places and regions is influenced by developments towards a more international economy based on electronic networks.

Methods and data

In the initial stage of these surveys interviews were made with people involved in ICT issues of ABB and Volvo. Interviews had also been performed in the pre-studies during spring 1991 concerning the use of ICT within the ABB Group and the Volvo Group.[1] These pre-studies were

---

[1] These studies "SJÖBERG, E (1991) The use of ICT within the ABB Group — a geographical perspective and LORENTZON, S and SJÖBERG, E (1991) The use

based on information collected from document studies and interviews carried out at ABB Data AB in Västerås and Volvo Data in Göteborg. The results from these studies were the starting point for this survey.

The information in this study has been collected at the plants of Ludvika and Skövde. At Ludvika the documentation is based on the information flows from ABB HV Switchgear AB. The company is one out of five ABB-companies with their headoffices at Ludvika. At Skövde interviews and documents were originally performed at the division of engines for cars but were later broadened to the total plant.

The surveys include different kinds of communication; telephone, fax, electronic mail, mail and business trips (reflecting face-to-face connections). Information of the companies is based on two periods; during 1991 and March 1992. The latter is seen as a representative period of activity. At the plant of Ludvika the main research period started 10 days later and was prolonged 10 days in April. The surveys, however, are performed as continous processes since contacts were established in connection to the pre-studies of spring 1991. The methods and data are also discussed along with the presentation of the flows of communication from ABB HV Switchgear at Ludvika and Volvo at Skövde.

A short presentation of companies, plants and places

ABB - Ludvika

The ABB Group[1] is one of the world s largest electrical engineering group of companies. It is owned by the Swedish company ASEA AB and the Swiss company BBC Brown Boveri Ltd, who have a 50 percent sharehold each. The ABB Group was created through a merger of the electrotechnical activities of ASEA AB and BBC Ltd in January 1988. The two companies, long time rivals, had very similar structures of production. The fusion was completed at extreme pace. Less than five months after the merger had been declared the new organization was presented and 500 new managers appointed. Through the merger ASEA AB gained market-shares in Europe within the EC-countries,

---

of ICT within the Volvo Group — a geographical perspective" were presented at the meeting of the IGU-commission "Geography of Telecommunication and Communications" at Göteborg in June 1991.

[1] The presentation of the companies is based on the papers "SJÖBERG, E (1991) The use of ICT within the ABB Group — a geographical perspective and LORENTZON, S and SJÖBERG, E (1991) The use of ICT within the Volvo Group — a geographical perspective" delivered to the meeting of the IGU Commission "Geography of Telecommunication and Communications" at Göteborg in June 1991.

where the company had only been represented to a limited extent earlier.

After the merger the headoffice of ABB Group holding company - ABB Ltd - was located to Zurich, Switzerland, away from the ASEA and BBC headquarters which were located to Västerås and Baden respectively. From a Swedish point of view this meant that the town of Västerås lost its former strong position in the hierarchy. On the other hand the Swedish influence on the fusion dominated. The far-reaching decentralized organizational pattern within ASEA became the model of the new ABB-structure.

Geographically the ABB Group is broken down into sub-groups or companies in the industrialized countries and regions in the developing countries. In Sweden the mother company ABB Asea Brown Boveri AB is located to Västerås. ABBAB has some 46,000 employees, out of which 33,000 in Sweden, in 130 companies. The main production units in Sweden are in Västerås, Ludvika. Finspång and Stockholm (see Figure 1).

The ABB group has production units in some 40 countries worldwide. Following the matrix-organization one unit will have the global responsibility for each specific Business Area. There are several Business Areas under each Business Segment. Here should be noted that the main production units within the segment of Power Transmission are located to Ludvika (Sweden), Västerås (Sweden), Mannheim (Germany), Drammen (Norway), Stockholm (Sweden), Zurich (Switzerland) and Raleigh (USA). This survey concerns the information flows from HV Switchgear, which is a Business Area within the Business Segment Power Transmission. The study refers to the Swedish part of HV Switchgear with focus on ABB H V Switchgear AB at Ludvika.

The plant at Ludvika has had predecessors. In 1893 the first 3-phase transmission for electricity was built and the succesful result attracted capital. In 1900 a company was founded with the sight towards the world market. After reconstructions in 1906 and 1908 the company was merged with ASEA in Västerås in 1916 (Ludvika kommun 1989).

Technical research and development of products for high voltage have become characteristics of Ludvika (Ludvika kommun 1988). More people (3 200 persons) are also working at ASEA Brown Boveri than at any other type of activity in the commune (Ludvika kommun 1991).

The company at Ludvika is included in ABB business area "high voltage switchgear". This area also comprises the following companies; ABB Hochspannungstechnik AG (Zurich/Switzerland), ABB

Figure 1: *Communes of 20 or more employees at ABB (excluding ABB Fläkt) in Sweden 1991.*[1]

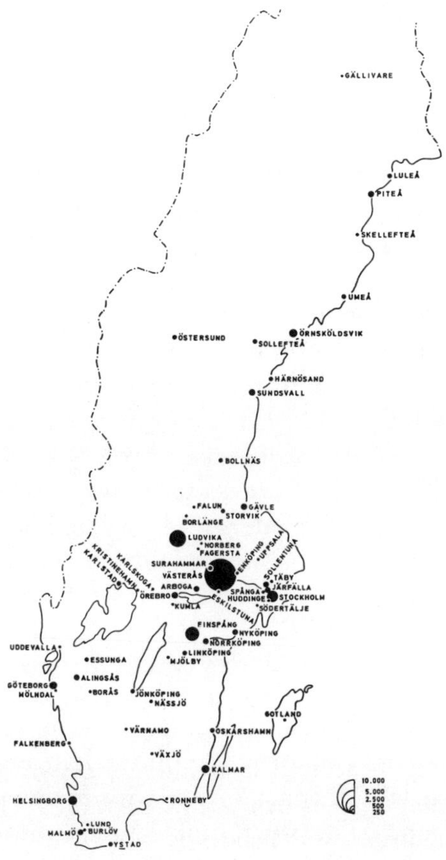

Schaltanlagen GmbH (Mannheim/FRG) and ABB Power Transmission Inc.(Greensburg; PA/USA). Thus there is similar production of swittchgears at other places within ABB as at the plant of Ludvika (HV Switchgear 1990).

Ludvika is located at the lake of Väsman in the middle parts of Sweden in the county of Kopparberg (see Figure 2). Within Ludvika commune there are more than 300 lakes in a hilly landscape dominated by forest (Ludvika kommun 1988). In a distance of 50 km from Ludvika the town Borlänge (47 000 inhabitants) can be reached. Borlänge forms

---

[1]Source: Data compiled from Asea Brown Boveri AB. Public Affairs and Communications, 1992-06-18.

an urban area together with the administrative center and biggest town of Kopparberg; Falun (close to 54,000 inhabitants). The number of inhabitants in Ludvika is about 29,000 to be compared with 289,000 in the county. Ludvika is the third largest commun of the county (Kopparbergs län 1991). In a functional view it can be noted that the distance from Ludvika to the head office of the Swedish holding company Asea Brown Boveri AB in Västerås is 117 km and to the head office of one of the owners of ABB - ASEA AB in Stockholm - is 223 km (Nordbeck 1976, Sjöberg 1991). (The other owner is BBC Brown Boveri Ltd with head office in Baden. The holding company - ABB Asea Brown Boveri Ltd - is located to Zurich).

Ludvika has a tradition within the iron industry. A starting point for this activity was the foundation of the ironwork at Ludvika by the king Gustav Vasa in 1555. In the surroundings of Ludvika a lot of ironworks were founded. During the 19th century, however, economies of scale meant the closure of many ironworks. Even the ironwork at Ludvika was closed down at the end of the century. New technological methods of producing iron turned the interest of production to the minerals of Grängesberg; nowdays located within Ludvika commun. The production at this mine has also been closed down in 1990 (Ludvika kommun 1988, Ludvika leder, nr 4/1991).

The refining within the steel industry and the forest industries generates transportation of goods. A lot of these transports as well as the traffic through the county is taken care of by the railway. Another important generator of traffic to and from the county of Kopparberg is the tourism. The consequence is primarily car traffic. The standard of the roads of the most important relations, e.g to Stockholm, are good. However, some relations are not satisfying. This concerns the roads to the north and to the region of Oslo. These shortages mean that the county of Kopparberg is outside the mainstream of the road traffic. The number of interregional railway connections have been diminishing during the last years even if the connection between Ludvika and Västerås has been improved by the new commuter train "Bergslagspendeln". In the national and regional perspectives Ludvika belongs to the bigger functional area of Falun-Borlänge. The airport of Borlänge/Falun links - by Arlanda Airport at Stockholm - the area to other parts of the world (Kopparbergs län 1987, 1989).

Figure 2: *The location of Ludvika in the county of Kopparberg with marking of the infrastructure of transportation.*

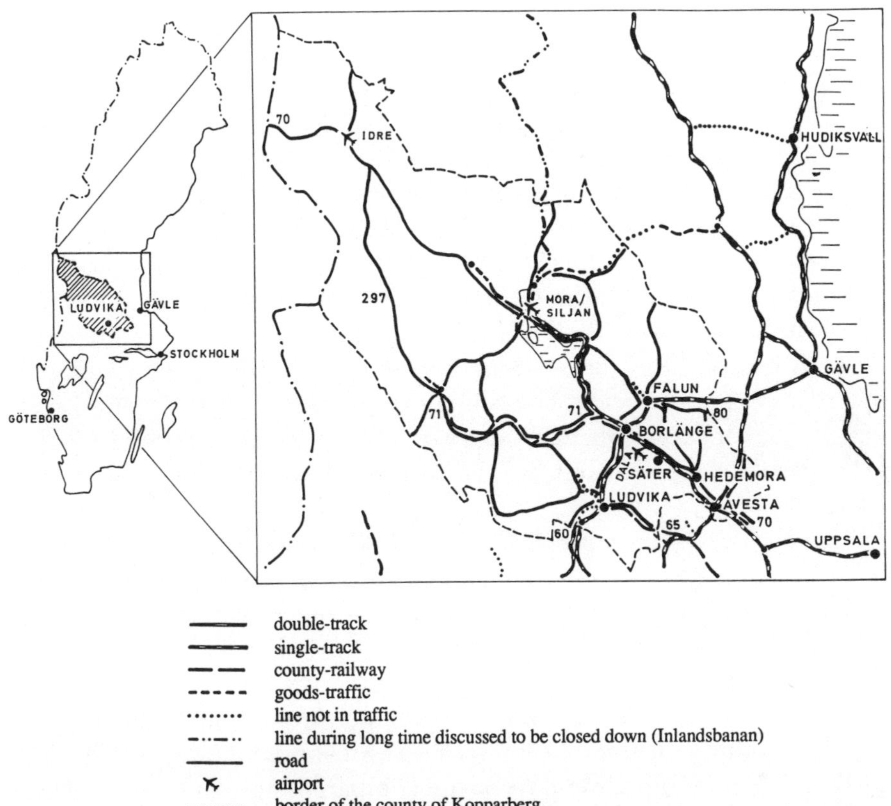

double-track
single-track
county-railway
goods-traffic
line not in traffic
line during long time discussed to be closed down (Inlandsbanan)
road
airport
border of the county of Kopparberg

The five headoffices of ABB at Ludvika can be seen as the spider of different networks. A center of power transmission has been established. A lot of attention is also paid to R&D. Thus ABB represents an important resource of competence. The position of Ludvika as a world metropol of power transmission is strengthened by the Swedish Transmission Research Institute AB (owned by ABB and Vattenfall). The commune of Ludvika and other organizations are also active in order to stimulate the development of the area. An example is the plans of a future city built on the idea of both ICT and the integration of work and living in beautiful surroundings (Ludvika leder, nr 4/ 1991).

Volvo - Skövde

The Volvo Group is the largest industrial enterprise by turnover in the Nordic countries with cars and trucks as main products. AB Volvo commenced business as a wholly- owned subsidiary of AB Svenska Kullagerfabriken (SKF) in 1926 in Göteborg (Sweden), where the Group still has its headquarter and main plant. The first Volvo car left the assembly line in April 1927. Today the Group accounts for one percent of the total car production worldwide and Volvo Trucks is the second largest manufacturer of trucks over 16 tonnnes in the world.

In 1990 talks with the French Renault Group resulted in an alliance between the two companies. The alliance — organized in a crosswise ownership — includes the business areas Cars, Trucks and Buses and concerns mainly production and product development. Volvo and Renault had earlier from 1979 an agreement on industrial cooperation in the passenger car field. The two companies are very different market-wise; while Volvo has its main share of sales in North America, Sweden and Great Britain Renault has its main markets in France, Spain and Italy.

The Volvo Group consists of around 30 companies in Sweden and some 25 companies in other countries. At the end of the year 1990 the Volvo Group had about 69,000 employees out of which 47,000 were employed in Sweden. Today the Volvo Group has two mother coun-tries; France and Sweden. The holding company of the group, AB Volvo, has its headoffice in Göteborg and another Group office in Paris. A policy committee and two committees for cooperation are also located to Paris. The dominating part of the companies and employees within the Volvo Group is found in Sweden. The main assembly plants are found in Torslanda (Göteborg, Sweden), Gent (Belgium) and Born (Netherlands). In Sweden the biggest production plants (more than 1,000 employees) are found in Göteborg (assembly line), Skövde (engines), Olofström (sheet-metal), Trollhättan (aircraft engines), Köping (gear boxes, rear axles), Umeå (truckcabins) and Kalmar (assembly line). See Figure 3.[1] The importance of Volvo in Göteborg is reflected in the number of employees. Nearly 24,000 persons, that is about 50% of the employees in the Volvo Group in Sweden, are working in Göteborg. In Skövde about 5,000 persons, corresponding to 10% of the employees in the Volvo Group in Sweden, are working at the Volvo-plant.

---

[1]Source: Data compiled from Volvo Annual Report 1991.

The plant at Skövde was founded in 1868 as a foundry and engineering workshop. In 1908 the production of "Pentaengines" started. In the middle of the 1920 s "Pentaverken" was a well established company; especially at production of boat-engines. The program of products was expanded when Volvo became intrerested in buying car-engines. The deliveries increased and in 1930 Volvo bought the "Pentaverken" (Volvo 1927—1990, AB Volvo Annual Report 1962). In 1935 the "Pentaverken" was incorporated with the mother company AB Volvo and got the name "Volvo Skövdeverken" (Ellegård, supporting documents 1983). Thus the production of engines at the plant of Skövde was early integrated to the units of control and production at Göteborg.

Later many changes of production systems and of the Volvo organization have been performed. The latest changes include the development towards a customer oriented structure of the organization as well as changes of the control of the production. Thus from 1992 Volvo in Skövde is submitted to the headoffice of engines located to Göteborg. The new organization consists of a manager of engines and a manager of transmission. The alliance between Volvo and Renault motivated these alterations (interview S Brännberg 1991-11-07).

Skövde is located in the western parts of Sweden (see Figure 4). The distance by road to Göteborg (the main city of western Sweden) is 158 km and the distance to Stockholm (the capital) is 340 km (Nordbeck 1976). The surroundings of Skövde are characterized by agriculture and forest areas. Skövde - centrally located - is the biggest town (about 48,000 inhabitants) of the county of Skaraborg. Within a 50 km circle there are 200,000 people (Skövde - mitt i Skaraborgs län, Skövde kommun 1991). The central places of the county are organized in a hierarchical manner with Skövde as the central place. The county is characterized by small scale activities. Most of the inhabitants live in small places; of the total number of 275,000 people 198,000 live in 82 places. Only 5 of these places have more than 10,000 inhabitants (Skaraborgs län, 1991).

The county of Skaraborg is a part of western Sweden and thereby strongly connected to Göteborg (the second largest city of Sweden). At the same time the county is in many ways connected to Stockholm. Thus the number of passenger trips by railway are mainly oriented towards Stockholm. The railway between Göteborg and Stockholm — opened in 1862 — was also an important factor for the development of Skövde as an industrial town.

Figure 3: *Communes of 20 or more employees at Volvo in Sweden 1991.*

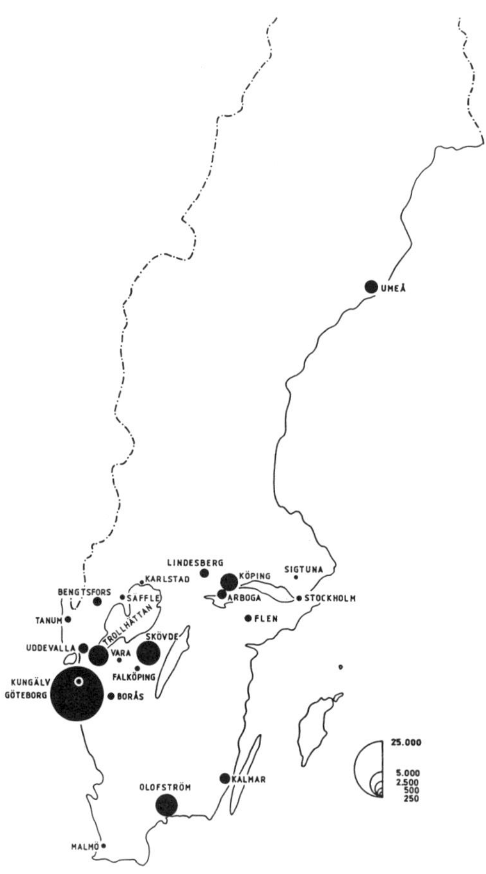

Other industrial factors are the minerals of limestone and granite, which are the base of the production of building materials like concrete and materials of insulation. The industry in Skövde today, however, is dominated by Volvo. Skövde is also characterized by the many employees in military activities (Skövde - mitt i Skaraborg 1991).

From the view of transportation is noted that the county of Skaraborg — by its central situation — often is used for by-passing traffic. Two streams of traffic are dominating. They connect the county with Göteborg and Stockholm. One stream flows on road E20 (former E3) and the other on the railway. Skövde is located along the railway and the distance to the road E20 is 25 km. In the regional perspective, however, Skövde is the central place of the county. Skövde has a hub function regarding bus-connections. This function together with the location along the railway between Göteborg and Stockholm give Skövde a competitive position within the national transportation system. The introduction of high-speed trains with stops in Skövde has further strengthened this position. It is also possible to go by plane from Skövde to Stockholm. The international traffic from the county of Skaraborg is mainly taken care of by the airport of Landvetter outside Göteborg (Skaraborgs län, 1991). There is an ambition within the county of Skaraborg to shape contact intensive environments. Prerequisites are the excellent transportation facilities as well as the college of Skövde (mainly economic education). Included in the strategy is the shaping of a creative center, located at the college, in order to cross different fields of competence. The purpose is to reach effects of synergy. These possibilities will be increased by the building of a traveller-center at the railway station located some hundred meters from the college (Kreativt center/Skaraborg, 1992).

The use of ICT within ABB in Ludvika[1]

In 1990 the number of employees at ABB HV Switchgear AB at Ludvika was 1,026. The sales were 1,346 million Swedish crowns (about 250 million US dollars in July 1992). The final customers of the products of ABB HV Switchgear are big power generating companies located all over the world. Time of delivery is often 6—7 months after the contract has been signed. The regular customer is another ABB-company. The deliveries come mainly from Europe of which a big part from Sweden.

The R&D within ABB is organized according to the philosophy that R&D should be located close to the production. This is also a reality since 95 percent of all R&D is performed by the companies themselves (Sjöberg 1991). The responsibility of R&D in the Business Area HV Switchgear is located to Ludvika.

Economic reports are sent from Ludvika to Zurich. A file of results is sent every month by the reporting system ABACUS. Every quarter of the year a more comprehensive report is sent including figures as well as notes. The systems of orders and inventories at ABB HV Switchgear are linked to a big computer at Västerås. Thus the transmission of data mainly consists of traffic between Ludvika and Västerås.

---

[1] The results are based on DRAKENBERG, O (1992) Kommunikationsflöden från ABB HV Switchgear i Ludvika (working-paper to be published at the department of human and economic geography, Gothenburg University, in August 1992).

Figure 4: *The location of Skövde in the county of Skaraborg with marking of the in-frastructure of transportation.*

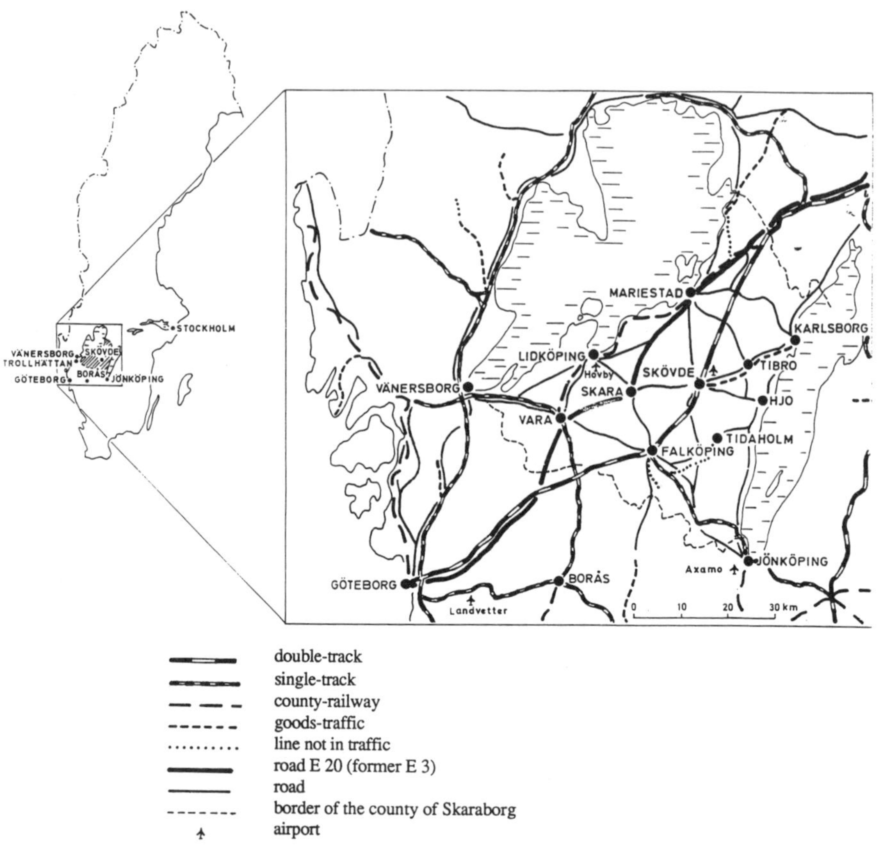

▬▬▬	double-track
▬▬▬	single-track
▬ ▬ ▬	county-railway
-------	goods-traffic
··········	line not in traffic
▬▬▬	road E 20 (former E 3)
▬▬▬	road
-------	border of the county of Skaraborg
⊀	airport

The structures of the customers and the suppliers

The ABB Switchgear is characterized by a great international dependence. Although the Swedish market was the most important in 1991 around 85 percent of the sales went abroad. The value of the orders differ. The deliveries to the Swedish market are usually of less value than in average. An explanation is that the Swedish power generating system is well established. Thus the sales often concern exchange of old products. In general most of the sales go to one place in each country in Europe. For example to Cordoba in Spain, Odense in Denmark and Mannheim in Germany went to each place more than 10 percent of the sales. The counterpart in these places is often another ABB-company.

Most of the suppliers are located to Sweden. About 40 places in Sweden are representing the location of suppliers. A big part (about 30%) of the delivery-value comes from the local area of Ludvika. From Europe goods are bought from i.a. the Ruhr-area and the area around Zurich. The number of important places of suppliers in Europe are limited to about 15.

The flows of communication

This section considers the flows of communication by telephone, fax, electronic mail (memo), mail and business trips from ABB HV Switchgear. The number of telephone calls, fax and business trips are based on surveys during the period 1992-03-19—1992- 04 10, while the use of memos are based on a survey performed during two weeks. The use of post is founded on the collection of all mail during two days and a sample from the more than 40 collecting places within the area of ABB at Ludvika. Telex like video conferences are excluded. They are used very seldom in spite of the fact that there is a fullequipped video-conference station in Ludvika. The transmission of data is also excluded as it is performed by Västerås, which makes it impossible to identify the final destination of messages.

The number of telephone calls (all except within the switchboard and mobile telephones) were 13,256. The calls were registered by the Swedish Telecom. More than half of these were local (Ludvika area) and are not included in the following presentation of calls to different places and countries. An assumption is that the local telephone calls are mainly private. Even when these are excluded eight out of ten of the calls are within Sweden. Most of the foreign calls are to Europe with emphasis on Germany, Switzerland and Norway. As is shown in Figure 5 a geographical pattern can be distinguished[1] in Europe (outside Sweden); the Nordic capitals and a belt from Telford in Great Britain to Milano with distinction of the important ABB-places Mannheim, Baden and Zurich.

In the same manner the use of fax was registered by the Swedish Telecom. The number of fax was 3,028 with three out of four messages sent abroad. Continents far away from Sweden like North- and South America, Asia and Australia were receivers of 25 percent of the fax. Looking upon different countries most of the fax are within Sweden

---

[1]The map shows places that have received more than 5 calls. The places on the map represent 95.7% of the telephone traffic from ABB/Ludvika to Europe during the period 1992-03-19—1992-04-10.

Figure 5: *The telephone traffic (in percent) from the ABB-plant at Ludvika to places in Europe during the period 1992-03-19—1992-04-10.*

(30%) followed by Germany (7%), Canada (6%), Switzerland (6%) and Italy (5%). But the fax messages go to many countries. Not less than 28 countries got at least one fax a day. A European belt can be identified from Telford in Great Britain to Milano in Italy. The important ABB-places Mannheim, Baden and Zurich as well as Milano are receivers of many fax. See Figure 6.[1]

Electronic mail is registered within ABB by the so called memosystem. It has more than 18,000 potential users. The system is built up continuously. The presentation of this survey, however, is limited. In

---

[1] The map shows places that have received more than 3 fax. The places on the map represent 87,4% of the fax traffic from ABB/Ludvika to Europe during the period 1992-03-19 - 1992-04-10.

this case a questionnaire was brought to all memo-users in order to note all messages sent to receivers outside Ludvika. But just 20 percent of the users answered, which makes it hard to draw conclusions. In spite of this some results of the material can be presented. About a fourth of the messages (325 altogether) went to Sweden and a fifth to the USA. Bulgaria (6%) and Hungary (3%) are among the other countries, which indicate the use of memos between many partners.

The figures from the survey of the mail-distribution must be read cautiously as the study was performed during a too short time to make it possible to draw reliable conclusions. The result, however, indicates similarities to the geographical pattern of the use of the telephones and fax.

The presentation of the geographical distribution of the business trips imply a remark. It is common to go to Västerås in a rented car. This means that the trip will not be registered as specification of travelling. With this remark it can be noted that the number of business trips were 157 and performed mainly by car within Sweden and by plane to places outside Sweden. Half of the number of trips were in Sweden. Germany, Great Britain and Switzerland were the most frequent destinations abroad. Västerås and Stockholm are often destinations in Sweden. Also when flying abroad mostly the airports of Västerås and Stockholm (Arlanda) are used. Business trips are common to places in Germany and to the pronounced destination in Switzerland; Zurich.

The use of ICT within Volvo in Skövde

In 1991 the number of employees at the plant of Skövde[1] was 4,887 (Volvo Årsredovisning 1991). The same year the sales amounted to 4 284 million Swedish crowns (about 800 million US dollars in July 1992). A lot of investment has been made during the end of the 1980s and the beginning of 1990's including new methods of production as well as new choices of materials. Thus engines are made by aluminium at the new production line (officially opened in October 1991) located to what is called the "eastern factory". At the introduction of these engines ("white engines") the latest technology and new ways of management have been launched. The production at the "western factory" (in operation since 1974) is based on production methods available during the 1970s ("red

---

[1] The results are mainly based on HAHN, I (1992) Kommunikationsflöden från Volvo Skövde (working-paper to be published at the department of human and economic geography, Gothenburg University, in August 1992). This section is mainly based on interviews with S BRÄNNBERG 1991-11-07, 1991-11-28.

Figure 6: *The fax traffic (in percent) from the ABB-plant at Ludvika to places in Europe during the period 1992-03-19—1992-04-10.*

engines"). A consequence is a division of the production towards a heavy sector based on traditional cast iron technique, while other production is mainly based on aluminium as input.

At the same time the wish to reduce the costs and raise the quality has contributed to more system deliveries. The subcontractors have to raise their competence. A consequence is a reduction of the number of subcontractors. The number of deliverers to the "red engine" is about 250 to compare with 160 to the "white engine". Of these subcontractors 15—20 are unique for the new production line. This development means that former assembling at the Volvo plant at an increasing degree is performed by subcontractors. This development also means that big subcontractors are building new systems of subcontractors.

Since the "eastern factory" was built the production of engines in Skövde is organized in two profit-centers. One of them is the new "eastern factory" and the other one the old "western factory". The plant at Skövde is a subcontractor within Volvo-Renault. From 1992 Volvo in Skövde is also submitted to the headoffice of engines located to Göteborg.

These organizational changes have gone hand in hand with the changes of the prerequisites to use ICT. The prerequisites to treat information have changed from the large scale techniques of the 1960 s to the possibilities of today to deal with a lot of information in small units. At the same time the possibilities to transmit information have increased substantially. Thus during the 1960s Volvo used the so called VIS-system (Volvo Information System). This system was based on big solutions. Different functions should be adjusted to this system. Another system SATS (Skövdeverkens Anskaffnings- och Tillverkningssystem) founded on the same idea with a central control unit was used during the early 1970s. Continously this structure has changed towards focus on the single human being. Computer languages adjusted to the needs of the consumers have been developed and increased the possibilities to change the organization in a decentralized direction.

The former approach with big systems including demand of a lot of programming work, however, in many cases still binds the treatment of information to old technology. This situation makes it hard to transform the information systems to the demand of new functional solutions. Therefore established systems are often barriers to the challenges met by the industry. The use of ICT is a prerequisite to be able to compete on an even more international market. At the same time it is important to be aware of the cooperation between systems and users. The mutuality is very clear. The behaviour of the human beings is decisive of the possibilities to perform different systems.

The R&D of engines is taken place at Göteborg. Looked upon in a production technical way, however, Skövde is a harbour of imports launching advanced technology, that to a higher degree tends to be brought from Italy instead of Germany. But Skövde alone represents also a great part of the technical innovation.

It should be noted that the alliance between Volvo and Renault was shaped in a situation when Volvo had developed the engine made by aluminium. Thus Skövde had a strong competitive position. A noteable result of this position is the engines ordered by Volvo- Renault from the plant of Skövde to be delivered during the period 1994—2004 at a value of about 12 billion Swedish crowns (about 2.2 billions US dollars in July 1992).

The structures of the customers and the suppliers

The fact that the plant at Skövde is within the production system of Volvo-Renault limits the structures of customers and suppliers. Thus, the plant receives delivery plans once a month by mail and by filetransmission. These plans are in detail one month ahead and contain a prognosis for 60 weeks. Göteborg is the most important place as receiver of engines followed by Gent, Kalmar and Uddevalla. The explanation is that assembly plants of both cars and trucks are located to Göteborg and Gent, while assembly plants for cars are located to Kalmar and Uddevalla.The orders received from the customers mean that plans of deliveries are sent to the subcontractors to the Skövde plant. The biggest suppliers of the production of truck engines are connected with the Odette-file, while a third of the suppliers to the production of car engines get their orders by the Odette-file. The idea is that the Odette-file will be integrated in the calculating-system of the suppliers. Today there are just some suppliers that are able to use this system.

The structure of suppliers is geographically more split up than the structure of customers. The plant at Skövde gets material from 250—300 suppliers. About 100 of these are located to Sweden (Brännberg 1991-11-07, 1991-11-28). Sweden and Germany stand for about 35 percent each of the value of the deliveries. But there are big differences concerning the number of deliveries. Sweden stands for nearly 60 percent of the number of deliveries to the plant at Skövde, while the corresponding figure for Germany is less than 20 percent. In Sweden the suppliers are mainly located to two belts; one horizontal belt stretching from the Norwegian border to the Stockholm area and another diagonal belt from the western parts of Sweden (around the city of Trollhättan) to the southeastern coast (the county of Blekinge). In Europe many suppliers are located along a broad band stretching from the southern parts of Germany across Netherlands to Midlands. The most important place of deliveries is Stuttgart, which is explained by the location of Bosch.

But the structure of subcontractors has changed. During the 1960s Great Britain was a more important deliverer than Germany. Another change that has taken place is that the suppliers tend to be located to more peripheral countries. Today e.g. 8-10 companies in Japan sell to Volvo in Skövde. These deliveries came earlier from the USA. In some cases, however, it is hard to change supplier. This situation exists concerning e.g. ignition systems. In this "high-tech" field Bosch has a very strong position and other companies have difficulties to compete. A general trend is that more deliveries come from abroad (Brännberg 1991-11-07, 1991-11-28).

The flows of communication

This section considers the flows of communication by telephone, fax, electronic mail (memo), mail and business trips from the Volvo-plant at Skövde during March 1992.

The number of telephone calls registered at the switch-board at the plant were 45,011 excluding the local area of Skövde. Skövde is excluded as most of these calls are assumed to be private. About nine of ten calls are within Sweden. The foreign calls are in general bound for Europe (corresponding to about 8% of the calls) reflecting the location of suppliers and customers. Germany is the most important receiver of calls (besides Sweden) followed by Great Britain and Italy. With the exception of these countries and Sweden the telephone is used to only one or some places in each country. About 15 places in Europe and 70 places in Sweden often receive calls (see Figure 7).[1] The flows of calls are highly correlated to the location of suppliers, while the flows don t seem to follow the location of customers. The county of Skaraborg receives many calls, which may be explained by the contacts to local/regional suppliers not integrated to the production system and calls assumed to be private.

The use of fax was measured by the registration of the number of messages sent from about 30 fax-devices corresponding to approximately 99 percent of the total number of fax, excluding the use of memofax (fax sent by memo) as the destination is unknown. The memofax stands for about 11 percent of the total number of fax. The number of fax sent during March 1992 was 2,525 of which nearly 70 percent was domestically. Nearly a quarter of the fax abroad was sent to Europe with Germany (10%) as the most important receiver followed by Great Britain (4%), France (3%) and Italy (3%). Fax is common as a mean of communication to about 40 places in Sweden and about 20 in Europe. The traffic is well correlated to the structure of suppliers. Paris and Turin, however, are overrepresented. A part of the explanation of the contacts to Italy is the fact that the assembly line in the "eastern factory"

---

[1] The map shows places that have received more than 20 calls. The places on the map represent 91% of the total telephone traffic from Volvo/Skövde during March 1992.

Figure 7: *The telephone traffic (in percent) from the Volvo-plant at Skövde to places in Sweden during March 1992.*

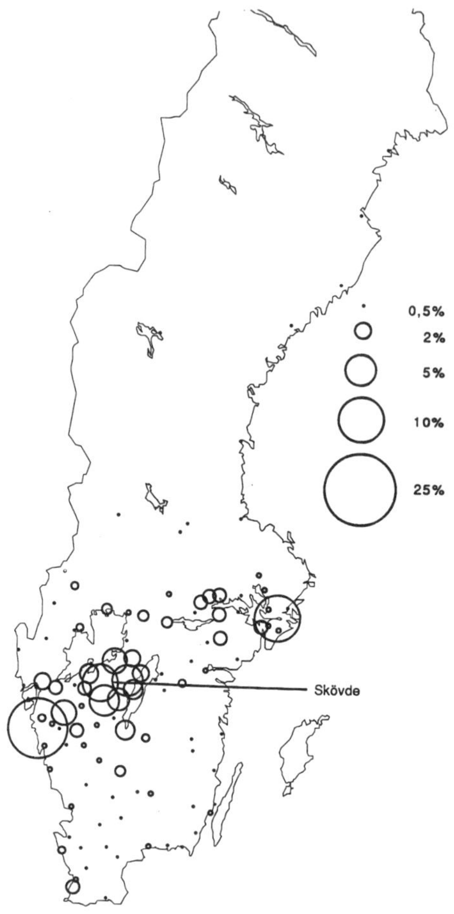

was made in Turin. The geographical distribution of the fax sent from Skövde is illustrated in Figure 8.[1]

The registration of electronic mail (memo) takes place at Volvo Data at Göteborg. The number of externally sent memos have been reduced by memofax and memotelex as the final destinations are unknown. These memos represent only 1,5 percent of the externally sent memos. About 40 percent of the total number of memos are registered as external. Most of the use of electronic mail at the Volvo plant takes place within and between the companies at Skövde. The number of memos

---

[1] The map shows places that have received more than 3 fax. The places on the map represent 86% of the total traffic of fax from Volvo/Skövde to Europe during March 1992.

sent externally during March 1992 was 43,599. About 98 percent of these messages have as destination the Swedish units of Volvo. Gent, Lyon and Paris are the most important counterparts abroad. The geographical distribution of memos is limited as the electronic connections are mainly installed to other Volvo companies.

The mail sent from the plant was sorted in seven geographical areas. About 20 percent of the mail is sent to the county of Skaraborg. The area around Göteborg has a similar portion and about 10 percent of the letters are sent to Stockholm. The importance of Skaraborg can be explained by all the messages sent to the employees concerning mainly salaries but also other type of information e.g at illness. Mail to other parts located far away from Skövde contains to a high degree delivery-plans sent to suppliers once a month.

The survey of the business trips includes all the train-, plane- and boattrips. Information of these trips were obtained by SJ (the Swedish railway) and by a travel agency. The registration of the number of business trips made by car was performed by a questionnaire. In average the answers correspond to 64 percent of all cars. Within the most used categories - rented cars and division cars - the frequency of answers was 83 percent. The destinations of the business trips are mainly places in Sweden (86% of all trips) with a strong orientation towards western parts of Sweden with Göteborg in an outstanding position (34% of all trips). The most important places abroad are located to Germany (7% of all trips) followed by Belgium (2% of all trips) and France (1% of all trips).

Final remarks

The surveys of ABB HV Switchgear at Ludvika and Volvo at Skövde presented here are examples of information flows from two medium-sized places integrated to the production systems of TNC's. Even if the companies are oriented towards different markets some common remarks can be made.

- The contacts are most intensive within Sweden followed by other european countries. Germany has an important position.
- The telephone is the most common means of communication. Concerning the Volvo plant at Skövde a remark can be made. The use of electronic mail is nearly as common as the use of telephone as a means of communication.
- There are big possibilities to substitute one means of communication with another. Fax is a common substitute for both mail and telephone. In the former case the time saving is the decisive factor and

Figure 8: *The fax traffic (in percent) from the Volvo plant at Skövde to places in Europe during March 1992.*

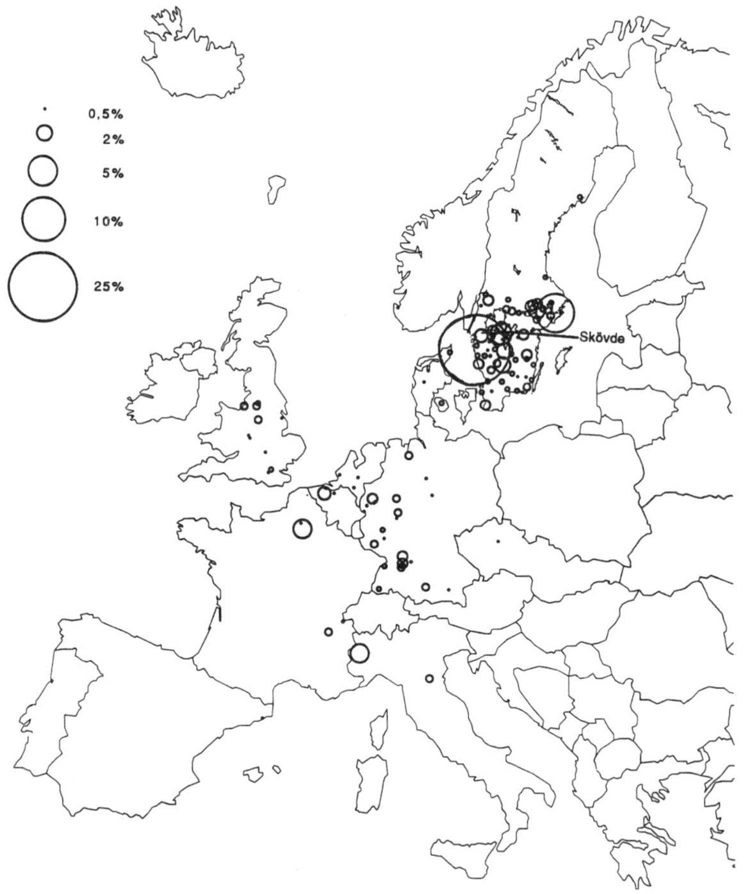

concerning telephone the accessibility is often a factor influencing the use of fax. In many cases electronic mail can substitute fax and mail. In the future the use of EDI is expected to take over a lot of the communication now performed by mail or fax. The costs are also a reason to use EDI.

• The companies need different means of communication. Business trips and contacts by telephone are important means of communication to establish confidence and make it possible to solve problems in a short time. Electronic mail and fax are needed when the receiver is hard to reach, e.g. at time differences. EDI makes it easier at routine orders, while transmission by mail is needed e.g at bigger deliveries. Except the possibilities to avoid time differences the saving of trans-

mission time is an important argument for using electronic mail or fax. This argument is emphasized at transmission over long distances.
• The structure of communication is not only directed towards customers or suppliers. Besides there are needs of contacts within the group of companies of ABB and Volvo.

This structure of communication is here seen in a geographical perspective. Both Ludvika and Skövde are medium-sized places that can offer agreeable environments. The infrastructure of Ludvika and Skövde admit communication of all means. The possibilities to use ICT are also prerequisites for both Ludvika and Skövde - located in the periphery of Europe — to be integrated in TNC:s. But there are differences in the infrastructure between the two places; mainly concerning the accessiblity of public transport. In the regional perspective Skövde is centrally located in the county of Skaraborg. Skövde is also located along the railway connecting Göteborg and Stockholm. Ludvika has a less favourable position both regionally and nationally.

There are also differences in the function of the two places within the organizations. The plant at Ludvika has a strong position in R&D within ABB, which can be seen as a result of the long tradition of competence in the high voltage field. The plant of Volvo in Skövde is on the other hand strongly connected to the research performed at Göteborg in spite of the fact that knowledge from engines has been built up during a long time. This could have been the origin for the shaping of local/regional R&D. The location of R&D to Ludvika indicates that, in spite of Ludvika s relatively bad infrastructure of transport, R&D can be performed outside great urban areas. It also indicates that the telenet has been built up in accordance with the demands of the TNC's.

However, it should be noted that the needs of infrastructure for transportation of goods differ between the two companies. The plant at Skövde is integrated in the well-established transportation system of Volvo with just-in-time deliveries, while the production at Ludvika is more oriented towards separate products. With regard to the fact that Volvo has a big share of its production located at Sweden (an unique situation among Swedish companies working abroad) it is important to be located in accordance with the Swedish transportation system. At the same time it can be noted that manufacturing in Sweden in many cases means a competitive disadvantage explained by the fact that the biggest markets are abroad and many deliveries take place from other countries.

In order to strengthen the competitive power places try to build up new networks based on the specific local/regional prerequisites. This aspect has become more important as a consequence of the development towards companies linked together by both material- and information flows. An important approach is to shape networks with the purpose to reach synergi effects. Another approach is to become more competitive within a special field by strengthening the nodal position in specific networks. An example of the former case is the focus on the college at Skövde as an important actor in shaping new networks, while the location of Swedish Transmission Research Institute to Ludvika is an example of how Ludvika gets a stronger position in the field of power transmission. Strategic roles are thus played by companies, different organizations and authorities. Great attention is paid to the possibilities to improve the competitive power by investing in infrastructure of transportation and ICT.

But still the issue is left. What are the possibilities for the medium-sized places located in the periphery of Europe to compete with the more centrally located places in Europe? Thus a further step of the study is to investigate the prerequisites for other medium-sized places in Europe to be competitive in comparison to Swedish places. The study also gives possibilities to compare the needs of communication at the development towards more integrated TNCs influenced by changing prerequisites for using ICT.

References

AB Volvo Annual Report 1991.

ANDERSSON, Å.E och U STRÖMQUIST (1988) *K-Samhällets Framtid*. Prisma.

ASEA BROWN BOVERI AB (1992) Public Affairs and Communications, 1992-06-18.

Brännberg, Sture — Personal interview. Materials Manager. Volvo Car Componenets Corporation, West Plant, Skövde (1991-11-07, 1991-11-28).

CLAVAL, P (1990) A Critical Review of the Centre-Periphery Model as Applied in a Global Context in Shachar, A and Öberg, S (eds), *The World Economy and the Spatial Organization of Power*. Avebury, Sydney.

DICKEN, P (1990) Transnational Corporations and the Spatial Organization of Production: Some Theoretical and Empirical Issues in Shachar, A and Öberg, S (eds), *The World Economy and the Spatial Organization of Power*. Avebury, Sydney.

DRAKENBERG, O (1992) Kommunikationsflöden från ABB HV Switchgear i Ludvika (working-paper to be published at the department of human and economic geography, Gothenburg University, in August 1992).

DUONG, P (1991) Mondialisation Logistique et Circulation de l In ormation. Le cas de l'industrie cimentiere et du Groupe LAFARGE COPPEE. Paper delivered to the meeting of the Commission: Geography of Telecommunication and Communication of the International Geographical Union, June 4-7 1991, Göteborg, Sweden.

ELLEGÅRD, K (1983) Supporting documents. Department of human and economic geography, Gothenburg University.

FORSSTRÖM, Å and LORENTZON, S (1991) Global development of communication: a frame for the pattern of localization in a small idustrialized country in Brunn, S.D and T.R Leinbach (eds), *Collapsing Space & Time — Geographical Aspects of Communication & Information.* Harper Collins Academic. London.

GODDARD, J. B (1990a) *The Geography of the Information Economy.* Centre for Urban and Regional Development Studies. University of Newcastle upon Tyne. Newcastle.

GODDARD, J.B (1990b) Positioning Older Industrial Regions in Relation to the Emerging Information Economy: the Case of North-East England in Hebbert, M and Hansen, J.C (eds), *Unfamiliar Territory — The Reshaping of European Geography.* Avebury, Sydney.

HAGSTRÖM, P (1990a) Unshackling Corporate Geography. *Geografiska Annaler,*

HAGSTRÖM, P (1990b) New information systems and the changing structure of MNCs. in *Managing the Global Firm.* Edited by C. A. Bartlett, Y. Doz and G Hedlund. Routledge. London and New York.

HAGSTRÖM, P (1991) The "Wired" MNC. The role of Information Systems for Structural Change in Complex Organizations. Institute of International Business (IIB), Stockholm School of Economics.

HAHN, I (1992) *Kommunikationsflöden från Volvo Skövde* (working-paper to be published at the department of human and economic geography, Gothenburg University, in August 1992).

HV SWITCHGEAR (1990) *ABB Business area High Voltage Switchgear.* Publication No. DE THS 1001 88 E.

KOPPARBERGS LÄN (1989) Transportvision Dalarna. Länsstyrelsens styrelse beslut 1989-12-18.

KOPPARBERGS LÄN (1991) Länsstyrelsens prognos 1991 över sysselsättning och befolkning. Regionalekonomiska enheten 910529.

KOPPARBERGS LÄN, LÄNSSTYRELSEN (1987) Transportvision Dalarna. Sammanfattning av systemskiss, etapp 1, diskussionsunderlag/remissmaterial.

KREATIVT CENTER/SKARABORG (1992).

LANGDALE, J. V (1989) The geography of International Business Telecommunications: The Role of Leased Networks. *Annals of the Association of American Geographers.* Vol. 79, No. 4.

LANGDALE, J. V (1991) Transnational Corporations and the Adoption of Information and Communications Technologies in the Asia-Pacific Region. Paper delivered to the meeting of the Commission: Geography of Telecommunication and Communication of the International Geographical Union, June 4-7 1991, Göteborg, Sweden.

LORENTZON, S. and SJÖBERG, E (1991) The use of ICT within the Volvo Group - a geographical perspective. Paper delivered to the meeting of the Commission: Geography of Telecommunication and Communication of the International Geographical Union, June 4 -7 1991, Göteborg, Sweden.

LUDVIKA KOMMUN (1988) *Jubileumsåret 1988.*

LUDVIKA KOMMUN (1991) *Välkommen till Ludvika.* 1991-02.

LUDVIKA LEDER (1991) Nr 4, extra februari 1991, högskoleextra.

NORDBECK, S (1976) *Vägavstånd i Sverige.* Svenska Åkeriförbundet. Stockholm.

PORTER, M. E (1990) *The Competitive Advantage Of Nations.* New York: The Free Press.

Series B, Human Geography. Volume 72 B, Number 1, 1990.

SHACHAR, A. and ÖBERG S (1990) *The World Economy and the Spatial Organization of Power.* Avebury, Sydney.

SJÖBERG, E (1991) The use of ICT within the ABB Group - a geographical perspective. Paper delivered to the meeting of the Commission: Geography of

Telecommunication and Communication of the International Geographical Union, June 4- 7 1991, Göteborg, Sweden.
SKARABORGS LÄN (1991) *Kommunikationsstrategi, Länsstyrelsen i Skaraborgs län.*
SKÖVDE - MITT I SKARABORG (1991) Skövde 1991.
TÖRNQVIST, G (1990a) Det upplösta rummet - begrepp och teoretiska ansatser inom geografin. Red. A Karlqvist. Nätverk. *Teorier och begrepp i samhällsveten-skapen.* Gidlunds, Institutet för Framtidsstudier.
TÖRNQVIST, G (1990b) The Swedish System of Cities in a Changing Technical Environment in Hebbert, M and Hansen, J.C (eds), *Unfamiliar Territory — The Reshaping of European Geography.* Avebury, Sydney.

9 Formation and Maintenance of Knowledge-Based Networks – The Case of University Contact Patterns

Hans Ouwersloot and Piet Rietveld

The formation of communication networks has been stimulated by the increase in the quality and range of telecommunication services and the increase in the speeds of transport. This has led to the emergence of strongly interdependent systems of regions which in certain cases may threaten the autonomy of particular regions. In the present paper special attention is paid to knowledge-based networks. A conceptual framework is developed to analyze the formation and maintenance of such networks. Empirical results are presented for contact patterns of scientists. It appears that, although the importance of distance has been reduced due to the improvements in the transport sytem, distance continues to play an important role in knowledge-based networks. Other important variables determining the formation of networks concern the language skills of potential contact partners, as well as their scientific status. We observe clear signs of decreasing utilities of adding new nodes to one's network. Finally, attention is paid to substitution and complementarity of face-to-face contacts versus telecommunication in contact patterns of scholars.

Introduction.

During the last decades the quality and range of telecommunication services have improved, while at the same time the tariffs have decreased. Similarly, communication has been greatly facilitated by the increase in the speeds of transport, a process which already started in the nineteenth century, and which did not come to a halt until now. These developments have enabled the formation of extensive communication networks.

On the basis of these developments one may expect a decrease of the importance of physical distance in communication networks. For example, the generalized (user) cost of telecommunication depends only to a limited extent on distance: the elasticity of tariffs with respect to physical distance is smaller than one in most countries. It also tends to be smaller than one in international telecommunication. In addition, the increasing value of time leads to a decrease of the relative importance of tariffs in generalized communication costs. Such developments stimulate the formation of systems of regions with a high degree of interdependence where physical distance plays a relatively modest role.

In physical transport, a similar tendency can also be observed, but in a more moderate way. For example in road transport, generalized transport costs (including travel time) continue to be approximately proportional to physical distance. However, the increasing importance of the travel time component for passenger transport has led to a shift towards faster transport modes such as air planes and high speed trains. In these systems the impact of physical distance is reduced to some extent since one only has access at specific points in space (airports, railway stations). An additional factor which leads to a less direct relationship between physical distance and generalized travel costs is the emergence of hub and spoke systems which lead to relatively cheap connections (in terms of generalized travel costs per kilometer) when the origin and/or the destination coincides with a hub. These developments stimulate the formation of interdependent regional systems where certain nodes have particular advantages in terms of accessibility. These nodes have the potential to achieve a dominant role in the sytem which may threaten the autonomy of other regions.

One of the types of networks which have strongly benefitted from the improvements of transport and telecommunication are knowledge-based networks. Given the increasing importance of knowledge and information in the economy, knowledge-based networks deserve ample attention in the analysis of interregional interdependences. A weak position in such networks will endanger the autonomy of regions.

In the present paper we will study the formation and maintenance of communication networks. This will be done by addressing contact patterns of scholars working at universities. As indicated by Fischer et al. (1992) relatively little research has been carried out in this field.

The structure of the chapter is as follows. We formulate a conceptual framework for the analysis of contact decision behaviour of scholars, then empirical results are presented of a stated choice approach to university contact decision behaviour. We then analyze existing contact patterns of about 600 scholars from 5 university cities. Issues of substitution and complementarity between contact modes (face-to-face contacts versus telecommunication) are discussed afterwards, followed by conclusions.

A conceptual framework for analyzing knowledge-based networks.

Contact patterns are the result of both individual and collective decisions. The relative weight of these factors may vary strongly among decision contexts. For example, contact patterns of individuals working in a firm with communication partners outside the firm will be strongly dependent on decisions taken at the top of the firm concerning the firms with which to collaborate. In universities the weight of the individual component may be expected to be much larger. Universities do not have a hierarchical structure compared with firms, so that the scope for individual initiatives is much larger. Nevertheless, it is also here that collective policies will play a role in individual contact behaviour. For example, financial and non-financial incentives may vary strongly among universities and departments. It is therefore reasonable to conceptualize contact behaviour of university scholars as the result of individual choices which take place within a set of constraints which are partly determined by the university/faculty where the scholar is working.

Knowledge-based contact behaviour takes place for a variety of motives related to the production and dissimination of knowledge. The following motives can be mentioned:

Collection of inputs in knowledge production.

For knowledge production one needs new ideas which can be collected by visiting lectures or conferences. Data collection may also give rise to university contact behaviour. This may lead to visits of places where data are stored, but also to places where field work occurs.

Collaboration in the production of research outputs.

As indicated by Beckmann (1992) scientific collaboration as revealed by joint authorship appears to be rapidly growing. An important reason is the improvement of transport and communication services mentioned in section 1. Collaboration involves the exploitation of positive externalities in knowledge production which leads to a higher quantity and/or quality of scientific products. It leads to longer publication lists of individuals and the demonstrated ability of scholars to collaborate is usually evaluated in a positive way.

Dissemination of knowledge

Particularly in the scientific arena, this is an important motive for scholars to travel and to communicate. This leads to travelling to give guest lectures or to present papers at conferences.

Coordination of knowledge-based contact patterns.

This is a motive with a secondary character. In order to have a smooth functioning of scientific contact patterns one needs certain institutions such as scientific associations, scientific journals, organizational committees and steering committees. For a proper functioning of these institutions face-to-face contacts and telecommunication are indispensible.

Contract research

When universities are involved in contract resarch scholars may have to visit actual and potential principals in order to secure present and future funding. In addition to these motives which have a clear link with knowledge formation as such, one can also mention some other relevant motives of scholars to be involved in contact behaviour. One motive is that scholars — like many other people — may like travelling from time to time. A similar motive may be that scholars like to visit certain attractive places. Still another motive for scholars to visit scientific meetings is social: it is nice to see old friends.

Other factors

It is clear that in most cases a mixture of motives will be relevant. Note especially that scientific conferences often have a multi-purpose character: scholars visiting them are usually driven by several of these motives.

The above motives for undertaking university contacts give rise to measurements of various types of benefits. For example, giving guest lectures may improve one's status, doing collaborative research leads to longer publication lists, visiting principals may generate research money, etc.

These benefits have to be traded-off against the costs of establishing and maintaining contacts. These costs are measured partly in money terms. Travel budgets of universities are limited, so that travelling sometimes means that one has to use one's own sources. One may expect a tendency that junior staff members with low income and low status find it difficult to secure sufficient travel money. The reverse may be true for senior staff menbers who are high in the hierarchy. In terms of time constraints one often observes a very different situation. Senior staff members usually have many more administrative duties which makes it difficult to find time to travel. For junior staff members time constraints are usually less severe. Both junior and senior staff members have to trade off the utility of contact activities with the travel costs and especially the opportunity costs of time.

One way to reduce the costs of communication for a certain person is to receive guests rather than to visit other people. For telephone contact a similar strategy can be followed since it is usually the person who calls who has to pay the bill. Not much is known about how partners agree on a visiting pattern. In certain cases one observes that an implicit rule is obeyed, i.e., that there is symmetry in the visit patterns: first A visits B, then B visits A, etc. In other cases one may observe asymmetric solutions: A always visits B, but B never visits A. This may be the result of a rational calculation, for example where B is very busy and has no time to travel and compensates A for his travel costs. Another relevant factor here is the utility of the contact. If the utility for A is larger than for B, person B may not be prepared to have the contact unless person A visits him. Another factor influencing visit patterns is the social or scientific status of the persons involved: it is often the person with the lower status who is expected to visit the person with the higher status. Unfortunately, the data available in our case study only concern the outgoing visits and telephone contacts of people so that it is not possible to discuss symmetry issues in this paper. Nevertheless, it is important to mention this aspect of communication patterns, because it is easily overlooked.

In this contribution we will pay special attention to the decision to add new partners in one's contact network. A conceptual framework of contact decision behaviour concerning adding new nodes in the network can be found in Figure 1 (cf. Fischer et al. 1992). Major groups of variables relate to:

- *Existing personal contact network.* This relates to both the size of the existing network and the orientation. As will be discussed in section 3, it is reasonable to expect that the utility of adding a node to one's network is decreasing as the size of the network grows.
- *Personal characteristics of scholar.* Variables such as position, age and gender may play a role in decisions whether or not to extend a net-

Figure 1. *A conceptual framework for contact decision behaviour*

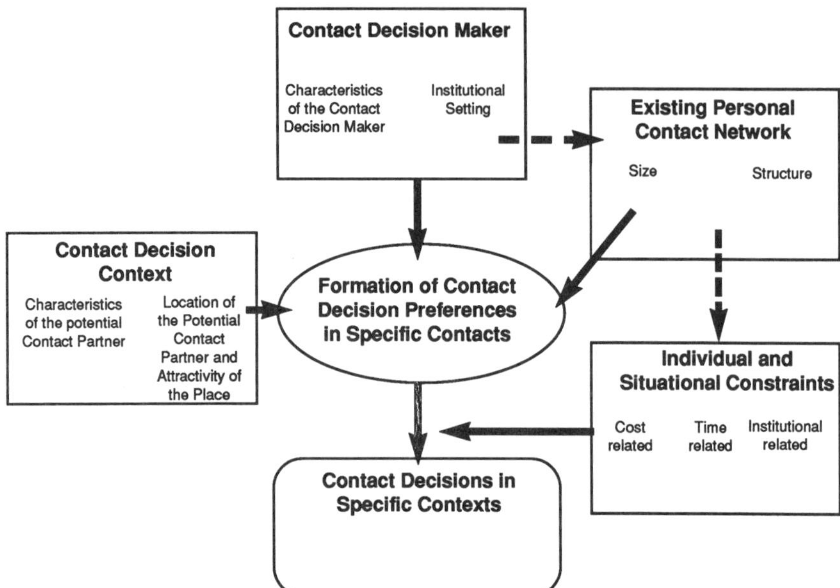

work. Time constraints and travelling budgets usually differ strongly among individuals.

- *Institutional setting.* Organizational cultures may vary strongly among universities, faculties or departments. Some faculties have incentive systems which clearly support exchange activities, other faculties are much more inward oriented.
- *Features of potential contact partner.* Relevant features include the scientific status, language capabilities, and locational aspects related to the attractivity of the city where the contact partner works.

In the next section we will carry out an empirical analysis of contact decision behaviour of Dutch scientists.

An analysis of network extension in academia

Data

During 1990 and 1991, at a number of universities in Europe a survey was carried out among scientists about communication and travel. The header of the questionnaire was "University Contact Patterns".[1] It consisted of the following five parts: personal background data, availability and use of communication media, actual contacts (telephone calls and visits), a contact decision and a media choice decision. The background information on individuals that was collected was not very detailed. Data were collected on affiliation (4 categories), position (3 categories), age (5 categories) and gender. The contact decision part consisted of one question, describing a hypothetical situation in which the respondent had to decide whether he would accept an invitation of another scientist or not. The conditions of the situation were varied and each respondent had to answer this question repeatedly

Data were collected at five universities: Amsterdam, Zurich, Vienna, Loughborough, and Liverpool. Although for the former three the questionnaire was held at more than one university,[2] the distinction in five locations is maintained. In this way minor differences in the way the questionnaire was actually carried out — interviews or not, specific ways of coding — are captured in differences between location. The total number of observations was 621 (149 from Amsterdam, 125 from Zurich, 188 from Vienna, 77 from Loughborough, and 82 from Liverpool).

The contact decisions part of the questionnaire is used to study what factors influence the decision whether or not a certain node is included in the network. The following hypothetical situation was described:

Imagine that you receive an unsolicited invitation from a full professor who you know to be a leader in your field to collaborate in the writing of a book. This person is based in Lyon (France) and you discover that his command of English is very poor. He offers to pay half of the costs of a visit to Lyon — a city that you have already been to in the preceding year — for a face-to-face meeting in order to discuss the proposal. Because of prior commitments on his part the meeting would have to take place during term time and would in-

---

[1] This questionnaire was held in the context of the NECTAR working group "Barriers to Communication". NECTAR was an ESF-sponsored research project on Communication and Transport.

[2] For instance the Amsterdam data come from 2 universities, those of Zurich from 3.

volve you in substantially rearranging your teaching and administrative duties. Would you go?

The only answers allowed are 'yes' and 'no'. The bold faced characteristics are varied, in a binary form. In this way, "full professor" is opposed by a "junior academic", a "leader in your field" by "someone you never heard of before", "Lyon" by "Mexico City" and "very poor English" by "extremely good English".

The above mentioned question is part of a stated choice approach. It means that respondents are confronted with a hypothetical choice situation in which a number of relevant variables are controlled. An advantage of the stated choice approach is that it is not hindered by difficulties such as the impact of uncontrolled variables, the occurrence of multicollinearity, or uncertainties about the choice set. This makes it rather easy to estimate the coefficients of the choice model. The alternative approach would be to use revealed preference data on actual decisions which gives rise to the above mentioned difficulties, but has as a major advantage that one does not have to worry about the question to which extent the estimation results are applicable in real decision situations (cf. Henscher et al., 1988).

In this section only the Dutch data are used based on responses of two universities (Vrije Universiteit and University of Amsterdam). Each scientist was asked to make the above described decision 4 times, of course with varying values for the state variables. Thus 149 persons managed to provide almost 600 observations on the contact decision.[1]

Estimation

Before presenting the results of the estimations we pay attention to one particular aspect of the conceptual scheme presented in Figure 1: the impact of the existing network on the decision to add a node to the network. It is important to know how the utility of a potential node is influenced by the size and the structure of the present network. An interesting contribution to this question is given by Burt (1990). Our reformulation of his theory leads to the hypothesis that the utility of having a network is additive separable with respect to coherent groups of nodes, but with diminishing benefits to the number of nodes within these groups. To put it simply: Burt suggests that the utility of one extra node in — for instance — France is independent of the total number of nodes in the

---

[1] This repetition of observations on the same respondent causes some econometric peculiarities which are treated in Ouwersloot and Rietveld (1992). Here no further attention is given to this.

network, but dependent on the number of nodes already in France. All nodes in France are considered as a group, leading to the same (sort of) benefits. But the benefits of the French nodes are different from the benefits of the group of German nodes. Since there are 'structural holes' between the groups it is likely that the French can provide other information than the Germans and vice versa.

Put it differently: nodes are considered as groups each leading to some source of utility. The utility function of the respondent is linear additive with respect to these sources of utility. However, an extra node in a group will only have a diminishing marginal increase in using the source associated with each group.

Burt's model is appealing within a scientific framework. It is not unreasonable to assume that certain groups share a common stock of knowledge, for instance resulting from a specific research paradigm, and also that the access to this knowledge increases with each contact laid with members of this group, though in a decreasing rate. The difficult point however is the operationalization of the concept of a 'group' in this context. Given our data we chose to consider scientists from one country as a 'group'. The data, resulting from the stated choice question presented above were used in a binary probit estimation. The outcomes are presented in Table 1. The likelihood ratio test shows that the equation as a whole is significant, but the pseudo R2 values are low. Three types of variables can be recognized as used in the estimation and we will discuss them accordingly.

The first group refers to the (expected) cost and benefit of exploiting the potential node as such. Cost variables are PLACE, ENGLISH -both referring to the characteristics of the invitor[1]-, and NATLANG -referring to the respondent. PLACE (Mexico = 1) represents costs that can be associated with establishing a new link. The negative estimate is expected. ENGLISH (good = 1) and NATLANG (1 if the respondent speaks the tongue of the home country of the invitor, 0 otherwise) represents some elements of non-monetary cost: poor english or native-tongue skills may result in difficulties in communication. The magnitude of the parameters suggest that English skills are more important than speaking French or Spanish respectively. These results underline the importance of language differentials as a barrier to communication. It is especially

---

[1] The hypothetical scientist who "invites you to collaborate in the writing of a book" will be denoted the invitor, while the person who is invited will be called the respondent. Note that this distinction is important since characteristics of the respondent and invitor may be the same, and thus variables like ENGLISH can refer to both.

Table 1: *Probit analysis of node decision*

Parameter		Estimate	St. Error
Constant		-1.56	(.30)*
PLACE		-.50	(.12)*
ENGLISH		.50	(.12)*
NATLANG		.31	(.14)*
POS_GOE		.53	(.14)*
REPUTATION		.76	(.12)*
Vrije Universiteit		-.28	(.14)*
Faculty	Alpha	.19	(.14)
	Beta	.60	(.18)*
Sex (1 if male)		.43	(.19)*
Age	≤ 30 year	.07	(.25)
	31—40 year	.17	(.18)
	41—50 year	.08	(.17)
Node in place		-.46	(.22)*
Number of nodes		-.06	(.04)
Log likelihood		-316.3	
Log liklihood at constand		-378.2	
LRT (14 dof)		123.8*	
Pseudo R^2		16.4%	

Notes: Dependent variable = 1 if respondent accepts invitation, 0 otherwise; Number of observations: 591 (yes—200, no—391); An "*" means significant at 5% level.

in knowledge-based networks that language differentials will play a role as a disincentive to communication. From empirical research on other types of communication (telephone contacts in general, telex contacts, trade) a similar result is found (cf. Brcker, 1984 and Rietveld et al., 1993). Language differentials remain to play a role as barriers to trade, even when all kinds of physical and economic barriers to trade are removed as is presently the case in Europe.

The result for the PLACE variable also deserves attention. It means that distance is important in establishing the network since it is related to travel time and costs. In general this will lead to what we will call hierarchical patterns: most respondents will have domestic nodes, many will have nodes in other European countries, and some will have a network expanded all over the world.

Related to benefits, two variables are defined, viz. the position of the person to be visited relative to the position of the respondent POS_GOE, and the REPUTATION of the invitor (leader in your field=1). POS_GOE equals 1 if the formal position of the invitor is at least as high as the position of the respondent. For instance when the respondent is full professor, and the invitor is junior academic, POS_GOE equals 0, but when the respondent is an assistant professor, POS_GOE is always 1. Since relatively more benefits can be expected from collaborating with a higher positioned person, the positive sign is in accordance with our expectations. For REPUTATION the rationale is similar, but with respect to the informal qualification. Thus the resulting positive parameter is according to expectation. Moreover, our intuition is confirmed which suggests that reputation is more characteristic of expecting fruitful cooperation than a formal higher position, as the estimate of the former is larger.

The second group of variables is included to take account of all kind of effects which are not of prime interest in this research, but may nevertheless be important. In particular different attitudes between institutes, faculties or departments may exist concerning travelling and having contacts with colleagues abroad (cf. Spangenberg, 1989). We also control for differences between the sexes, and between young, and older scientists. We indeed find that the variables of this category affect the estimations. We find that scholars at the Vrije Universiteit are less inclined to accept the invitation to collaborate than are scholars working at the University of Amsterdam. Scholars at the Beta faculties have a higher propensity to accept the invitation to collaborate than scholars at ALFA and GAMMA faculties. Male scholars will accept invitations earlier than female scholars. There may be several interpretations of this result. One is that female scholars tend to have less ambitions. Another one is that for female scholars time constraints may be more severe since in households with more than one person working it is usually the female partner who does the larger share of the household activities, including the care for the children (Kruythoff, 1992).

Finally we included two variables related to the existing network. We find that the existence of a node in the group of the invitor indeed significantly reduces the probability that the respondent accepts the invitation as predicted by Burt's model. We also find that the number of group-nodes has a negative (though not entirely significant) effect on the same probability, as was suggested by our interpretation of Burt. Obviously these results affirm the hypothesis that there are decreasing marginal utilities of having contacts, especially when these contacts refer to groups with which there is already a good connection.

We conclude that the estimations point to the appropriateness of the conceptual scheme formulated in section 2.

Existing Networks

After the stated preference approach employed in section 3, we now turn to a revealed preference approach by analyzing actual contact networks of scholars. A possible way to measure the size of a network of a scholar would be the total number of scholars from different nodes with which the scholar had a face-to-face contact during the past period. The available data do not allow to use this definition; the best proxy available is the total number of visits during last year. This obviously will give rise to an underestimate of the size of a scholar's network, but it is the best proxy available (for a discussion refer to Ouwersloot, 1993).

In the analysis of existing networks we used data from the five university places mentioned above. Sixteen potential categories of destinations have been defined: Austria, Belgium/Luxembourg, Eastern Europe, France, Germany, Italy, the Netherlands, Spain/Portugal, Switzerland, United Kingdom, Rest of Europe, the USA, the rest of America, Asia, Africa and Australia/New Zealand. This aggregation was partly forced by some minor encoding differences between the 5 versions of the questionnaire, and partly by the consideration that the number of visits on lower aggregation levels were simply too low to perform sensible analyses. In terms of networks, these 16 destinations are the potential nodes of a scientist's network.

In the analysis we will distinguish between three types of nodes: the domestic node, the European node and the worldwide node. The domestic node is the Netherlands for the Dutch sample, Austria for the Austrian sample etc. The European nodes are all other European nodes, of which there are 10 for each sample, and the worldwide nodes are the remainder.

We will analyze the existing networks from two perspectives. In the first place we consider the orientation of the network: is the majority of the contacts domestic, are they in Europe or do they spread out all over the world? Our second research question concerns size. How large are the networks, and what determines their size? When the scientist has a domestic node, he is said to have a domestic network. When he has a European, resp. worldwide node, then he has a European, resp. a worldwide network. Thus, a scientist can have both a domestic, and a European and a worldwide network, or any combination of these.

Figure 2: *Venn-diagram of network orientation*

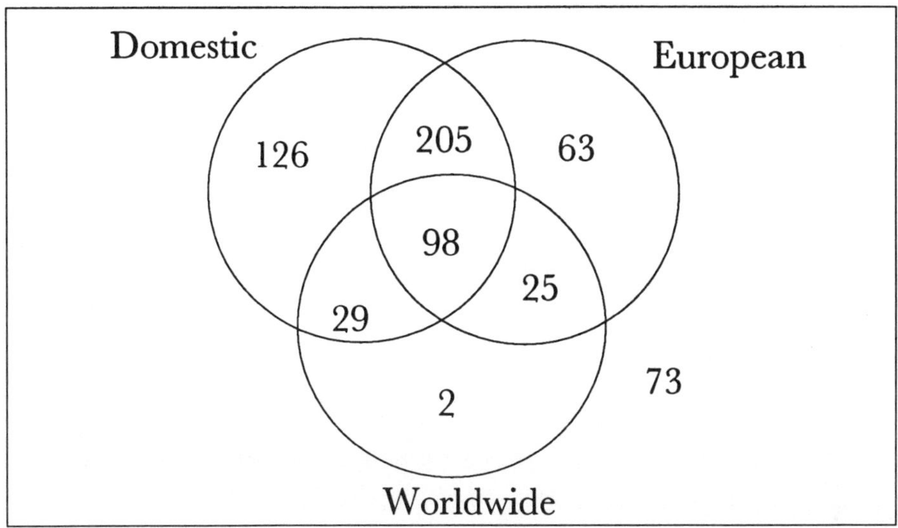

Figure 2 shows a Venn-diagram of the distribution of all respondents in the sample when the three sets are defined as respondents having a domestic, European, respectively worldwide network. Thus 73 scientists have no network at all, whereas 98 of them have a "complete" network with nodes in their own country, in other European countries and in any other continent.

Table 2 shows the same results, split up by the five reporting universities.

The categories numbered 1, 2, 4, and 8 in Table 2 are following the hierarchy idea introduced in the previous section. Approximately 80% of the respondents report networks which are in line with this model.

Table 2 also shows some interesting discrepancies from the hierarchical pattern. Swiss and Austrians appear to have relatively many nodes in Europe (besides their home country), while respondents from Loughborough and Liverpool have comparatively many contacts outside Europe.

Table 2: *Network structure for all places*

	Amster-dam	Switzer-land	Austria	Loughbor.	Liverpool	*Total*
No net-work	4.7	17.6	15.4	10.4	8.5	*11.8*
Domestic	19.5	13.6	11.2	35.1	39.0	*20.3*
European	5.4	11.2	18.1	2.6	6.1	*10.1*
Dom + Eur	43.0	32.8	31.9	26.0	24.4	*33.0*
World-wide	-	-	-	1.3	1.2	*0.3*
Dom + WW	4.0	4.0	1.6	9.1	9.8	*4.7*
Eur + WW	2.0	7.2	6.9	-	-	*4.0*
Complete	21.5	13.6	14.9	15.6	11.0	*15.8*
n=	149	125	188	77	82	*621*

A possible explanation would be that the Swiss and Austrians have many contacts in Germany (the Swiss respondents were from universities in the German speaking part of Switzerland), and that the English have a bias towards other English speaking countries like the USA or to their former colonies like Canada and Australia. A closer inspection of the data reveals that this explanation indeed holds true for Switzerland and Austria, but not for the UK. This result underlines the importance of language similarity for Switzerland and Austria. For the UK it indicates that in academia, the UK is not as strongly integrated into Europe as the other European countries: UK scholars have a stronger worldwide orientation.

The size of the network simply is the number of nodes as defined before. Table 3 gives a frequency distribution of the whole sample, for the scientists with a worldwide network, and for the rest. The average number of nodes is 2.3; the variance is large: some scientists visited as many as 8 or more nodes in a year. The average number of nodes visited by scholars with a destination outside Europe (worldwide) is twice as large as that of scholars without a worldwide orientation.

Table 3: *Frequency distributions of network size*

# Nodes	All	Non Worldwide	Worldwide
0	73	-	-
1	161	160	1
2	151	118	33
3	98	66	32
4	63	31	32
5	38	13	25
6	18	6	12
7	11	0	11
8	6	0	6
9	1	0	1
10	1	0	1
Total	*621*	*394*	*154*
Average # nodes	*2.34*	*2.08*	*4.10*

To analyze these data more thoroughly, we assume that the number of nodes of a scientist's network is Poisson distributed with parameter λ:

$$\Pr(nodes = k) = \frac{\exp(-\lambda)\lambda^{k}}{k!} \qquad (1)$$

Then the parameter λ is assumed to depend on independent variables:

$$\lambda = \exp(\mathbf{X}'\beta) \qquad (2)$$

where $\mathbf{X}$ is a vector of independent variables, viz. characteristics of the respondent. The estimation results are presented in Table 4 (for technical details refer to Ouwersloot, 1993).

The parameter estimates require careful interpretation. What is estimated is the parameter λ of the Poisson distribution, explained by a number of independent variables, see eq. (2). This means e.g. that a positive parameter for the variable sex, means that c.p. the parameter of the Poisson distribution according to which the number of nodes for men is distributed, is larger than for women. Fortunately the parameter of the Poisson distribution has a straightforward interpretation as it equals the mean of the distribution. Thus on average men have larger networks than women. This mean is modelled in such a way that it depends on the independent variables in an exponential way.

With these remarks in mind it is clear that the effect of network orientation is indeed positive and significant. Respondents with an intercontinentally orientated network have on average 2.05(=exp(0.719)) as

Table 4: *Poisson estimation of network size*

Variable	Estimate	Stand. error	
Constant	.040	.152	
Orientation	.719	.058*	
Age < 30	-.134	.123	
Age 30—40	.158	.089	
Age 40—50	.161	.075*	
Full professor	.412	.080*	
Assoc professor	.187	.076*	
Sex (male=1)	.126	.096	
Alpha	.098	.107	
Beta	.092	.088	
Gamma	.059	.088	
Amsterdam	.251	.104*	
Switzerland	.091	.111	
Austria	.177	.102	
Liverpool	-.086	.119	
Log liklihood full model			-1020.4
Log liklihood with constant only:			-1185.7
Liklihood ratio test statistic (14 dof):			165.3*
Pseudo R^2:			13.9%

Notes: Dependent variable: Number of nodes according to 'visits-definition'; Number of observations: 621; An "*" means significant at 5% level

many nodes as those with a European orientation. Notice that this comparison has to be stated in multiplicative terms because of the chosen model.

Age is also important: scholars between 40 and 50 years visited the largest number of nodes compared with other age groups. The formal position of staff members also plays a role: full professors and associate professors have clearly larger networks than assistant professors (50% and 20% higher, respectively).

Network Use

An existing network can be used in two ways: the scientists can visit each other; or they can communicate, using telecommunication media. In this section we use data about visits and about telephonic interaction, visits and calls for short.

Two opposing theories exist to describe the effect of the increased availability of telecommunication means on travel behaviour (see e.g. Salomon 1986). One says that telecommunication decreases the need to exchange information in face-to-face meetings thus reducing travel. The other theory argues that telecommunication makes it easier to start up and maintain more contacts thus leading to an increase in travel. We will refer to these theories as the substitution and generation theory respectively.

Table 5 is the most elementary form to present the data that can reveal something about a trade-off between visits and calls. This cross-tabulation shows for each respondent-node combination if there has been a call and/or visit. Given 621 respondents and 16 destinations, the sum of the cell entries is 9936.

Table 5. *Visit or Call trade-off*

	Call No	Yes	*Total*
Visit No	7834	651	*8485*
Yes	526	875 (223)	*1451*
Total	*8410*	*1526*	*9936*

If the generation hypothesis holds, the number in the right-lower cell should be relatively large, but when substitution takes place the bias would occur in the left- lower and right-upper cells. This bias can be measured as the difference between the expected values, which would be found when visiting and calling would happen completely independent of each other, and the observed values in the cells. The expected number in the visit&call cell is given in parentheses in the table and it is obviously much less than the observed number. Since this is a 2x2 table, the expectations in the visit&no-call and no-visit&call cells are larger than the observed values. So, Table 5 gives support to the generation hypothesis: telecommunication lowers the thresholds to visit each other, which is revealed by a simultaneous increase in both ways of interaction.

Cross-tabulation is a simple and statistically poor technique. Therefore we report in Table 6 about some estimations using the Poisson model again. Recall that this model assumes that the number of calls follows a Poisson process with a parameter that is (among others) dependent upon the number of visits paid to the same destination. This model has already been discussed in section 4 and we use a similar parameterization.

Table 6 shows the estimation for all respondent-node combinations for which either a call or a visit was reported. In Table 5 we find that there are 2,102 of such combinations. The estimation shows that visits

Table 6: *Poisson estimation of visit-call trade-off*

Variable	Estimate	Standard error
Constant	.76	.09*
Visits	.028	.0010*
Age ≤ 30	-.07	.080
Age 31—40	.13	.053*
Age 41—50	.07	.045
Full. prof	.26	.049*
Assoc prof	-.13	.047*
Sex	-.15	.056*
Alpha	.19	.069*
Beta	.24	.059*
Gamma	.34	.056*
Amsterdam	-.28	.055*
Switzerland	-.54	.064*
Austria	-.39	.055*
Liverpool	-.56	.069*
Number of Nodes	-.045	.0091*

Note: Log likelihood full model (-4631.0); Log likelihood constand only (-4958.5); LRT (13 dof) 654.9*; Pseudo R^2 (6.6%); Dependent variable: calls; Number of observations: 2102; An "*" means significant at 5% level

has a positive effect on the mean of the Poisson distribution. It is small, but also significant. Each visit to a node results on average in an increase in the number of calls with 2.8%.[1]

Concerning the other parameters, we note that the negative estimate for the size of the network was expected since our dependent variable is calls for each node individually. Thus in larger networks the number of calls to each node slightly decreases. The time budget obviously becomes a more severe constraint when the number of nodes increases.

We conclude that we found some evidence of an overall generating effect, i.e. the advancing opportunities offered by telecommunications do not substitute travelling, but rather pave the roads to make more contacts which is revealed by a simultaneous increase in visiting and calling.

Conclusions

The formation of communication networks has been stimulated by the increase in the quality and range of telecommunication services and the increase in the speeds of transport. This has led to the emergence of

---

[1]The procentual increase equals exp(.0282) - 1 = 2.8%. A simple approximation is that for small numbers x, exp(x) approximately equals 1+x.

strongly interdependent systems of regions which in certain cases may threaten the autonomy of particular regions. In the present paper special attention has been paid to knowledge-based networks. A conceptual framework has been developed in section 2 to analyze the formation and maintenance of such networks.

In section 3 empirical results have been presented for decisions of scholars on adding nodes to their contact networks by scientists. It appears that, although the importance of distance has been reduced due to the improvements in the transport sytem, distance continues to play an important role in knowledge-based networks. Other important variables determining the formation of networks concern the language skills of potential contact partners, as well as their scientific status. We observe clear signs of decreasing utilities of adding new nodes to one's network.

In section 4 the spatial structure of existing networks in a number of European countries has been studied. Three main types of networks can be identified in this respect: 1—domestic only, 2—European, and 3—worldwide. Most scholars with a worldwide orientation in their network also have European and domestic nodes in their network. The number of nodes of scholars with a worldwide orientation is considerably larger than of other scholars. Network size tends to grow with age (until 50 years), and scholars with a higher formal position tend to have larger networks. Male scientists tend to have larger networks than female collegues, although the difference is not entirely significant.

Finally, in section 5 attention is paid to substitution and complementarity of face-to-face contacts versus telecommunication in contact patterns of scholars. We find some evidence of a complementarity effect in the sense that the number of calls scientists make is positively related to the number of visits they make, even if we correct for the impact of other relevant variables. Another conclusion of the analysis is that scholars with larger networks tend to use them less intensively (or maybe more efficiently): this is probably caused by the tightness of timebudget constraints.

References

Beckmann, M.J. (1992) Spatial aspects of knowledge networks: the case of scientifc collaboration at a distance, conference paper 1992-10, Institute for Posts and Telecommunications Policy, Tokyo, Japan.

Brcker, J. (1984), How do international trade barriers affect interregional trade?, in: A.E. Andersson, W. Isard and T. Puu (eds.), *Regional and Industrial Development Theories*, North Holland, Amsterdam, pp. 219-239.

Burt, R.S. (1990), *Tertius Gaudens - a study of structural holes as social Capital,* unpublished paper.

Fischer, M.M., R. Maggi and C. Rammer (1992), Stated preference models of contact decision behaviour in academia, Papers in Regional Science 71, pp. 359-371.

Henscher, D.A., P.O. Barnard and T.P. Truong (1988), The role of stated preference methods in studies of travel choice, *Journal of Transport Economcs and Policy* 22, pp. 45-58.

Kruythoff, H.M. (1992), *Tweeverdieners vergeleken,* Urban Networks, Delft.

Ouwersloot, H. (1993), Networks of Scientists, Paper presented at the Netcom symposium on Networks, Washington, August 1992

Ouwersloot, H. and P. Rietveld (1992), Stated Choice Experiments with Repeated Observations, unpublished paper.

Rietveld, P., J. van Nierop & H. Ouwersloot (1993), *Barriers to International Telecommunication,* Systemi Urbani, forthcoming.

Salomon, I. (1986), Telecommunications and Travel Relationships: A review, *Transportation Research* A 20, pp. 223-238.

Spangenberg, J.F.A. (1989), *Economics of Atmosphere,* Van Gorcum, Assen.

10 The Geography of Information Technology Infrastructure in Multinational Corporations

Edward M. Roche

The distribution of information technology in multinational corporations is complex. Understanding the dynamics of information systems in multinational corporations is complicated by the scale and complexity of the problem.[1] This paper devises a short-hand notation for expressing the distribution of technological infrastructure and the pattern of applications and their control. It assumes that two major external sets of variables influence the evolution of information technology in the MNC: (1) international organizations, and (2) restrictive policies of nation states. What is known now about the texture of information technologies in MNCs is discussed, with suggestions for future research. Of key concern is the interplay between these two families of variables. The nation state has generally acted as an *inhibitor* of international systems developments, whereas, variables associated with international organfization have generally acted as *accelerators*.

Multinational corporations and information systems

Multinational corporations (MNCs) account for most of the world's economic activity and *intra-firm* trade at the international level is greater than all other trade. Multinational corporations also use most of the information technology in the world. Most MNCs have operations in many countries of the world, carry on a wide variety of activities, including marketing, research & development, and manufacturing. In addition they operate many layers of management and control according to product line, geographical area, and requirements for manufacturing coordination. Sustaining these types of complex operations on an international scale requires a large and sophisticated information system.

---

[1] An early version of this chapter was presented at The Japan Society for Management Informatics, International Conference on Economics/Management and Information Technology, August 31-September 4, 1992, Tokyo, Japan

Understanding the scale and dynamics of information systems in today's mnc is difficult, primarily because of scale, complexity, and geographical distribution. We find mncs maintaining computer centers in dozens of countries, each with different types of installations and functions. Some systems are stand-alone, others are linked together into a global network. Many times the level of decentralization of control over investments in information technology make even a basic accounting of inventory and expenditures on data processing difficult to appraise and hopelessly impossible to accurately calculate. In terms of complexity, we find so many different applications, spread across many geographical areas, operating in different languages, and performing a variety of tasks driven by firm strategy, divisional and product structure, and operational requirements. A good sized mnc may have several *hundred* separate data processing centers, scattered around the world, each in their way responsible for the day-to-day functioning of the business.

General functions of information systems

Some of the earliest research concerning information technology and the multinational corporation appears in antonelli (1984)[1] who studied the emerging effects of international telecommunications systems. For Japanese perspectives, see Masuda (1985), Ishikawa (1990), and Imai (1991a,b) who examines "techno-globalism". Hagström (1990) and Ledin (1990) reviewed the use of information technology in the mnc for defensive and offensive strategies. Bakis (1987a,b) studies global geographic distribution of functions. Mookerjee and Cash (1990) examined the distributed infrastructure of regional bank processing in foreign exchange trading. Butler Cox (1991) study sketches out the linkages between distribution of applications and databases as a function of different MNC strategies. Ives and Jarvenpaa (1991), Deans (1991) and Palvia & Saraswat (1991), Karimi and Konsynski (1991) have studied the key management issues. Daniels, et al (1991) described the external pressures leading to globalization of information systems. Giga (1986) highlighted new trends in application of telecommunications. Daniels and Frost (1991) discussed the various steps a company might go through in managing the transition to a global information system. Gurbaxani and Whang (1991) have touched upon the role of information systems in lowering the cost of "accessing international markets." Clemons et. al (1991) suggested that international technology linkages

---

[1]The references at the end of this paper are suggestive of the inter-disciplinary approach needed to understand this problem.

may enable a firm to become a "virtual global corporation" by building cooperative alliances to coordinate service internationally.[1]

Headquarters-Subsidiary and Subsidiary-Subsidiary Coordination

Coordination between headquarters and subsidiaries and between subsidiaries themselves may be he most fundamental function of information technology in the multinational corporation. New information technologies (electronic mail, voice mail, teleconferencing, digital facsimile, distributed processing, etc.) are changing the nature of communications within the MNC, yielding more potential for transparency in decision taking, and considerably tighter coordination. In addition, inter-subsidiary coordination may be enhanced as subsidiary-subcontractor or subsidiary-customer relationships are further informated.[2]

Headquarters-subsidiary coordination and subsidiary-subsidiary coordination will be notated as:

$$C^{h \leftrightarrow s} \text{ and } C^{s \leftrightarrow s}$$

respectively, as variations of general coordination C. We can also distinguish other types of coordination between the firm and its business partners, suppliers and customers, at the general corporate or subsidiary level.

It should be noted that in the case of coordination between a corporate headquarters, one or more regional headquarters, and subsidiaries, the information and telecommunications systems are *internal* to the firm, and are thus under budgetary and technical control. In contrast, the telecommunications networks which link the multinational with its customers, suppliers or business partners are *external* in nature, and as a result, it is more difficult to exercise precise technical and managerial control.[3]

Two classes of *external* relationships are known as Inter-Organizational Systems, notated as *IOS*, after the work of Konsynski. See Table 1.

---

[1] The work of Eric Clemons is closely tied to studies of international equities and other financial markets.

[2] See Henry Bakis and Yolande Combes "Towards corporate networks — a conflict of cultures" in this volume.

[3] One result of this might be that the technical nature of *external* networks tends to be less sophisticated than that of *internal* networks. In order to build inter-organizational systems, firms are forced to accept a *least common denominator* in terms of technical sophistication until such time as it is possible to use more sophisticated services promised by such technologies as broad-band ISDN and Asynchronous Transfer Method.

Table 1: *Coordination functions within the multinational corporation*

	Types of Coordination	
	Headquarters Controlled	Subsidiary Controlled
Subsidiaries	$C^{h\leftrightarrow s}$	$C^{s\leftrightarrow s}$
Customers	$C^{h\leftrightarrow cus}$	$C^{s\leftrightarrow cus}$
IOS — Business Partners	$C^{h\leftrightarrow bp}_{IOS}$	$C^{s\leftrightarrow bp}_{IOS}$
IOS — Suppliers	$C^{h\leftrightarrow sup}_{IOS}$	$C^{s\leftrightarrow sup}_{IOS}$

The nature of the information which flows through the international information technology systems changes according to its underlying function. We can distinguish several characteristics of coordination information. Coordination-oriented information systems are more likely to utilize distributed database technology and involve complex exchange of highly-structured information. The use of highly-structured information is indicative of an *internal* information system which is within the control of the firm. In addition, the flows of this highly-structured information tend to be *regular* in nature — it is easily possible to predict how much volume of international traffic will be carried over the global telecommunications system.

Corporate Intelligence Systems

The literature on corporate intelligence has emphasized the need of the MNC to scan its environment for many types of information which can influence its ability to do business. In addition to 'standard' information on market trends and competitors, other more esoteric areas of coverage might include political risk assessment, economic trends, host government policies, security threats (such as terrorism), and general developments in the realm of culture.

In contrast to the information which is used for coordination purposes, corporate intelligence information is different. Because the nature of the information is that it is primarily *external* to the firm, it has a ir-regular nature. The heterogeneous nature of external information raises many issues of how it can be handled through computer systems, how it can be collected (translated), synthesized, and communicated. It is clear that the design of the information system will be different from that used for coordination functions. It is a considerably more difficult problem because it is more difficult to handle irregular information in a computer system. Corporate intelligence systems I., are more likely to be centralized, and involve sporadic reporting, which means that the telecommunications traffic will be of a *bursty* nature. In other words, there may be only a trickle of information flowing into the firm on a particular issue or region of the world, then should there be a crisis, an emergency, or some substantive change in circumstances, the firm requirements for critical information will increase by an order of magnitude or more.

It is clear, therefore, that the underlying principles for design of corporate intelligence systems are quite different from general coordination systems.

Internalization Theory and Efficiency in Transactions Processing

Internalization theory is used to (partially) explain the rise of the multinational corporation, as writers such as Dunning took the basic theories of Coase and extended them to encompass the multinational corporation. A firm grows by *internalizing* economic transactions which previously were carried out on the open market. As the firm is able to sustain economic transactions at a reduced cost, it can be more efficient than the market and pocket the difference in the form of economic rent and profits. Internalization T raises the question of how transaction costs, particularly on a comparative basis, can be used to ensure global information systems provide the lowest cost base against the competition.

It is possible to think of information technology and telecommunications systems within two specific aspects of internalization — general internalization and information internalization.

General internalization occurs when the international information technology system is used to improve the overall efficiency of the firm, and operate itself more efficiently than the general market. On the other hand, *information internalization* can be suggested as being related to how information technology is used as the primary engine is minimizing the costs of information processing.[1]

Information Technology-Based Firm-Specific Advantages

One explanation of why firms engages in foreign direct investment (FDI) instead of just exporting the goods and services it produces holds that they set up operations overseas when they have some type of advantage

---

[1]General internalization is important for any type of firm, however, information internalization is critical in *information-intensive* firms such as those found in the financial services sector, which the cost of transactions is a basic indicator of firm profitability.

(a Firm-Specific-Advantage F) — capital or technology — in the target national market. For example, advantages of capital or technology. The methods to understand what specific component(s) of competitive advantage are accounted for by global information systems (as opposed to marketing, technology, manufacturing, capital, or management skill and other advantages) are not well understood.

The search for firm-specific advantages deriving solely from information technology F^{IT} may be a long one, more likely to yield highly visible success in the service sector than in manufacturing. The key question is whether information technology and telecommunications systems can be of such benefit to the firm that they overshadow all other factors of advantage for the firm. If this is the case, then an information technology based FSA may have been identified.

In the financial services sector, the design and implementation of information systems is at the heart of the competitive experience. In some trading situations, the creation of new financial services products is based completely on information technology.

Physical infrastructure

Composed as it is of hundreds of types of components, the physical infrastructure of the MNC — computers, memory devices, peripherals, networks, etc. — can be viewed with four units of measurement: 1—distribution of data processing centers, 2—distribution of employees within the information systems function, 3—the distribution of processing power, including mainframes, minicomputers, personal computers, servers, workstations, etc., And 4—the amount of corporate memory, the capacity of the direct access storage devices. Each of these factors can be assessed by its amount of internationalization I, given as its distribution with respect to the home country of the mnc.

Applications infrastructure

The applications infrastructure of a multinational information system can be measured by examination of 1—application family, 2—family composition, 3—operational distribution of an application as measured by geographical distribution of 3a—database, 3b—application software, 3c—end-user display screens.[1]   Applications are distributed according

---

[1]There are hybrids of these categories, but these are assumed away for now.

Table 2: *variables of information technology infrastructure*

Infrastructure variables	
Variable	Notation
Centers The number of data centers in each region	Θ for major data centers Φ for regional centers Ω for smaller centers
Employees	Λ for number of employees at any specific location
Dasd	M for the amount of direct access storage devices
Mips Processing power	μ measured by millions of instructions per second
Percent of internationalization	I - the level of resources located outside of the home-country.

to their physical location within the infrastructure, divided up into 4a—central Θ, 4b—regional Φ, and 4c—local subsidiary Ω.[1]

Geography of information and applications

These factors related to infrastructure are useful in showing the basic layer of distribution in the firm. For example, they can be analyzed according to different geographical locations. There are at least two approaches to doing this type of measurement. One approach iso focus on political economy variables. In this case, measurement of the geographical distribution of the infrastructure would be accomplished by measurement of the presence or absence of these resources in different countries or regions of the world. For example, this type of analysis might help shed light on why multinational corporations do not engage in a substantial amount of technology transfer to developing countries.

A second type of measurement would focus on the abstract geographical and network analysis of the information technology and telecommunications system. Using this approach, a point-by-point analysis of the distribution of infrastructure would be carried out, without direct reference to the political (nation state) location of the resources. This would be more appropriate for a firm-level analysis, as it would help the

---

[1]Although this method of analyzing the geographical distribution of information technology within the multinational corporations can provide a satisfactory organizing principle, it is thus far weak when there is a need to understand how the firm is organized along product lines.

analyst determine the operational characteristics of an individual information system.

Geographical distribution of applications

It is also crucial to understand the geographical distribution of information. Within a multinational computer system, information is carried through the infrastructure and transmitted globally as part of the applications making use of it. Application, however, are not single entitles. Rather, multinational corporations have *dozens* of major applications. One technique of understanding the variety of software applications within an organization is called *portfolio analysis*. This type of analysis is a tool which may be used to study groups of families of applications. A related approach is suggested here.

The first step is to divide up the applications used in the multinational corporations in to different broad-based groups, which are called *application families*. Using A_{type} to notate a major family of applications, we can distinguish at a minimum financial control, human resources & personnel, inventory control & logistics, marketing, research & development, and corporate intelligence, respectively as:

$$A_{fin},\ A_{\lambda},\ A_{d},\ A_{mk};\ A_{rd},\ A_{CI} \cdots A_{N}.$$

This is not a complete list of application families, and we would expect a slightly different pattern between any two firms in the same sector and a *very* different pattern between firms in different economic sectors.

An example of an application family is financial reporting and control. Although the fundamental purpose of this type of application is clear, in reality, the financial reporting and control application within a firm is composed of a series of sub-units making up the portfolio. In other words, the financial reporting application is actually composed of many different individual applications. We may say the major application family is composed of different application fragments:

$$a_{n}:\ \forall \underbrace{A_{N}}_{family} \exists \underbrace{|a_{i}, a_{ii} \cdots a_{n}|}_{fragments}.$$

It is necessary for any analysis to consider fragments on a case-by-case basis because each fragment can be characterized by how it is distributed across the physical infrastructure of the multinational information system, and it is generally unlikely that any two fragments are alike.[1]

In order to understand the geographical distribution of applications and information, the characteristics of each application must be matched against the physical infrastructure. A key element of this analysis is the assumption that for physical distribution Θ, Φ, and Ω are mutually exclusive for each application fragment a_n

Centralized infrastructure and decentralized information

A peculiar fact about the relationship between a telecommunications and information technology infrastructure and they information which they are holding and processing is that *their is no direct relationship — they are somewhat independent of each other*. If one examines the information technology infrastructure in a multinational corporation and finds that it is heavily centralized, it is wrong to assume that information *and the way in which it is accessed* is also centralized.

For argument purposes, assume the application being studied is a global inventory system. All of the data processing is done in a single location.[2] The processing is done on a large mainframe computer located near corporate headquarters. All of the key data, and the applications which serve the system is co-located with the mainframes, since they are responsible for the processing. Under these circumstances, most would agree with a characterization of this system as being completely centralized. However, in terms of the *access to information* this may not be the case.

If this is a global inventory system, it is necessary for it to process information regarding the location of spare parts and goods in many different shipping and storage areas around the world. Under these circumstances, the system uses a large international telecommunications network to provide a nervous system linking terminals and other end-user devices, such as bar code readers, to the central computer center. From any of the locations around the world, it is possible for someone to access the data and applications located on the mainframe computer. In this case, what the user get is a telecommunications-based window to the databases and applications found on the mainframe, even though this

---

[1] As a working hypothesis, we can assume that after an extensive analysis is done of the characteristics of different fragments, it will be possible to group them according to one or more characteristics. This is, however, a matter for research in the future.
[2] An example of this type of system is that of the company *Caterpillar* found in Edward M. Roche, *Managing Information Technology in Multinational Corporations*.

access is being provided from locations around the world. Therefore, the system is both *centralized* and *decentralized* at the same time. The data and applications are centralized, but the access to them is decentralized. One measurement or indicator of access is the existence of a *screen* of data. This is abbreviated as *Sc*.

By examination of each application fragment, a characterization can be made as to whether the location of data, application, or screens is either centralized, regionalized, or localized (*e.g.* fully distributed). For distribution of database, application, and end-user display screens (D, Ap, and Sc), if the database of an application fragment is neither centralized or regionalized, it must be localized:

$$[D\Theta \to 0] \wedge [D\Phi \to 0] \Rightarrow D\Omega.$$

According to the definitions and assumptions in this model, this type of exclusivity holds for each of the application fragment descriptors D, Ap, and Sc — they can not have contradictory characterizations simultaneously:

$$a_n \begin{bmatrix} D\Theta \vee D\Phi \vee D\Omega \\ Ap\Theta \vee Ap\Phi \vee Ap\Omega \\ Sc\Theta \vee Sc\Phi \vee Sc\Omega \end{bmatrix}.$$

A completely centralized application fragment

$$a_n[DASc\{\Theta\}]$$

would be rather rare because it would indicate that not only the processing and data was co-located, but that access was concentrated at the center as well[1]. A more common arrangement would be represented by our example of the centralized inventory management system. This is the most common form of "classic" centralized application fragment, with widespread access from remote terminals, characterized by:

$$a_n[DA\{\Theta\}, Sc\{\Omega\}].$$

---

[1] This type of arrangement might be characteristic of an executive support system intended for managers at the headquarters level, but designed so that *only* headquarters locations have access to the information. Even though this type of application is feasible, as a percentage of the total data processing within the vast infrastructure of the multinational corporation, it could represent but only a small part and share.

Environmental forces and evolution of multinational information systems

The fundamental question which must be answered is "what are the environmental factors which have provided the environment in which international information systems have developed — and how does the nature of these forces transmitted into the shape of the evolving information system?"

Part of this answer[1] lies in the system of regulations which govern the use of information technology. The *regime* provides the great context in which multinational firms build and operation their global information systems. Although there are many ways to characterize these external factors, a political science and political economy system of classification can provide a first approach to the question.

Two classes of factors define the environmental forces: 1—the nation state (country) factors, 2—the international organizational factors, notated *NS* and *IO* respectively (Roche, *et. al*, 1992). To study the impact of these factors of necessity requires a certain amount of generalization. International organization factors refers to the impact on the international environment of various international organizations, part of the united nations system. These giant bureaucracies have played an important role in shaping the texture of the post war period, and this is also true of the quarter of a century after the development of the digital computer. Various international organizations are composed of membership of nation states, who many times have goals and values different from the international community or from other nation states. One could say that an important role of international organization is to to provide a conduit for channelling conflicts into avenues for peaceful resolution. The high amount of variability from one nation state to the other virtually guarantees differences in their approach to information technology.

---

[1] There are other factors which are of critical importance as well — they relate to the changing price-performance of technology and the various services, including telecommunications, which are used to support it. In addition, the changing strategies of the multinational corporation — use of product divisions, centralized management, matrix management, etc. — also have a very great impact as the eventual shape and texture of how information technology is used in the firm is heavily influenced by these factors, about which there is a large and established body of academis research. The economics of information systems will be integrated into this model in as a product of future research.

It is difficult and only remotely empirical to analyze the role of either *NS* or *IO* factors.[1] One example of an important international actor influencing how international information technology systems develop is the International Telecommunication Union $\left(IO_{ITU}\right)$ and its role in promoting the adoption of standards for telecommunication. Although it is not common to think of development of international technical standards as helping promote development of global information systems, there is no denying that the work of the ITU has acted as an *accelerator*. There are many other international organizations which have played important roles in other aspects:

- The *International Bank For Reconstruction And Development* has promoted the use of information technology in many parts of the world — particularly developing countries — by providing funding for computerization as part of its general development efforts in sectors such as transportation, and other.

- The *United Nations Industrial Development Organization* has worked hard over the years to bring together experts for planning of information technology, telecommunications, and electronics production in many regions of the world including the middle east, africa, latin america, and asia.

- The *International Standards Organisation* has promoted all types of standards for exchange of information at the international level, including edi, and has thereby done much to ease the transition to international systems, particularly those which are part of inter-organizational systems, external to the firm. Standards provide the least common denominator for computer communication systems.

- The *World Intellectual Property Organisation* has done much to promote a regime of protection of intellectual property, thus making it more profitable and less risky for firms, including vendors of software and information technology to expand their business around the world, thus helping the development and proliferation of international information systems.

There are many other examples of how various international organizations have played, and continue to play, an important role in the acceleration of international information systems. In some aspects, it is

---

[1]Some of the earliest work in quantification of non-quantifiable factors was done by Forrester at Harvard. Quantification of political economic variables has been called a *pseudo-science* by critics.

clearly difficult to quantify their effect, but it is not difficult to realize that a strong effect exists.

On the other hand, nation states have in many cases had the opposite effect on the development of international systems. Since countries are forced to promote policies which are in their own national interest, it is only logical that they do not take the same position as international organization. In the case of information technology, we find that the nation state has taken many steps which tend to act as an *inhibitor* against the development of international information systems. For example, controls on transborder data flow $\left(NS_{tdf}\right)$ have been a major inhibitor for some international applications. As with international organization, there are many factors which point to the effects of the nation state:

- Some countries have adopted *industrial policies* which are targeted at building up their computer, software, telecommunications or electronics industries. The import-restrictive policies which are usually part of these programs tend to inhibit the international diffusion of information technology.

- Countries which have adopted restrictions on *transborder data flow* have thereby placed limitations on international flow and thus on the ability of multinational corporations to build comprehensive international information systems, unless they use a distributed architecture.

- Some countries have regulations which impose stringent *administrative controls* on how data is processed, regardless of whether it has any international dimension. Countries such as Sweden, for example, have a government representative who regularly visits the data processing sites of companies to carry out an inspection. In these cases, the multinational is restricted in its freedom to choose alternative types and forms of data processing.

- Also various *national and cultural characteristics* of host countries can heavily influence how information technology is used, in particular the types of applications which are used or ignored. This too changes the scope of options available to the multinational corporation.

There are many other ways and specific examples in which the administrative controls or other policies of the nation state tend to inhibit the international diffusion and development of information systems. This model assumes that in general, the nation state acts as an *inhibitor* to international information technology.[1]

---

[1] It is recognized that some nation states take actions which subsidize or accelerate the introduction of information technology or the expansion of its use. The model

One of the key questions which must be examined is given

$$\uparrow IO \Rightarrow accelerator \, , \, \uparrow NS \Rightarrow inhibitor$$

Then "how can this be measured?" Failing precise or even proxy empirical measurement, these factors must be assessed at the general qualitative level to determine their impact on shaping the emerging structure of multinational information systems.

The geographical shape of information

Putting together a general reading of the literature as well as evidence from surveys and interviews with information systems professionals in multinational corporations, it is possible to make a series of statements regarding the geographical shape of information technology and information utilization in today's multinational corporation.

In terms of the number of installations involved n, we know that for a generalized model of the multinational corporation, the number of data processing sites is greatest at the local (nation state) level, that the number of regional sites is considerably less, and that the number of sites which are centralized for the entire company represent the smallest number of sites:

$$n\Theta < n\Phi < n\Omega \quad [1]$$

It also appears that processing power and storage tend to be centralized. The implication of this is that *independent of the international structure of information*, the physical infrastructure of data processing in the multinational appears to concentate a great deal of data storage and processing power near headquarters:[1]

$$\Theta(M,\mu) > \Phi(M,\mu) > \Omega(M,\mu) \quad [2]$$

---

assumes that although these counter-forces exist, they are considerably weaker than the *inhibiting* forces of various restrictive policies.

[1] There are several technical trends which mitigate against this conclusion. For example, the rapid increase in power, speed and complexity of the microprocessor has made it possible to put "mainframe power" workstations on each workers' desktop. Since this is the case, we would expect to see a rise in the amount of processing power outside of the headquarters locations of the multinational, because it is becoming increasingly easy for users to purchase inexpensive mips. The counter-argument to this observation is that the high-powered workstations and file servers have a tendency to be adopted first in the headquarters locations before they are dissiminated throughout the corporation, thus keeping the "balance" between the center and periphery.

A correlary to this observation concerns the amount of international distribution of other factors, such as how workers are "distributed" through the multinational enterprise, and how data processing centers themselves are distributed. We can say that the amount of *internationalization* is greater for employees and centers than for storage and processing power:[1]

$$I[(\Phi + \Omega)(\Lambda)] > I[M,\mu] \quad [3]$$

This has very significant implications for understanding how information technology is used in the multinational corporation. In means, in effect, that *physical infrastructure is centralized but information infrastructure is decentralized*. This illustrates the dis-connect between information and the computer and telecommunications platform upon which it is processed. It is also clear that the role of the regional center tends to mimic the relationship between headquarters and subsidiaries in that it has a lower internationalization for location of data processing centers:

$$I(\Phi) < I(\Omega) \quad [4]$$

The regional processing centers are smaller in number than the local centers, with the ratio many times being more than 50:1.

Geographical distribution of application families

Another aspect of this problem is the differing nature of application families. It has been known for some time that some applications, such as financial control, have strongly centralized aspects whereas applications such as marketing, since it has to adopt to local markets, tends to be decentralized and distributed in form and function. What we find is that different types of application families have different pattern for distribution of their application, data, and structure of access throughout the multinational.

For different application families, there appears to be a movement towards either centralization or decentralization, with financial control tending towards centralization, human resources towards localization, inventory logistics towards centralization, marketing towards regionalization from localization, research & development towards localization, with corporate intelligence also centralized.

---

[1]Local centers have the highest degree of internationalization of all: headquarters, Θ have zero.

Financial reporting and control

In the *financial control* application, we find that in general this is a headquarters-driven process. Information concerning financial performance — sales, production, expenses, etc. — are collected throughout the various subsidiaries of the multinational and then sent to headquarters for processing. It is common for only a few persons at the center of the corporation to have a clear view of the overall financial performance of their organization. There are, of course, many regional and local financial applications which are not operated from the center of the multinational, but we assume that they are in general support of the analytical objectives of headquarters. For financial control applications, we see a strong pattern of centralization:

$$A_{fin} \approx [D\Theta, Ap\Theta, Sc\Theta] \quad [5]$$

This strong pattern of centralization fits in with what we know about managerial control in the multinational corporation. Although many operations functions are decentralized, financial control remains under the tight control of headquarters.

Human Resources

In sharp contrast to the centralized nature of financial control in the multinational, the *human resources* application family is generally driven by local conditions. Different schemes of taxation, medical and retirement benefits, different currencies as well as other factors all mitigate against centralized applications, which can become very difficult to build if they must be designed to adjust to many different local variations in processing requirements. What we see, then, is that applications in the human resources area are decentralized:

$$A_{\lambda} \approx [D\Omega, Ap\Omega, Sc\Omega] \quad [6]$$

This complete decentralization is necessary in order to adapt the information system and its utilization to the many variations in local conditions.

Distribution and Logistics

The *distribution* application exhibits a mixed aspect of centralization and decentralization. Based on the application of Caterpillar, Federal Express, United Parcel Service and others, we can assume that distribution and logistics systems operate from a strong centralized infrastructure, but provide distribution of information out to the more distant extremity of the information system — not only to the remote subsidiary offices, but occasionally even beyond to customers, business partners, or other third parties. In this case, the distribution of display *screens* is highly localized:

$$A_d \approx [D\Theta, Ap\Theta, Sc\Omega] \quad [7]$$

This type of arrangement allows the most distributed access to the database, and is the most telecommunications-intensive of all the applications.

Marketing and sales

There is little evidence regarding the precise data processing characteristics of the *marketing and sales* application.[1] We know, however, that much sales and marketing activity takes place within the individual countries or regions of the world where a multinational conducts business. As a result, we can make a reasonable estimation that those data processing functions in support of sales are decentralized in nature.[2] However, since many sales programs are coordinated on a regional basis — Europe-wide, North America, Latin America, Middle East & Africa, etc. — it is likely that a strong regional processing application is resident in the system. On the other hand, like financial reporting, sales information, particularly pricing, may be coordinated from headquarters:

$$A_{mk} \approx \left[D\Theta, Ap\left(\begin{array}{c}\Phi\\\Omega\end{array}\right), Sc\Omega \right] \quad [8]$$

There is likely a strong *sectoral differentiation* for this application family. For example, in the pharmaceutical industry, pricing information may be decentralized to the regional or even local levels in accordance with the dictates of various national health plans.

---

[1] There is no published research in this area.
[2] An exception to this estimation may be represented by a centralized price-quotation database. Under this model, however, this would be classified as an application *fragment* rather than application *family*.

Research and Development

Study of the research and development function in the multinational has a long history. Multinationals have been criticized for failing to transfer technology and research expertise, because there is a tendency to keep more research efforts focused at headquarters. It is argued that whatever local research there is, it is oriented towards simply helping to adopt products to local conditions rather than towards basic research.

As a result we can approximate the research and development application family as being centralized or regionalized for data, with strong distribution of applications processing:

$$A_{rd} \approx \left[D\binom{\Theta}{\Omega}, Ap\Omega, Sc\Omega \right] \quad [9]$$

This type of arrangement allows each of the individual laboratories to get access to larger amounts of information and data than they would normally create on their own while at the same time maintaining autonomy. In many cases reported, the chief control over research and development resides at corporate headquarters, and yet this control must be exercised over many different general and focused purpose laboratories located in various locations around the world.

Corporate intelligence systems

The key function of corporate intelligence is to process a great stream of heterogeneous information relating to the environment in which the multinational must conduct business. Political events and trends, economic policies, security (terrorism) information and, perhaps most important, *information on competitors* are all examples of the types of information needed by the strategic planning cadres within the multinational corporation.

There has not been much work on studying the information technology aspects of corporate intelligence systems. It is known that they can be built to model the government intelligence systems in place, although they can not be as advanced. This is irrespective of the significant amount of writing on corporate intelligence.

It appears that in terms of environtal scanning and assessment, much of the data is kept in the local environment, but that the operation and maintenance of the information system is located at the center of the corporation. Corporate intelligence is communications-intensive and is built upon a need to quickly relay useful and critical information from the periphery of the corporation to the appropriate set of decision-makers at the center.

$$A_{CI} \approx [D\Omega, Ap\Theta, Sc\Omega] \qquad [10]$$

Under these circumstances, the data and access to screens of information is decentralized, but the overall application for corporate intelligence lies at the center of the system.

Application fragments

A slight complication arises when the different families of applications are broken down into their fragments, characteristics of which may vary considerably. Although the application family as a whole may have fixed characteristics, such as decentralized access to different information screens of the system, this may not, and probably does not, hold true for the application fragments of which it is composed. Individual application fragments may have completely different and even contradictory characteristics.

A key to understanding the overall shape and texture of information technology within the multinational corporation is the comprehension of the composition and individual characteristics of the application fragments.

An example of how the application family might be composed of a series of application fragments which have different characteristics might be found in the human resources area — some MNCs maintain centralized files of "high profile" employees which supplement localized data processing activities found in individual nation states:

$$A_{\lambda} \approx \left[a_{\lambda_1} \begin{bmatrix} D\Theta \\ Ap\Theta \\ Sc\Theta \end{bmatrix}_{\underbrace{}_{highprofile}}, a_{\lambda_2} \begin{bmatrix} D\Omega \\ Ap\Omega \\ Sc\left(\dfrac{\Phi}{\Omega}\right) \end{bmatrix}, \cdots a_{\lambda_n} \right] \qquad [11]$$
$$\underbrace{}_{local\,/\,regional}$$

There is not evidence at this time available to document the shape and texture of the many application fragments found within the complex information systems of the multinational corporation, but this technique offers one approach to understanding the problem.

This type of uneven relationship between application fragments is true for all application families A_N. In addition, there is substantial *sectoral differentiation* in which the relationship between fragments and their families is inconsistent. Given any A_N, and various business sectors S_N, then

$$S_1 A_N \neq S_2 A_N \cdots \neq S_N A_N.$$

This makes the problem even more complicated, as it insures that there is a very limited amount of generalizeability between different sectors and types of multinational corporations.

The nation state

As argued, the nation state has generally acted to inhibit the development of international information systems. Within the context of the world political system, the forces of international organization and those of the nation state are in contradition with each other. As the influence of one increases, the influence of the other decreases:

$$\uparrow IO \propto \downarrow NS.$$

$\uparrow IO$ has allowed an acceleration of internationalization of multinational information systems, whereas $\uparrow NS$, associated with such factors as transborder data flow controls, privacy regulations, interconnection standards, or other inhibitory factors, has tended to induce MNCs to decentralize their multinational information systems. Each of these factors, along with many others are each in themselves separate and controversial areas of study, and it is difficult to create a specific schema which would allow quantification of the impact of these different forces.[1] As an analogy to the application family—fragment model, we can conceive of the different nation state inhibitors as being fragments within the overall context of the role of the nation state.

---

[1] The quantification of political forces is difficult, but can be done using a series of index numbers which are based on qualitative assessments. Although this is not a precise method, and is more subjective that many would like, nevertheless it is a method which can shed light upon the relative strength of each of the forces, and help in determining possible outcomes given hypohetical situations.

$$NS_N \approx \begin{bmatrix} NS_{tdf} & NS_{prv} \\ \underbrace{NS_{tel}} & NS_n \end{bmatrix} \quad [12]^1$$

inhibitors

These different political and economic forces exercised at the level of the nation state combine together to create the environment in which international information systems must operate.

International organization

The environmental factors associated with international organization have been accelerators. The work of the International Telecommunication Union (ITU) in promoting standards, of the World Intellectual Property Organization (WIPO) in protecting technology secrets, the work of the World Bank (IBRD) in financing infrastructure projects with information technology and telecommunications components, and the work of organizations such as IEEE also in standards have all tended to act as accelerators in the spread of multinational information systems in the past quarter of a century. Like the inhibitory factors which are components of NS_N, the IO_N family also breaks down:

$$IO_N \approx \begin{bmatrix} IO_{ITU} & IO_{WIPO} \\ IO_{IBRD} & IO_n \end{bmatrix} \quad [13]$$

accelerators

Once again, it is necessary to warn the reader about the difficulty in assigning empirical quantitative measures to the forces of international organizations. At best, these can only be approximations of reality, but useful in determing the general pattern of causality.

Partial general causality model

This leads to a general causality model in which the environmental factors influence distribution of infrastructure and application fragments, leading to specific parameters for required application families, which in turn enable different international business functions:

---

[1] Although there are nation state accelerators, it is assumed that nation state factors are primarily negative and inhibitory. The same is true for the later discussion of international organization factors, which are assumed to be accelerators. *Note:* There are many more nation state factors than mentioned here. These are only for illustration purposes.

$$
\underbrace{\begin{bmatrix} IO_N \\ \Updownarrow \\ NS_N \end{bmatrix}}_{\text{environ}} \leftrightarrow \underbrace{\begin{bmatrix} Sc \\ Ap \\ D \end{bmatrix}}_{\text{frag}} \rightarrow \underbrace{\begin{bmatrix} \Theta \\ \Phi \\ \Omega \end{bmatrix}}_{\text{phys}} \rightarrow \underbrace{[A_N]}_{\text{family}} \rightarrow \underbrace{\begin{bmatrix} C & I \\ T & F^{IT} \end{bmatrix}}_{\text{IBfcns}} \qquad [14]
$$

In terms of its explanatory power, this model has both strengths and weaknesses. On the positive side, it does set forth a series of relationships which show how the infrastructure of both information technology as well as information itself is geographically distributed. This in itself should enable analysts to understand the distribution of resources. In addition, it gives a tool which helps to categorize the different patterns of infrastructure distribution into units which themselves are functions of the specific applicatons which are being supported. Within this context, the use of the concept of applications fragments and families gives a powerful tool to explain how different applications can have contradictory characteristics simultaneously. Finally, the model points the way towards the need to bring into the analysis the different environmental factors set up by the complex interplay of nation states and international organizations.

On the other hand, there are difficulties in working with this model. First, it is difficult to collect comprehensive data on all of the details under consideration. Second, the general environmental factors — international organization and nation states — must be estimated by subjective methods to determine their values, and this makes their correlation with the empirical measurements of infrastructure more suspect, but not necessarily inaccurate. Third, it difficult to precisely define the relationship between application fragments and families.

These concerns about the model raise questions about the need for further research.

Directions for further research

Field tests and empirical measurements

More work needs to be done to engage in measurements of the information structure of a multinational corporation in order to test further the viability of the different hypotheses and observations put forth herein.

Develop economic variables to understand drivers of change

We know that over time international information systems are going through drastic changes, much of it driven by economic factors — either the general economics and competitive situation for the company or the rapidly changing price/performance characteristics of information systems themselves and the rapidly dropping costs of international telecommunications in a few key retions of the world. After time-distributed measurements are taken, it should be possible to understand more about the logic of the dynamics of change and transformation in the infrastructure.

References

Multinational Information Systems

Roche, Edward M. *Managing Information Technology in Multinational Corporations* (New York: Macmillan, 1992)

Deans, Candace. and Dennis Kane. *International Dimensions of Information Systems and Technology*. Boston: PWS Kent, 1991.

Butler Cox plc. *Globalisation: The IT Challenge.* (Hampshire, U.K.: The Amdahl Executive Institute, 1991).

Roche, Edward M., Seymour Goodman and Hsinchun Chen. The Landscape of International Computing. *Advances in Computers* (Spring 1992)

Headquarters Subsidiary Coordination

Bartlett, Christopher A. and Sumantra Ghoshal. Managing Across Borders: New Organizational Responses. *Sloan Management Review* Fall 1987. pp.43-53.

Egelhoff, William G. "Strategy and Structure in Multinational Corporations: A Revision of the Stopford and Wells Model" *Strategic Management Journal*, Vol. 9, 1-14 (1988)

Perlmutter, Howard V. The Tortuous Evolution of the Multinational Corporation *Columbia Journal of World Business* January-February 1969.

Doz, Yves and C.K. Prahalad. "Patterns of Strategic Control Within Multinational Corporations" *Journal of International Business Studies* Fall 1984. pp.55-72.

Gates, Stephen R. and William G. Egelhoff. Centralization in Headquarters-Subsidiary Relationships. *Journal of International Business Studies* Summer 1986. pp.71-92.

Mascarenhas, Briance. The Coordination of Manufacturing Interdependence in Multinational Companies. *Journal of International Business Studies* Winter 1984. pp. 91-106.

Corporate Intelligence Systems

Ghoshal, Sumantra and Seok Ki Kim (1986). Building Effective Intelligence Systems for Competitive Advantage. *Sloan Management Review* Fall 1986. pp. 49-58.

Herring, Jan P. (1988). Building a Business Intelligence System. *The Journal of Business Strategy* May/June 1988. pp.4-9.

Keegan, Warren J. "Acquisition of Global Business Information" *Columbia Journal of World Business* March-April 1968. pp.35-41.

Arvai, Ernest Stephen. "Eliminating the Lag in International Reporting" *Information Strategy: The Executive's Journal* Vol. 3, No. 2, Winter 1987, pp. 43-44.

Attanasio, Dominick B. (1988). The Multiple Benefits of Competitor Intelligence. *The Journal of Business Strategy* May/June 1988. pp. 16-19.

Beauvois, John J. International Intelligence for the International Enterprise. *California Management Review* 1960-1961. pp.39-46.

Eells, Richard "Multinational Corporations: The Intelligence Function" *Columbia J. of World Business* November-December 1969

Murray, J. Alex. "Intelligence Systems of the MNCs" *Columbia Journal of World Business* September-October 1972. pp.63-71.

Firm Specific Advantages

Clemons, Erik K. and Bruce W. Weber. "London's Big Bang: A Case Study of Information Technology, Competitive Impact, and Organizational Change" *Journal of Management Information Systems* Spring 1990, Vol. 6, No. 4. pp.41-60.

Karimi, J. and Benn Konsynski "Globalization and Information Management Systems" *Journal of Management Information Systems.* Vol.7., No.4., Spring 1991.

Michael J. Earl. Exploiting IT for Strategic Advantage -- A Framework of Frameworks. Oxford Institute of Information Management. Research paper RDP 88/1.

Internalization Theory

Casson, Mark C. "Transaction Costs and the Theory of the Multinational Enterprise" in Alan M. Rugman, Ed. *New Theories of the Multinational Enterprise* St. Martin's Press, New York, 1982. p.37.

Dunning, John H. and Peter J. Buckley. (1977) International Production and Alternative Models of Trade. in *The Manchester School* pp. 392-403.

Teece, David J. "Economies of Scope and the Scope of the Enterprise" *Journal of Economic Behavior and Organization* 1 (1980) 223-247.

Rugman, Alan. "Internalization and Non-Equity Forms of International Involvement" in Alan M. Rugman, Ed. *New Theories of the Multinational Enterprise* St. Martin's Press, New York 1982. p.10.

Nation States and the Multinational Corporation

Doz, Yves L., Christopher A. Bartlett, and C.K. Prahalad. "Global Competitive Pressures and Host Country Demands: Managing Tensions in MNCs" *California Management Review* Spring 1981, Vol. XXIII, No.3, pp.63-74.

Sauvant, Karl P. Transborder Data Flows and the Developing Countries. *International Organization* 37, 2, Spring 1983 pp. 359-371.

Das, Ranjan. Impact of Host Government Regulations on MNC Operations: Learning from Third World Countries. *Columbia Journal of World Business* Spring 1981. pp.85-90.

Encarnation, Dennis J. and Louis T. Wells, Jr. Sovereignty en Garde: Netotiating with Foreign Investors. *International Organization* 39, 1, Winter 1985. pp. 47-78.

Guynes, Jan L., C. Stephen C. Guynes and Ron G. Thorn, "Conquering International Boundaries That Restrict the Flow of Data" *Information Strategy: The Executives Journal* Vol. 6, No. 3, Spring 1990, pp. 27-32

Heitzman, James, "Information Systems and Development in the Third World" *Information Processing and Management* Vol. 26, No. 4, 1990, pp. 489-502.

Kim, W. Chan. Competition and the Management of Host Government Intervention. *Sloan Management Review* Spring 1987. pp.33-39

Rowan, Richard L., and Duncan C. Campbell, The Attempt to Regulate Industrial Relations through International Codes of Conduct. *Columbia Journal of World Business* Summer 1983. pp. 64-72.
Vernon, Raymond.   Multinational Enterprises and National Governments: Exploration of an Uneasy Relationship. *Columbia Journal of World Business* Summer 1976. pp.9-16.

11 Regional Development of Telecommunications in Hungary

Ferenc Erdösi

The telegraph has been a state monopoly since its introduction in 1847 while the telephone service became a part of the national post service after 17 years of its appearance.

Mass communication was a part of postal services — radio since 1925 and television since 1955. This situation has partly changed recently when the telephone, the telegraph and other telecommunication facilities were separated from postal services. In 1990, a new organization the Hungarian Telecommunication Company (MATAV) was formed. Radio and TV broadcasting do not belong to postal services any more but they are managed by the Hungarian Broadcasting Company which still under state ownership. However, with revision to the legal system, there exists a possibility for breaking the state monopoly and for carrying out a partial privatization.

State ownership had some impacts on the spatial structure of telecommunication because the market economy (from the middle of the 19th century until 1848/49) was under the predominance of central decisions and preferences. During the communist era (between 1949 and 1989) network developments were carried out by preferences harmonizing with the ideolögy of the Hungarian Communist Party.

The development and diffusion of traditional telecommunication services

The gradual separation of telegraph from the railway system

The *telegraph* as the first electronic device of telecommunication at first had to follow the railway system because it was mainly used for railway traffic regulation. As a result not only railway but most of the public telegraph offices were functioning only in settlements lying along railway lines even in the last 30 years of the nineteenth century. See Figure 1. The busy Danube ports were also connected with cables and some riverside settlements also had telegraph facilities. The transport servicing and infrastructural function of telegraphs was mainfested in the small

Figure 1: *Districts of post and telegraph offices, 1873*

Note: 1—post office; 2—telegraph office; 3—railway station; 4— villages without postal services; 5— railway line; 6—postal district border

participation of county seats and district centers in telegraph network from settlements having no railway access. (Not all the railway stations even some bigger ones had telegraph service at that time). On the other hand, smaller telegraph offices provided only very restricted public services.

The Hungarian railway system had a greater monocentric feature than the French one with the aim of facilitating the intensive development of Budapest for national political-economic interests. As the telegraph system was following railway structure it had also a monocentric macrostructure. The telegraph was gradually spreading and later on it was installed in every village. By the beginning of our century, public telegraph offices became independent from the railway system and they provided an almost homogenous service.

The spatial division of telegraph offices did not reflect general regional development but rather the population—size structure of settlements. (Figure 2). For economic reasons, there were neither telegraph nor post office services in villages with population of several hundred persons. While the Hungarian Plain — the region of medium or large villages (with a population of 5—28 thousand) 95 per cent of villages had a post office and 80 per cent had telegraph services. The other (hillside

Figure 2: *Post and telegraph offices and settlements with telephone service*

Note: 1—post office center; 2—post office branch; 3—post and telegraph office; 4—railway telegraph station; 5—telephone; 6—villages without postal services; 7—railway station; 8—postal district border

and mountainous) areas with their small village system had these services in 85 and 65—70% in 1913.

The average service area of a telegraph office has greatly diminished. The dominance of railway-side telegraph offices was only 55 per cent. In many cases, telegraph services were not functioning in the largest village-center of a post-office area but rather in small villages lying along major railway lines.

There were less telegraph offices than there were post offices. For this reason mainly in small village territories, the territorial system of post and telegraph offices did not coincide, (or there were only some coincidences) and they formed a homogenous unit only in some areas.

The spatial diffusion of the telephone

From the beginning, the telephone was mainly used rather for private than public purposes. That is why in a market economy for a long time its spatial diffusion was determined by concrete needs having come from economic development, dynamics, income, professional and educational reasons. The role of state in the spatial diffusion of telephone service was small. It was only restricted by the public administrational status of the given settlement. Military aspects were not regarded in network development.

This has resulted in serious spatial inequalities in telephone services. Following the high representation of industrial, trade and service sectors in Budapest telephone services were highly concentrated in budapest. there were also great differences in the tertiary and quaternary functions of regonal centers, rural centers and agricultural areas (agricultural towns, villages, farms) too.

The "socialist planning system" was characterized by the predominance of the productive sector (with forced extensive industrialization) and by the negligence of infrastructural development. The communist dictatorship highly restricting personal freedom ad individualism considered the telephone as a means of contact between state companies, offices and institutions. To provide telephone services for private flats was not a primary target of the government. (Except for party and government leaders and highly-positioned party personalities who were connected to each other by sometimes a secret coded direct telephone access). Mátyás Rákosi the former communist leader's slogan Hungarian workers do not need "telephone services" had a consequence of not installing telephone into private flats. There were only some telephone boxes in streets available for making public telephone calls.

Although the importance of infrastructure namely telecommunicational development was several times mentioned in different medium-term plans from the 1960s (just only for increasing productivity) Hungary took one of the last positions in telephone service. (This is true not only in the absolute number of telephone-sets but in the number of sets connected to long-distance and international network also in the rate of digital networks too.)

In Central Europe, telephone was first used in Budapest, the leader of infrastructure development. Even in the biggest rural towns the telephone was first used only for local calls. It was used for interurban calls since 1908. For a short time the term of "interurban" expressed the very essence of its meaning — the connection between urban settlements. The introduction of telephone services into villages mainly into hamlets was a very slow process. The map of the 1913 situation (Figure 2) indicates greater differences in the spatial diffusion of telephone-stations than telegraphs. There were more of them in the Hungarian Plain. In the south and southwestern parts of Hungary, telephones were installed only in cities, in the largest villages, in the villages of Lake Balaton, at railway centers and in some smaller villages. (Having the role of a mi-

croregional enter.) Despite the villages of Northeastern Hungary were
not larger than those in South and South-eastern Hungary there were
more telephone lines installed in the villages of Northeastern Hungary
before the First World War because of mines and industrial companies
which were situated on the spot. There were also more villages with
telephone stations inthe North Hungarian region with higher agricultural and industrial production and more populated villages than those
in the north-eastern, south or south-western regions.

Due to the increase in the number of post offices facilitated by the
starting of road traffic between the First and the Second World War,
almost all the villages of the Hungarian Plain had postal services. In
other parts of Hungary, the development could only reduce the number
of micro-regional post offices (providing services for 3—4 in extreme
cases for 6—7 villages). The use of the telephone was following this pattern. *It was only villages with postal services that were linked up to the national telephone network.*

After the Second World War, the telephone was installed into villages
with no postal services too, so by the middle of the 1950s, with electrifi-
cation, the telephone was installed into every Hungarian village. The
development of the telephone network did not serve only for private
purposes. Instead, it was used for emergency calls or contacting higher
administrative bodies and authorities.

Slow quantitative developments were followed by qualitative ones
with the introduction of inter-urban remote calling systems in the 1970s.
A greater development was made by the introduction of digital telephone exchanges in 1990.

Regional differences in telecommunication

The offer and demand of telecommunication services depend on the
types (sectors) of telecommunication. The traditional but still appopriate
telegraph service like any other mailing services was determined by regional demand but there is a heavy demand for telephone services concerning both the absolute capacities and their spatial division. Thus the
possibilities and regional aspects of telephone services largely depend on
the relative density of telephone stations (the number of network nodes)
also with the type and direction of calls. For technical reasons the spatial
diffusion of telecommunication services like the telex or facsimile is also
restricted now.

The telephone

The growth of telephone services in counties between 1965 and 1991 based on the relative number of telephone stations has been an interesting point of study.

The first valid figures on the spatial division of the telephone among counties were published in 1965. Thus the latest figures should be compared with them. The development of telephone services between 1965 and 1990 has the following spatial features:

* The increase in telephone stations took place in Budapest five and one-half times quicker than in rural areas.
* There were not great differences among counties in the level of development. The largest figure was 2.6 times, the second largest figure was 1.4 more than the smallest one. The difference was less than 13 per cent among two-thirds of the counties. The greatest improvement was made in Komárom being the most industralized count, in Bács-Kiskun drawing the largest personal incomes from agriculture, in Vas largely affected by the Austrian shopping tourism and in Csongrád having the largest residential contribution to developments.

The relatively smallest improvement was made in Szolnok being still an agricultural county of large villages in spite of its industrialization, in Baranya being a mining county of small halets, in Fejér having various industries on its territory and in Szabolcs-Szatmár being the most underdeveloped county of Hungary.

There are only some cases when county differences can be explained by their funtional features. However, in most cases the comprehensive plans of regional development, the declared preferences and the hidden (but generally known) dispreferences are not manifested in services.

The telephone — spatial differences based on county indicators

The traditional statistical indicator of telephone services is the number of telephone stations per population. It is indicated for each county in Figure 3. Here we can see an almost equal service in the Transdanubian and East Hungarian regions while there is a strong underdevelopment in the Hungarian Plain.

The number of telephone stations per population is enough only for a quantitative analysis. *It has a great influence on the real value and quality of services whether calls are made through manual or automatic switches.*

Figure 3: *Telephone service indicators in the 19 counties of Hungary including budapest in 1990.*

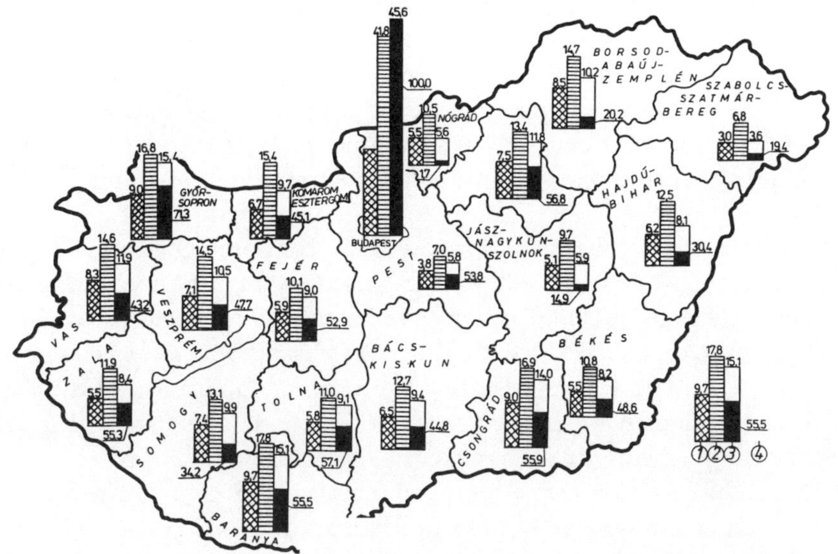

Note: 1—number of public telephone stations, trunks/100 residents; 2—total number of public telephone stations (including trunks and extensions); 3—complex telephone indicator (number of lines multiplied with the percentage of settlements with remote access; 4—percentage of settlements with remote access within the county.

In long distance calls, another difference can be observed based on the possibility of making international calls. Manual switches are the most primitive types of service (used mainly in small hamlets) operating only in the daytime (8—16 or 6—20) hours.[1]

Villages with non-stop telephone switches belong to a higher category. To simplify the very essence of the trend, our further analysis is based on researches made in the category of home long-distance calls (which is including the possibility of making international calls, but it is not true inversely!)

In the middle of the 1980s, to make long-distance calls was possible only from Budapest and some of its agglomeration — from county-seats, from some additional 2—3 towns in each county and from some micro-regions. Budapest was the natural starting point of diffusion. The qual-

---

[1]If the telephone is out of service-time or in case of vis maior a car should be used to contact the destination of emergency calls.

ity of long-distance calls depends on the improvement made in digitalisation. The rate of digital telephone exchanges compared to the total is going to increase from 8 per cent in 1990 to 29 per cent in 1993. The largest coherent telephone exchange zones were built along the Western borders of Hungary mainly for tourism.

In spite of these developments the majority of long-distance calls will still be made by the use of analog techniques in 1993. At the same time, the majority of rural residents must still use the primitive manual switch system.

This is true not only for peripheral areas, but some central, relatively advanced, territories as well. See Figure 4. For a better and single demonstration of regional differences in telephone services we have made a complex analysis *with the integration of quantitative and qualitative* indicators. Based on figures resulting from the multiplication of the density of telephones with the percentage of settlements connected to the international network, we can make the following conclusions:

- *Regional and complex indicators put the Transdanubian region to the first rank.* (11.0) It is followed by the North-Hungarian region — 10.4, but the indicator of the Hungarian Plain — 7.8 shows a backward situation.

- *There is a loose functional correlation* between the level of *industrialization* and the level of telephone services.

- *There is a very strong correlation between relative personal income tax and the level of telephone services.* It appears that telephone services largely depend on incomes.[1]

- Settlement conditions, having some consequences on incomes, have a role of a strong negative correlation[2] between the quantitative indicators of telephone services and the *rate of rural population.* This means that smaller rates of rural population will produce almost the same rate of telephone growth. At the same time, *the average population size of villages has almost no role in the quantitative and qualitative factors of telephone services.* (r=0.5477 and r=0.2988) There is a large difference among county indicators. The largest figure of Borsod-Abaúj-Zemplén 17.2 is almost five times more than the lowest figure of Szabolcs-Szatmár which measures 3.6 only.

- *The provisional indicator of Budapest with its 100 per cent long-distance service rate is more than four imes more than the indicator of rural long-distance services.* This is also true in the case of quantitative indicators showing two and a half times more telephones in Budapest than in rural areas.

---

[1]Correlation: r = 0.8003
[2]Correlation: r = -0.7991

Figure 4: *Areas with remots access inter-urban telephones at the end of 1993 excluding Village Program*

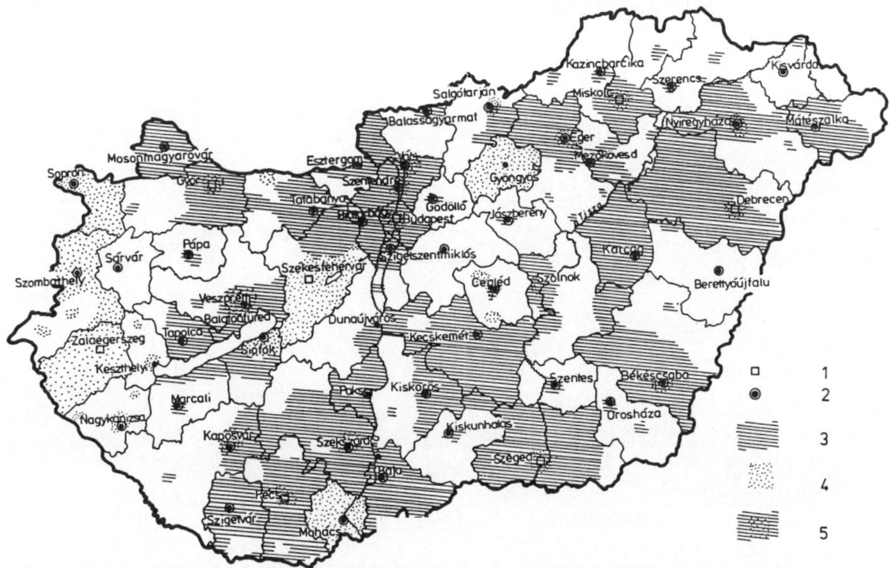

Note: 1—secondary center; 2—primary center; 3—analog system; 4—digital system; 5—mixed analog and digital system.

Another indicator of this advantageous telephone situation is that two-fifths of the total public telephone boxes are situated in Budapest. It is also important from the qualitative point of services that the automation of main telephone exchanges is 100 per cent, while in the case of rural exchanges, it is 88.5 (79.9). It is even smaller in the case rural subcenters 84.3). The advantages of Budapest in telephony are confirmed by the introduction of a Westel radiotelephone system which connects 3,000 subscribers since 1990 in Budapest.

The telephone — the features of telephone services according to city categories[1]

There is a strong interdependence between telecommunication services and urbanization. Cities meeting functional infrastructural requirements with a traditional historical background and development have better telephone conditions as well in comparison with those apparently lucky settlements that were given the rank of town without any well-established reasons just only for excessive parochialism or resulting from good personal contacts with government administrational executives.

---

[1] Based on telephone stations per 100 residents.

Table 1: *Telephone service indicators based on urban categories*

Urban categories	Trunk lines per 100 residents
Size categories	
2 million residents (Budapest)	22.81
Cities larger than 100,000 up to 250,000	13.16
Medium cities 60,000—100,000	13.70
Medium cities 30,000—60,000	7.82
Small towns 10,000—30,000	6.47
Mini-towns smaller than 10,000	6.62
Functional Division	
Capital (Budapest)	22.81
County seats	13.35
"Socialist cities"	9.47
Old (heavy) industrial centers	12.00
Cultural centers (Church administration centers)	7.08
Tourist and recreation centers	12.39
Agricultural centers	4.66
North-eastern agricultural centers in Hajdú-Bihar and Szabolcs-Szatmár counties	3.48

Multiple categories can be set up for the evaluation of regional differences in telephone service. The main elements can be recognized by analysis of *the number of residents and functional categories*.

The number of telephone stations does not directly follow the number of residents, it has rather a terraced line pattern. Apart from the gap between Budapest a metropolis of 2 million and our rural cities of 100,000 residents, there is another gap at the level of 60,000 persons. We can hardly find greater differences in the category of middle-size and big cities and if there is any it is in favour of cities with 60,000—100,000 residents. See Table 1. It is because of the rapid and spectacular development of some county seats during the 1970s and the early 1980s, perhaps as a "compensation" for their inferiority complex.

There are also no significant differences in the number of telephones in the category of cities below 60,000 residents: it is almost zero in case of small and mini-towns but the situation is not much better in middle-size cities.

Functional researches did not include every city of Hungary — typical or cities with mixed functions were moitted from the research. In the hierarchy made by the number of telephones, Budapest takes the first position, country seats take the second one. They are closely followed by cities with the function of tourist and holiday centers and there is a smaller difference between them and the old industry centers. The average number of telephone stations in the last three categories is almost the same but there is a large gap between them and the new "socialist cities" built on village sites. They are lagging far behind our traditional industrial cities, but the situation is worse in small-town size cultural centers, fulfilling church administrative functions as well.

Agricultural towns are the last in this ranking. It is true mainly in case of East Hungarian agricultural towns, particularly for those in Hajdú-Bihar county.

This hierarchy is harmonizing with the hierarchy of general infrastructural service. There is a significant deviation in case of "socialist cities" having the best parameters in general infrastructural services and housing. The parameters of their service infrastructure are also above the national average but on the other hand they suffer from significant shortages in telephone. There are no explanations for the extreme differences within this category: While Kazincbarcika (17.8) and Leninváros (20.7) centers of the chemical industry have a top position on the other hand in spite of their political-economical preferences Dunaújváros a metallurgical center (5.4), Ajka with its aluminum industry (5.7) should be satisfied with the service level of agricultural towns. The telephone service level in Oroszlány (8.0) and Várpalota (5.4) mining centers is also far below the national average. Cultural centers, fulfilling church administrative functions as well, have relatively better infrastructural conditions, mainly in the fields of education, health systems and commercial services. Unfortunately, telephone services are "lagging behind" in these areas.

Despite the fact that the Hungarian Telecommunication Company has been offering some special telephone services that make everyday life and administration easier for a long time it has aroused only a moderate interest. There was a decrease in the use of time, bet-game and message services since 1970, there is a stagnation in the use of wake-up and weather information services. There was a growth only in the use of different "enquiries" providing factual and information services. There was also some growth in the use of music and tell-tale services. Although the lessening interest for some services can be explained by the emergence of TV and radio, but its main reason is that the Hungarian society has only a low level burgeois mentality and telephone culture.

Figure 5: *The spatial division of short-distance, operational, CB stations and of Westel radio telephones with international call facilities in 1991.*

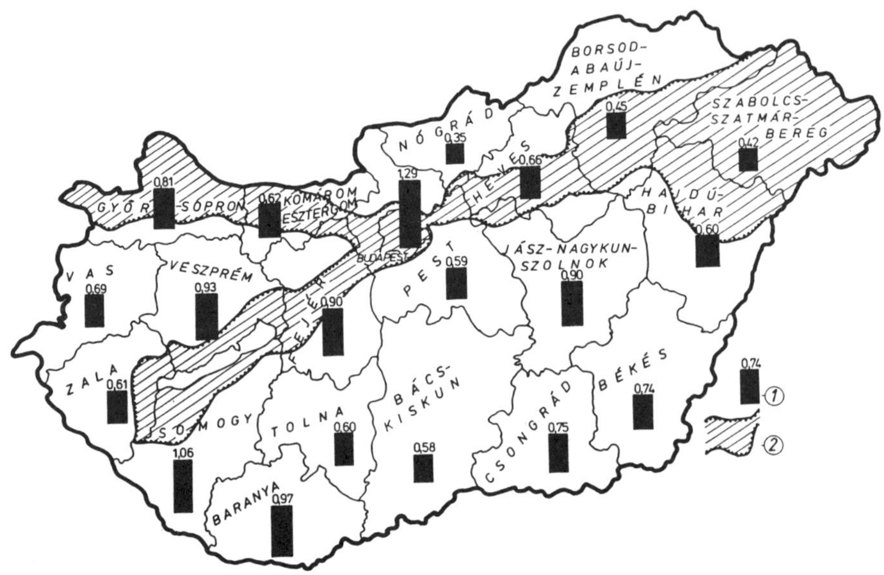

Note: 1—CB stations/1,000 residents; 2—areas with Westel connection along international routes and highways.

The spatial features of CB radio diffusion

Among the socialist countries of Eastern Europe, the use of short-distance CB radios was licensed first in Hungary since the middle of the 1970s. At first 65 per cent of the total CB sets was in public ownership but today the majority of CB sets are in private hands. Besides its basic organizational functions, keeping contacts between dispersed industrial units, and agricultural farms, it was used by private holders — taxi drivers, retailers gardeners, etc. — to ease the difficulties caused by telephone shortages. Due to these factors the number of private CB sets was ten times more in the 1980s than in the 1970s. Almost half of the total CB sets are located in Budapest, another 35—38 ercent are in the biggest rural towns, another 12—15 percent are in small towns while they are hardly used in villages. Villages are too small to maintain a CB center.

The regional division of CB sets in Hungary shows a higher relative number of sets in the Transdanubian region than in the Eastern one. See Figure 5.

Figure 6: *The spatial division of telex and telefax stations in 1991.*

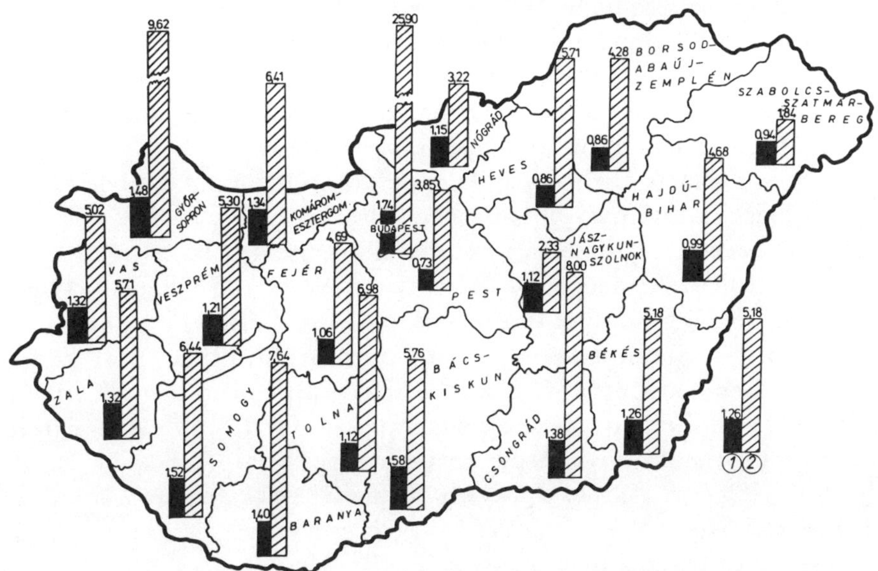

The spatial diffusion of new text-, data- and photo transmission facilities

The traditional text transmitting telegraph has lost its primary importance with the emergence of the telephone and the facsimile.

Most of the telexes are located in the West Hungarian region. This region is closely followed by the Hungarian Plain and the third rank is taken by the North-Hungarian region.

The county indicators of telex services are different from the telephone. Despite the general expectations, telex is not an alternative to the telephone. See Figure 6. During funtional analysis, we could not discover any rules because *extreme values occur both in industrialized and non-industrialized countries.* In spite of the fact that telex services are not available for private users there is a weak correlation between the use of telex services and income conditions.

The practical value of the *facsimile*, a new invention in written telecommunication having been used in Hungary since 197 was first recognized by banks, partly because of their aptitude for innovations partly because of the ability to pay the high costs of buying a facsimile, but the share of large industrial-, trading-, transportational-, and tourist firm centers was also high.

There are 20 times more facsimiles now than 5 years ago. The growth of the facsimile was quicker in rural areas than in Budapest. From technical points, it is only its remote calling facilities that serve as a differentia specifica in spatial diffusion.

Despite the facts, the share of budapest from the total number of facsimile devices is still over 50 per cent. However, only a *small number of settlements can benefit* from the advantages of this trend.

This results in a deeper "gap" between cities and villages. While more than half of the rural facsimile stations are located in county seats, the majority in regional centers, one-third are in other rural towns. One-hundred and fourty two from the total of 166 towns has at least one facsimile, and the share of villages compared to this is only one-eighth. There is a facsimile only in 9 per cent of villages.

On the other hand, the spatial division of facsimile is concentrated in more aspects. The predominance of Budapest is followed by the predominance of county seats, the Budapest agglomeration and the villages of Lake Balaton.

Comparing with the Hungarian Plain the advantages of the Transdanubian and the East-Hungarian regions are manifested in the greater number of facsimile both in urban and rural but mainly in rural settlements. It is so, in spite of the fact that there are more ventures specialized for the purchase of facsimile in the big village network of the Hungarian Plain than in the small village system of West- and North-Hungary.

The majority of rural towns having almost the same or more facsimile rate than county seats is located in the Transdanuban region. However, the facsimile rate in borderline areas is not dominating over the other parts of the West-Hungarian region which was against our general expectations. Facsimile services are not available in large areas yet. See Figure 6.

It is very difficult to put into a direct correlation those very different urban indicators with possible factors. Even in case of county seats size categories do not seem to have an important factor on the relative number of facsimile stations. This is also true for other rural towns where not the biggest cities have the greatest number of facsimile stations.

There is not a strong correlation with the functional role of cities. Among the leaders we can find tourist centers, agglomeration cities, "socialist" industrial cities and traditional transport and trading centers having a great gravity force on other settlements.

Th greatest number of facsimile stations in Budapest is located in the central administrative district of budapest having an overwhelming predominance over the others. We can conclude from this multifold concentrated structure that in the first period of its diffusion facsimile serves for centralization purposes. It is not clear yet *when and how it can be used as a means of deconcentration and political-economic decentralization.* The interactive videotext service, providing not only passive information but offering active data-entry services for its users, was introduced into Hungary in 1989 so it looks back to a 2-year old history. Because of the high terminal costs, it is used only by public organizations but their number is also very small. It was 90 in 1989, 175 in 1990 — yet, 6,000 is expected by 1993.

Decodix videotext software was launched in Hungary in 1990, making it possible for the PC to serve as a videotext terminal. The accelerated development of videotext services is expected to take place after 1992. For the service of the French Minitel type terminals, the professional assistance of France Telecom company are expected.

Minitex service is available via telephone network, each subscriber has a private electronic mailbox. New user capacities were planned for the service of 500 subscribers. There were 428 actual users in the end of 1990. As a result of a growing interest capacities are planned for the service of 800 users in 1991. By the year of 1993, the expected number of Telebox and Minitex users is 2,500.

The spatial features of radio and TV broadcast service

There are 3 central (national) and some regional stations transmitting radio programs. Programs are transmitted by 12 FM stations and 9 AM stations. Although there is a great number of relay transmitters none of them can cover the whole area of Hungary. The Kossuth program is received on 93 per cent of the territory of Hungary by 96 per cent of the population. Petöfi program is received only on 67 per cent. This equates with 95 per cent and 76 per cent of the total population. The most backward areas of radio transmission are peripheral areas and, apart from some exceptions, they are at the eastern border of Hungary.

There are two television programs in Hungary. The first, still the main, program is received on 93 per cent of Hungary while the second program is received only on 78 per cent of Hungary with standard aerials. These areas include 95 per cent and 90 per cent of the total population.

Figure 7: *The spatial difference of TV sets and satellite broadcast areas.*

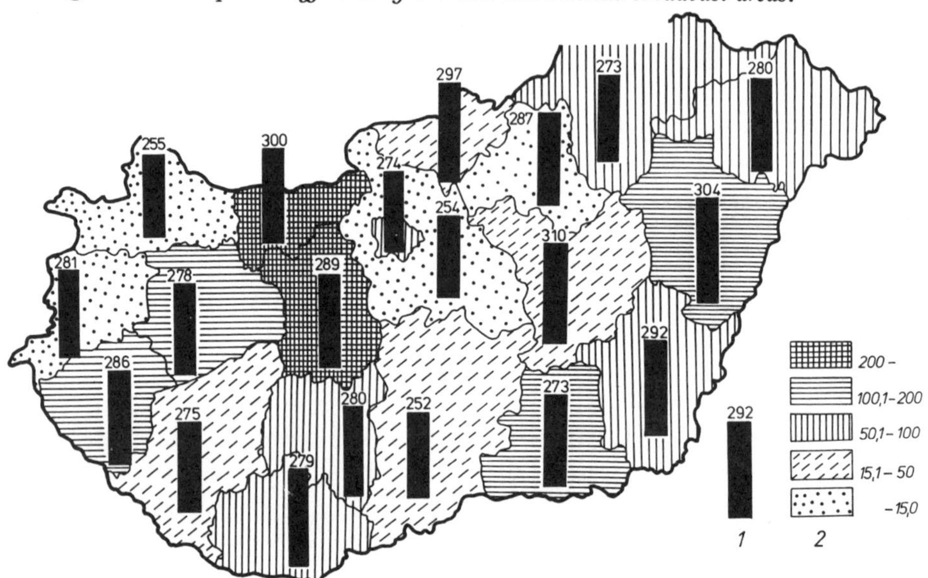

Note: 1—Number of TV subscribers/1,000 residents; 2—county indicator of flats connected to a satellite system per 10,000 persons.

The density of TV sets is hardly determined by incomes or by county urbanization level and except for a few cases the availability of foreign TV programs is not a motivating factor for the purchase of a second TV set. See Figure 7.

The diffusion of satellite programs can hardly be motivated by social-economic factors including the level of incomes. It is because privte satelite receivers are much more expensive than the joining costs of communal receivers. This latter is preferred in blocks of flats being the homes of not the richest people. This means that *now the regional spread of satellite receivers is rather determined by architectural means.* This is especially true in cities with blocks of flats. The initiative power of residents is another important factor. If there are no needs for communal systems, only a few users can receive satellite program. This would be the case in the borderland cities of West Hungary.

New features in Hungarian telecommunication policy after the political change

The negative consequences of the negligence of telecommunicational development were seen in the first half of the 1980s. There were several plans made for the acceleration of development but priority was given to telecommunication developments only in the new political system. The poor conditions of infrastructure are hindering the inflow of large foreign capital.

To create competitive conditions having positive impacts on quality and pricing, it was necessary to break the monopoly of the Hungarian National Post. The Hungarian National Post had the exclusive rights of providing telephone services.

The government launched a project starting from the 1st of January 1990 to break monopoly and to introduce a shared property system still ensuring the majority of holdings for the state. As a first step of this process, the Hungarian Telecom (MATAV) was separated from the system of the Hungaran post. Now the state has full property rights in this company but the share of foreign capital will be greater after 1992. Its institutional background appears in good order because the Hungarian Telecom was transformed into a share company. Some activities of the Hungarian Telecom are done by some smaller firms based mainly on private capital with the participation of the Hungarian Telecom. Examples include Contel Hungaria Telecom Ltd., The First Hungarian Telecom, Ltd., Westel Radiotelephone Ltd., etc. The Hungarian Post is no longer licensed for radio or television.

We can see the predominance of the state sector now but it is forced to carry out a competitive development and business policy. Based on competition and correct partnership, national interests should dominate over the business interests of the Hungarian Telecom organization. Both at the national as well as international level, it will still have a leading role in broadcasting. Based on tese principles it will take the responsibility of providing basic telecommunication services. It is true even in rural areas where the cost of services are high. This pluralization process will go on in the future: Some data transfer and telematic services with mobile telephone services will also be separated from Hungarian Telecom and they will be provided by independent companies.

The development of telephone services can only gradually take place with preferences harmonizing with national interests. The most important job now is to provide telephone services for thousands of small companies to facilitate privatization, a healthy business life and a strong market economy. The development of telephone services for individual subscribers, installation of telephones into individual flats, will be possible only after 1994.

Contributors

Henry Bakis
Directeur de recherche
à l'Université Paris IV-La
Sorbonne

Aharon Kellerman
Professor
Department of Geography
University of Haifa

Seamus Grimes
Lecturer in Geography
Department of Geography
University College Galway

Kenneth E. Corey
Office of the Dean
College of Social Science
Michigan State University

Peter Nijkamp
Jaap Vleugel
Faculteit de Economische
Wetenschappen en Econometrie
Vrije Universiteit
Amsterdam

Karlheinz Hottes
Geographisches Institut
Ruhr-Universität Bochum

Yolande Combes
Chargé de cours en communica-
tion à l'Université de Paris XIII-
Villetaneuse

Sten Lorentzon
Kulturgeografiska Institutionen
Göteborgs Universitet

Hans Ouwersloot
Piet Rietveld
Vrije Universiteit
Amsterdam

Edward M. Roche
Computing and Decision
Sciences
Seton Hall University
Information Systems Area
New York University

Ronald Abler
Executive Director
Association of American
Geographers

Ferenc Erdősi
Hungarian Academy of Sciences
Research Center on Regional
Studies

Index